THE SPIRAL STAIRCASE

Also by Karen Armstrong

Through the Narrow Gate

Beginning the World

The First Christian: St Paul's Impact on Christianity

Tongues of Fire: An Anthology of Religious and Poetic Experience

The Gospel According to Woman:
Christianity's Creation of the Sex War in the West

Holy War: The Crusades and Their Impact on Today's World

The English Mystics of the Fourteenth Century

Muhammad: A Biography of the Prophet

A History of God: The 4000-Year Quest of
Judaism, Christianity and Islam

Jerusalem: One City, Three Faiths

In the Beginning: A New Interpretation of Genesis

The Battle for God

Islam: A Short History

Buddha: A Penguin Life

THE SPIRAL STAIRCASE

KAREN ARMSTRONG

HarperCollins*Publishers*

HarperCollins*Publishers*
77–85 Fulham Palace Road
Hammersmith, London W6 8JB

www.harpercollins.co.uk

Published by HarperCollins*Publishers* 2004
3 5 7 9 8 6 4 2

Grateful acknowledgement is made to the Estate of
T. S. Eliot and Faber & Faber Ltd, for permission to
reprint an excerpt from the poem Ash-Wednesday,
from *Collected Poems, 1909–1962* by T. S. Eliot.

A catalogue record for this book
is available from the British Library

ISBN 0 00 712228 4

Typeset in Minion with Trajan Display by
Rowland Phototypesetting Limited,
Bury St Edmunds, Suffolk

Printed and bound in Great Britain by
Clays Ltd, St Ives plc

CONTENTS

PREFACE

This is the sequel to my first book, *Through the Narrow Gate*, which told the story of my seven years as a Roman Catholic nun. I entered my convent in 1962, when I was seventeen years old. It was entirely my own decision. My family was not particularly devout and my parents were horrified when I told them that I had a religious vocation. They thought, quite correctly as it turned out, that I was far too young to make such a momentous choice, but they allowed themselves to be persuaded because they wanted me to get it out of my system as soon as possible. I was usually quite a biddable child but I was anxious to test my vocation immediately, instead of waiting until after I had been to university, as my parents would have preferred. My unusual resolution in the face of their opposition impressed them, and they feared that I might spend my college years in a state of mulish obstinacy, failing to make the most of the opportunities of university life, and longing for it all to be over so that I could do what I really wanted. So, on 14 September 1962, I packed my bags and joined twelve other girls at the novitiate.

1

Why was I so determined to take this step? The motivation behind this type of decision is always complex, and there were a number of interlocking reasons. It is true that at this time I was very shy and worried about the demands of adult social life, but even though the religious life might seem a soft option, it was tough and I would not have lasted more than a few weeks if it had simply been a means of escape. I wanted to find God. I was filled with excitement and enthusiasm on that September day, convinced that I had embarked on a spiritual quest, an epic adventure, in the course of which I would lose the confusions of my adolescent self in the infinite and ultimately satisfying mystery that we call God. And because I was only seventeen, I imagined that this would happen pretty quickly. Very soon I would become a wise and enlightened woman, all passion spent. God would no longer be a remote, shadowy reality but a vibrant presence in my life. I would see him wherever I looked, and I myself would be transfigured, because, as St Paul had said, my puny little ego would disappear and Christ, the Word of God, would live in me. I would be serene, joyful, inspired and inspiring – perhaps even a saint.

This was, to put it mildly, an eccentric career option. I was almost the first student of my convent school to become a nun. Birmingham, my home town, was a materialistic place, where money was king. Most of my immediate family and friends were nonplussed – even slightly irritated – and I, of course, revelled in the sense of striking out and being just that little bit different. But I may have been more in tune with my times than I realized, since many of my generation, born in the last years or in the immediate aftermath of the Second World War, had the same inchoate yearning for transformation. Post-war Britain was not an easy place in which to grow up. We may have defeated Hitler, but the war had ruined us. Britain was now a second-rate power, and food, clothing and petrol were strictly rationed well into the 1950s. Because thousands of homes had been destroyed during the Blitz, there was a grave housing crisis. Our cities were scarred with desolate bombsites and filled with towering heaps of rubble. The centre of Birmingham was not completely rebuilt until after I left for the convent. After the war, we were in debt to the United States for three billion pounds, our empire was dismantled, and, though we were fed on a surfeit of films celebrating Britain's endurance and victory, nobody seemed prepared to look facts in the face, and decide what our future role in the world should be. Young Britons, like myself, who came to maturity in this twilight confusion of austerity, repression, nostalgia, frustration and denial, wanted not only a different world but to be changed themselves.

In 1948, 60 per cent of British people under thirty wanted to emigrate; we wanted to be somewhere else. Hence, as the music historian Jon Savage explains in *England's Dreaming: the Sex Pistols and Punk Rock* (1991), the quasi-religious fervour inspired by the Rock'n'Roll records that fell, like manna from heaven, between 1954 and 1959 on a country that had no tradition of Afro-American music. The unabashed rebellion and sexual explosiveness of these records seemed to promise a new world. They were 'so transforming that nobody who heard them could find a language to explain them except in the phrases of the songs themselves, which talked in tongues: "A Wop Bop A Loo Bop", "Be Bop A Lula".' People used to say of a record: 'It *sent* me!' as though they had been magically transported, without any effort of their own, to another place. In the world conjured up by Rock'n'Roll, nobody had to do National Service or listen to endless stories about the war. People could reject the self-sacrifice preached by their parents, live intensely, run wild, have sex, consume freely and 'do as much as they could as soon as they could'.

This might seem a far cry from the convent. But, in my own way, I shared what Savage calls the 'first time intensity' of my generation. The raw, disturbing beat of Rock'n'Roll had penetrated my convent school, even though I was neither able nor equipped to answer its summons. I did not like being a teenage girl in the 1950s. I was awkward, plain, bookish and unpopular with boys. I looked absurd in the fashions of the day: the wide swirling skirts, pert ponytails, and backcombed beehives. In 1961, the year before I entered the convent, my parents tried to entice me from my intended course by talking me into joining a young people's party at the Birmingham Catholic Ball. It was a ghastly affair. Encased in a stiff brocaded dress, with a skirt that stuck out aggressively, my feet squeezed into an agnoizing pair of pink stain shoes with long pointed toes, I was hobbled. On the few occasions when I was invited to dance, and grimly quickstepped, waltzed and fox-trotted with a herd of others, I felt like a prisoner going round and round the exercise yard. At one point, my partner and I left the main room, and for ten blissful minutes managed to escape. We weren't doing anything unlawful; we weren't smoking, drinking alcohol or kissing – just sitting on the stairs and talking – but a friend of my mother's pounced on me and frog-marched me back into the ballroom. I felt like a Victorian girl who had been compromised in some way. There had to be more to life than this.

Of course there were alternatives. We were told that, within reason, we could do anything we wanted: we could study, travel and have a career – until we got married. But even though I shrank from the appalling prospect of being an Old Maid, marriage did not look particularly appealing either, since most of the women

I knew spent their lives ceaselessly cleaning, baking and washing, chores that I detest to this day. When my father had business problems, my mother took a job, and started an interesting career in the medical school of Birmingham University. I could see how she blossomed in this new environment, but the cooking and washing-up still had to be done. By contrast, the nuns seemed remarkably unencumbered. They had no men to tell them what to do, they ran their own lives, and were, presumably, concerned with higher things. I wanted that radical freedom.

I was looking for the sort of transformation that others were seeking in Rock'n'Roll, an option that was closed to me. As a convent schoolgirl, I was protected from the street culture, and lived in a separate world from most of my fellow-countrymen and women. In the 1950s, most people in Britain still paid lip-service to religion, but Catholicism was beyond the pale. Its extravagant statues with bleeding hearts and crowns of thorns, its Latinate ritual, its Irish priests, and its orientation to Rome made it highly unBritish, and therefore suspect. Catholics lived in self-imposed 'ghettoes': we socialized together, went to separate schools, did not attend Protestant services, and were taught to hold aloof from the 'non-Catholic' mainstream. As a result of this upbringing, I think that many of us have never felt entirely English, and continue to feel outsiders in British society. My head was filled with the imagery of Catholicism, with the lives and example of its saints, and the soaring theatre of its liturgy. I too wanted to be 'sent', to experience an ecstasy that would lift me to a different dimension, to go to another place, and live more authentically than seemed possible in the world I knew. Like my peers, who loitered menacingly in the El Sombrero coffee bar in Birmingham, I too could reject the values of contempoary society. The cloister seemed a radical and daring solution. So while my peers 'opted out' in hippie communes, experimented with mind-altering drugs, or tried to change the world politically, I sought intensity and transformation in the life of a nun.

Needless to say, the convent was not what I expected. I entered in 1962 as an ardent, idealistic, untidy, unrealistic and immature teenager, and left seven years later, having suffered a mild breakdown, obscurely broken and damaged. This was nobody's fault, even though I assumed that the failure was entirely my own doing. I had embarked on the religious life at a particularly difficult moment, since my superiors were involved in a painful period of change, and were trying to decide what exactly it meant to be a nun in modern society. The Catholic Church was also seeking transformation in the post-war world. During my first few months in the convent, the Second Vatican Council convened in Rome. It had been summoned by Pope John XXIII to fling open the windows of the Church, and let the fresh air of modernity sweep through the musty corridors of the Vatican.

One of the areas tackled by the Council Fathers was the religious life, which urgently needed reform. Many of the orders were stuck in a traditional rut. Customs that had made perfect sense in the nineteenth century, when my own community had been founded, now seemed arbitrary and unnatural. Practices that had no intrinsic spiritual value but were cultural relics of the Victorian age had acquired sacred significance, and change was regarded as betrayal. The Council urged the religious orders to go back to the original spirit of their founders, who had been men and women of insight and imagination, innovators and pioneers, not guardians of the *status quo*. Nuns and monks should also let the bracing spirit of change invade their cloisters; they should throw out the rubble that had accumulated over the years and craft a new lifestyle that was in tune with the times.

This proved to be a monumentally difficult task. Nuns had to decide what was essential in their Rule, and then translate this into present-day idiom. But they themselves had been shaped by the old regime at a profound level and many found that they could not think in any other way. They could modernize their clothes, but they could not change the habits of their minds and hearts, which had been formed by a training that had been carefully designed in a different world and was meant to last a lifetime. For some, this was a time of great anguish. They saw a cherished way of life disappearing while nothing of equal value was emerging to take its place. I left the religious life in 1969, just ahead of a massive exodus of religious who left their convents and monasteries like flocks of migratory birds during the 1970s. The intense discussions surrounding the reforms had led them to call everything into question, even their own vocation. This, I believe, was a healthy development. The title of my first book, *Through the Narrow Gate*, comes from a text in St Matthew's gospel, in which Jesus tells his disciples that 'only a few' find the narrow gate that leads to life. By the end of my seven years in the convent, I had come to the conclusion that only a very small number of people could live up to the demands of a life that requires the entire subjugation of the ego and a self-abandonment that, I realized sadly, was beyond me. I knew nuns who beautifully enshrined this ideal, but I realized that I was not of that calibre. I suspect that many of those who left during the 1970s had also faced up to this hard truth.

So I arrived at my convent at a difficult juncture, and would be one of the last people to be trained according to the old system. The reforms set in motion by the Vatican Council came just too late for me. And I experienced the traditional regime at its worst. A young nun in those days had to undergo a long period of intensive training. In my order, we spent the first nine months as postulants, wearing a sober black dress with a little white veil, and practising selected portions of the Rule. The Postulantship was a period of probation, designed to test our resolve, and about half of us dropped out. I must emphasize that there was never any pressure to stay. We all knew that we were free to leave at any time, and often a girl would be sent home because it was clear that she was not suited to convent life.

At the end of the nine months, we received the habit and began two years in the novitiate. This was a particularly testing time, and we were often told that if we did not find it almost unbearable, we were not trying hard enough. My superiors should, therefore, have been delighted with me, because I spent a good deal of my novitiate in tears. As if to fend off unwelcome change, they had appointed a particularly conservative nun as Novice Mistress the year before I arrived. In *Through the Narrow Gate*, I called her Mother Walter. She was unswervingly devoted to the old ways, and revived many disciplines that her two predecessors had discarded as unsuitable for twentieth-century girls. The system she devised, I now believe, was extremely unhealthy, but I threw myself into it because I was convinced that the harder I found it, the sooner it would bring me to God. Much later I was told that several nuns had been concerned about what was happening in the Noviceship during those years. As I shall explain in the early chapters of this book, the system was a form of conditioning. It was meant to change us irrevocably and it did – in my case, for the worse. I suspect that pressure was brought to bear upon Mother Walter, however, because towards the end of my novitiate, she relaxed some of her draconian innovations. A new batch of novices had arrived who were older and more worldly-wise than my own set and they simply would not put up with some of her more outrageous rules. But again, the change came too late for me.

Yet Mother Walter, too, was undergoing a painful transition, watching the religious practices that she had known and loved for so long thrown aside. It must have been a period of great suffering for her. It would never, of course, have occurred to me at the time but I now suspect that she was not very intelligent, and therefore unable to understand the effect of some of her policies. I remember once that, towards the end of my Noviceship, when she was savaging us for what she regarded as a failure in obedience, I suddenly cracked and told her that I no longer knew what obedience really was. 'We seem to swing, like a pendulum, from one extreme to another,' I protested, 'from one disorder to another! One day we will be told off for not obeying absolutely to the letter, however absurd the command may be, and the next day we'll be in trouble because we *did* obey blindly instead of using our intelligence and showing initiative! What *are* we supposed to do? What *is* obedience?' I was astonished at myself, because we were never supposed to challenge our superiors in this way, especially while we were being reprimanded. My fellow-novices were gazing at me in dismay, clearly waiting for a thunderous riposte. But Mother Walter looked shocked, and for a moment was quite lost for words. She soon recovered herself, though the scolding she gave me was not up to her usual standard of scathing invective. But during those few seconds, while she fumbled for a suitable response, I could almost see an unwelcome insight breaking the surface of her mind, and forcing her to question the wisdom of her methods of training in a way that, perhaps, she had never done before.

Despite my difficulties, I was allowed to make vows of poverty, chastity and obedience for five years on 25 August 1965. It was a triumphant day. I felt that, like the heroes of myth, I had come through an ordeal and that things could only get better. I would soon get over the strains and tension that had made my life so miserable. Very quickly now, I would become mature and holy, and in five years' time, if all went well, I would take the final vows that would commit me to the society for life.

And at first, things did go well. After the Noviceship, we left the Mother House in Sussex and went to London for two further years of training, known as the Scholasticate. During the novitiate, we had concentrated on our spiritual lives. We had spent most of the time learning about prayer and the meaning of our Rule. Ironically, considering my aversion to domesticity, we also spent our days doing simple, manual tasks, though in the second year we had been permitted to read a little theology. In the Scholasticate, however, we began our professional training. Since our order was dedicated to the education of Catholic girls, most of us were destined to become teachers in one of the society's many schools. I had already completed the matriculation requirements for college, and it was decided that I should now prepare for the competitive entrance examinations to Oxford University, where the order had been sending nuns ever since women had been allowed to take degrees. For the next twelve months, I attended classes and tutorials at a 'crammer' near Marble Arch. My subject was to be English Literature. That meant that I had to take two three-hour papers in literature, one paper in English language and philology, two translation papers – one in Latin and the other in French – and a paper on topics of general interest. I loved it. I am a natural student and like nothing better than immersing myself in a pile of books. After the years of dreary domestic toil, I was in heaven. I also took a correspondence course in theology, scripture and church history.

In the autumn of 1966, I sat the entrance examinations for St Anne's College, Oxford, passed the first round, was summoned to interview, and to my own and my superiors' intense delight, succeeded in winning a place. In 1967, the Scholasticate completed, I arrived at Cherwell Edge in South Parks Road, the Oxford convent of my order, to begin my university studies. And my life fell apart.

Intellectually, everything was fine. I lived at the convent, but attended lectures and tutorials with the other students and did very well. I got a distinction in the preliminary examinations, which we sat in the spring of 1968, won a University Prize, and was awarded a college scholarship. So far, so good. But as a religious, I felt torn in two. My elderly superior was bitterly opposed to the new ideas, and I fought her tooth and nail throughout the entire year. I am sure that I was quite insufferable, but I found it well-nigh impossible to think logically and accurately in college, where I was encouraged to question everything, and then turn off the critical faculty I was developing when I returned to Cherwell Edge, and become a docile young nun. The stringent academic training I was receiving at the university was changing me at just as profound a level as the religious formation of the Noviceship, and the two systems seemed to be irreconcilable. I was also increasingly distressed by the emotional frigidity of our lives. This was one of the areas of convent life that most desperately needed reform. Friendship was frowned upon and the atmosphere in the convent was cold and sometimes unkind. Increasingly, it seemed to me to have moved an immeasurably long distance from the spirit of the gospels.

Nevertheless, I struggled grimly on. To say that I did not want to leave would be an understatement. The very idea of returning to secular life filled me with dread. At first, I could not even contemplate this option, which was surrounded with all the force of a taboo. But the strain took its toll and in the summer of 1968 I broke down completely. It was now clear to us all that I could not continue. Everybody was wonderfully kind to me at the end and, in a sense, this made it even more distressing. It would have been so much easier to storm out in a blaze of righteous anger. But my superiors let me take as long as I needed to make my decision. I returned to college, and after a term of heart-searching, I applied for a dispensation from my vows, which arrived from Rome at the end of January 1969.

Writing *Through the Narrow Gate* some twelve years later was a salutary experience. It made me confront the past and I learned a great deal. Most importantly I realized how precious and forma-tive this period of my life had been, and that, despite my problems, I would not have missed it for the world. Then I attempted a sequel: *Beginning the World* was published in 1983. It is the worst book I have ever written and I am thankful to say that it has long been out of print.

As its title suggests, this second volume attempted to tell the story of my return to secular life. But it was far too soon to write about those years, which had been extremely painful, even traumatic. I had scarcely begun to recover and was certainly not ready to see this phase of my life in perspective. Yet there was another reason for the failure of *Beginning the World*. At almost the exact moment when I sent the manuscript off to the publishers, my life changed completely in a most unexpected way. I started on an entirely new course, which took me off in a direction that I could never have anticipated. As a result, the years 1969 to 1982, which I had tried to describe in this memoir, took on a wholly different meaning. In that first, ill-conceived sequel, I had tried to show that I had put the convent completely behind me, had erased the damage, and completed the difficult rite of passage to a wholly secular existence. I had indeed 'begun the world'.

But I had done no such thing. As I am going to try to show this time around, I have never managed to integrate fully with 'the world', although I have certainly tried to do so. Despite my best endeavours, I have in several important ways remained an outsider. I was much closer to the truth at the end of *Through the Narrow Gate*, when I predicted that I would in some sense be a nun all my life. Of course, it is true that, in superficial ways, my present life is light years away from my convent experience. I have dear friends, a pretty house and money. I travel, have a lot of fun and enjoy the good things of life. Nothing nunnish about any of this. But although I tried a number of different careers, doors continually slammed in my face until I settled down to my present solitary existence, writing, thinking and talking almost all day and every day about God, religion and spirituality. In this book I have tried to show how this came about and what it has meant.

As soon as it was published, I realized that *Beginning the World* had been a mistake and that I would probably have to rewrite it one day. It was not a truthful account. This was not because the events I recounted did not happen, but because the book did not tell the whole story. The publishers were concerned that I should not come across as an intellectual. So I had to leave out any kind of 'learned' reflection. There could be no talk of books or poems, for example, and certainly no theological discussion about the nature of God or the purpose of prayer. I should stick to external events to make the story dramatic and accessible. I was also told to present myself in as positive and lively a light as possible, and, as I was still very unsure of myself as a writer, and assumed that my publishers knew what they were doing, I went along with this.

But most importantly, I *wanted* this cheery self-portrait to be true. It was, therefore, an exercise in wish-fulfilment, and, predictably, the result was quite awful. Today I can hardly bear to look at *Beginning the World*, which has a hearty, boisterous and relentlessly extrovert tone. It is like reading my life story as told by Ruby Wax.

The reality was very different. During those years, I did in fact live a great deal inside my head, and approached the world largely through the medium of books and ideas. To an extent, I still do. And I was not a lively, positive girl. Much of the time, I was withdrawn, bitter, weary, frightened and ill. And while I was writing *Beginning the World*, I was particularly scared – with good reason, because, yet again, my latest career had collapsed, and the future looked most uncertain. The book was badly conceived, and could be nothing but a distortion of an important and ultimately valuable period of my life.

And so I have decided to try again. We should probably all pause to confront our past from time to time, because it changes its meaning as our circumstances alter. Reviewing my own story has made me marvel at the way it all turned out. I am now glad that after all I did not simply 'begin the world'. Something more interesting happened instead – at least, I think so. T. S. Eliot's *Ash-Wednesday*, a sequence of six poems that trace the process of spiritual recovery, has been central to my journey. Ash Wednesday is the first day of Lent. Catholics have ashes sprinkled on their foreheads to remind them of their mortality, because it is only when we have become fully aware of the frailty that is inherent in our very nature that we can begin our quest. During Lent, Christians embark on six weeks of penitence and reflection that lead to the rebirth of Easter – a life that we could not possibly have imagined at the outset.

In Eliot's *Ash-Wednesday*, we watch the poet painfully climbing a spiral staircase. This image is reflected in the twisting sentences of the verse, which often revolves upon itself, repeating the same words and phrases, apparently making little headway, but pushing steadily forwards nevertheless. My own life has progressed in the same way. For years it seemed a hard Lenten journey, but without the prospect of Easter. I toiled round and round in pointless circles, covering the same ground, repeating the same mistakes, quite unable to see where I was going. Yet all the time, without realizing it, I was slowly climbing out of the darkness. In mythology, stairs frequently symbolize a breakthrough to a new level of consciousness. For a long time, I assumed that I had finished with religion for ever, yet, in the end, the strange and seemingly arbitrary revolutions of my life led me to the kind of transformation that, I now believe, was what I had been seeking all those years ago when I packed my suitcase, entered my convent and set off to find God.

Note: Some of the characters in this memoir have their own names. Those who prefer anonymity have pseudonyms.

Because I do not hope to turn again
Because I do not hope
Because I do not hope to turn
Desiring this man's gift and that man's scope
I no longer strive to strive towards such things
(Why should the agèd eagle stretch its wings?)
Why should I mourn
The vanished power of the usual reign?

Because I do not hope to know again
The infirm glory of the positive hour
Because I do not think
Because I know I shall not know
The one veritable transitory power
Because I cannot drink
There, where trees flower, and springs flow, for there is nothing again

Because I know that time is always time
And place is always and only place
And what is actual is actual only for one time
And only for one place
I rejoice that things are as they are and
I renounce the blessèd face
And renounce the voice
Because I cannot hope to turn again
Consequently I rejoice, having to construct something
Upon which to rejoice

And pray to God to have mercy upon us
And I pray that I may forget
These matters that with myself I too much discuss
Too much explain
Because I do not hope to turn again
Let these words answer
For what is done, not to be done again
May the judgement not be too heavy upon us

Because these wings are no longer wings to fly
But merely vans to beat the air
The air which is now thoroughly small and dry
Smaller and dryer than the will
Teach us to care and not to care
Teach us to sit still.
Pray for us sinners now and at the hour of our death
Pray for us now and at the hour of our death.

T. S. ELIOT
Ash-Wednesday, I.

~: 1 :~

ASH WEDNESDAY

I was late.

That in itself was a novelty. It was a dark, gusty evening in February 1969, only a few weeks after I had left the religious life, where we had practised the most stringent punctuality. At the first sound of the convent bell announcing the next meal or a period of meditation in the chapel, we had to lay down our work immediately, stopping a conversation in the middle of a word or leaving the sentence we were writing half-finished. The Rule which governed our lives down to the smallest detail taught us that the bell should be regarded as the voice of God, calling each one of us to a fresh encounter, no matter how trivial or menial the task in hand. Each moment of our day was therefore a sacrament, because it was ordained by the religious order, which was in turn sanctioned by the Church, the Body of Christ on earth. So for years it had become second nature for me to jump to attention whenever the bell tolled, because it really was tolling for me. If I obeyed the rule of punctuality, I kept telling myself, one day I would develop an interior attitude of waiting permanently on God, perpetually conscious of his loving presence. But that had never happened to me.

When I had received the papers from the Vatican that dispensed me from my vows of poverty, chastity and obedience, I was halfway through my undergraduate degree. I could, therefore, simply move into my college, and carry on with my studies as though nothing had happened. The very next day, I was working on my weekly essay, like any other Oxford student. I was studying English literature, and though I had been at university for nearly eighteen months, to be able to plunge heart and soul into a book was still an unbelievable luxury. Some of my superiors had regarded poetry and novels with suspicion, and saw literature as a form of self-indulgence, but now I could read anything I wanted, and during those first confusing weeks of my return to secular life, study was a source of delight and a real consolation for all that I had lost.

So that evening, when at 7.20 I heard the college bell summoning the students to dinner, I did not lay down my pen, close my books neatly and walk obediently to the dining hall. My essay had to be finished in time for my tutorial the following morning, and I was working on a crucial paragraph. There seemed no point in breaking my train of thought. This bell was not the voice of God, but simply a convenience. It was not inviting me to a meeting with God. Indeed, God was no longer calling me to anything at all – if he ever had. This time last year, even the smallest, most mundane job had sacred significance. Now all that was over. Instead of each duty being a momentous occasion, nothing seemed to matter very much at all.

As I hurried across the college garden to the dining hall, I realized with a certain wry amusement that my little gesture of defiance had occurred on Ash Wednesday, the first day of Lent.

That morning, the nuns would have knelt at the altar rail to receive their smudge of ash, as the priest muttered: 'Remember, man, that thou art dust and unto dust thou shalt return.' This *memento mori* began a period of religious observance that was even more intense than usual. Right now, in the convent refectory, the nuns would be lining up to perform special public penances in reparation for their faults. The sense of effort and determination to achieve a greater level of perfection than ever before would be almost tangible, and this was the day on which I had deliberately opted to be late for dinner!

As I pushed back the heavy glass door, I was confronted with a very different scene from the one I had just been imagining. The noise alone was an assault, as the unrestrained, babbling roar of four hundred students slapped me in the face. To encourage constant prayer and recollection, our Rule had stipulated that we refrain from speech all day; talking was permitted only for an hour after lunch and after dinner when the community had gathered for sewing and general recreation. We were trained to walk quietly, to open and close doors as silently as possible, to laugh in a restrained trill, and, if speech was unavoidable in the course of our duties, to speak only 'a few words in a low voice'. Lent was an especially silent time. But there was no Lenten atmosphere in college tonight. Students hailed one another noisily across the room, yelled greetings to friends, and argued vigorously, with wild, exaggerated gestures. Instead of the monochrome convent scene, black and white habits, muffled, apologetic clinking of cutlery, and the calm, expressionless voice of the reader, there was a riot of colour, bursts of exuberant laughter and shouts of protest. But, whether I liked it or not, this was my world now.

I am not quite sure of the reason for what happened next. It may have been that part of my mind was absent, still grappling with my essay, or that I was disoriented by the contrast between the convent scene I had been envisaging and the cheerful profanity of the spectacle in front of me. But instead of bowing briefly to the Principal in mute apology for my lateness, as college etiquette demanded, I found to my horror that I had knelt down and kissed the floor.

This was the scene with which I opened *Beginning the World*, my first attempt to tell the story of my return to secular life. I realize that it presents me in a ridiculous and undignified light, but it still seems a good place to start, because it was a stark illustration of my plight. Outwardly I probably looked like any other student in the late 1960s, but I continued to behave like a nun. Unless I exerted constant vigilance, my mind, heart and body betrayed me. Without giving it a second's thought, I had instinctively knelt in the customary attitude of contrition and abasement. We always kissed the floor when we entered a room late and disturbed a community duty. This had seemed strange at first, but after a few weeks it had become second nature. Yet a quick glance at the girls seated at the tables next to the door, who were staring at me incredulously, reminded me that what was normal behaviour in the convent appeared to be little short of deranged out here. As I rose to my feet, cold with embarrassment, I realized that my reactions were entirely different from those of most of my contemporaries in this strange new world. Perhaps they always would be.

There may have been another reason why I kissed the ground that evening. Ever since my dispensation had come through, many of my fellow-students and tutors had made a point of congratulating me. 'You must be so relieved to be out of all that!' one of them had said. 'It never seemed quite right for you.' 'How exciting!' others had exclaimed. 'You can start all over again! You can do *anything*, be anything you want to be! Everything is ahead of you!' It was true, in a sense: now I could fall in love, wear beautiful clothes, travel, make a lot of money – all the things that, most people assumed, I had been yearning to do for the past seven years. But I didn't feel excited or relieved. I didn't want to do any of the things that people expected. I had no sense of boundless opportunity. Instead, I felt, quite simply, sad, and was constantly wracked by a very great regret. When I pictured that dedicated Lenten scene in the convent, it seemed unbearably poignant because it was now closed to me for ever. I mourned the loss of an ideal and the absence of dedication from my new life, and I also had a nagging suspicion that if only I had tried just a little bit harder, I would not have had to leave. There had been something missing in me. I had failed to make a gift of myself to God. And so I felt like a penitent and, perhaps, when I kissed the floor that night, I had unconsciously wanted – just once – to appear in my true colours to the rest of the world.

In *Beginning the World* I described how I had threaded my way through the tables, flinching from the curious gaze of the other students, until I was rescued by a group who had become my friends and who had kept a kindly but tactful eye on me during the past difficult weeks. There was Rosemary, a cheerful extrovert, who was reading modern languages; Fiona, a gentler, more thoughtful girl; her constant companion Pat, who had been a pupil at one of the boarding schools run by my order; and finally Jane, who was also reading English. All were Catholics. All had some experience of nuns. Jane retained a great fondness for the kindly semi-enclosed sisters at her rather exclusive school. Pat had actually known me as a nun, since I had been sent to help out at her school in Harrogate. There were other people at the table for whom Catholicism and convents were alien territory and who clearly intended to keep it that way. In *Beginning the World*, I made them all tease me good-naturedly about my gaffe, question me about convent life and express shock and horror at such customs as kissing the floor, confessing faults in public and performing elaborate penances in the refectory. Maybe there was some discussion along these lines; certainly people were curious, up to a point. But I doubt that anybody was really very interested.

These young women had been quite wonderful to me. It had been Rosemary, Fiona and Pat who had marched me down to Marks and Spencer a couple of hours after my dispensation had come through and helped me to buy my first secular clothes. Rosemary had cut and styled my hair and all three had escorted me to dinner, my first public appearance as a defrocked nun. But they were probably wary of prying too closely into the reasons for what they could see had been a traumatic decision. I certainly had no desire to discuss the matter with them. In the convent we had been carefully trained never to tell our troubles to one another and it would never have occurred to me to unburden myself to my peers. And these girls had their own concerns. They too had essays to write; they were falling in love, and trying to juggle the demands of concentrated academic work with those of an absorbing social life. They were making their own journeys into adulthood, and now that the drama of my exodus was over, they almost certainly assumed that I was happily revelling in my new freedom, and were content to leave well alone.

I also knew that they could not begin to imagine my convent existence. Occasionally one of them would express astonishment if I inadvertently let something slip. 'My nuns weren't a bit like that!' Jane would insist stoutly. 'Your lot must have been abnormally strict.' Pat would look even more bewildered, because she and I had lived with exactly the same community, but her perspective, as a secular, was different. 'They were so modern and up-to-date, even sophisticated!' she would protest. 'They drove cars, were starting to go to the cinema again, and were changing the habit!' Both girls would look at me reproachfully, because I was spoiling a cherished memory. Nobody likes to be told that things were not as they imagined. But I was quite certain that my own order had not been particularly austere, and agreed with Pat that it had been far more enlightened than many. Most nuns had observed these arcane rituals, had kissed the ground, confessed their external faults to one another, and were forbidden to have what were known as 'particular friendships', since all love must be given to God. That was why the reforms of the Second Vatican Council were so necessary.

I also knew that, taken out of context, such practices as kissing the floor or reciting the Lord's Prayer five times, with your arms in the form of a cross, would seem sensationalist, exaggerated and histrionic. But in reality they became as normal to us as breathing, a routine part of our lives, sometimes even a little tedious. To speak of these things outside the convent would give a false impression. I had not left the convent because we had to do public penance, but because I had failed to find God and had never come within shouting distance of that complete self-surrender which, the great spiritual writers declared, was essential for those who wished to enter into the divine presence.

So I did not speak of my old life to anybody and most people assumed that I had, therefore, simply put the past behind me.

'Much better out than in,' Miss Griffiths, my Anglo-Saxon tutor said decisively, as we sat in her elegant college rooms drinking sherry one evening. 'You look much better out of that habit, my lamb. And, you know, however things turn out in the future, I'm certain you made the correct decision. If you come back to me in fifteen years' time and say "Look, five children and a divorce!" I shall *still* say that you were right to leave.'

This, of course, was quite true. There had been no other option. But as I looked around at the richly coloured William Morris curtains, the massive bookcases, and the oriental rug in front of the fire, I felt entirely out of my element. Every item of furniture, down to the tasteful ornaments glinting on the marble mantelpiece and the cunningly arranged lamps, had been designed for comfort and pleasure. In the convent, everything had been pared down to essentials: scrubbed floorboards, uncurtained windows, starkly positioned tables and chairs. Each was a perpetual reminder of how we too were to be stripped inwardly of any lingering attachment to the world, to people and to material objects, if we were to be worthy of God. Nevertheless, it was nice here, I reflected, the sherry blurring the room in a golden glow. Perhaps I could become a don one day, and have a pretty room like this, piled high with books. Perhaps I could dedicate myself to scholarship, as I had once devoted myself to the disciplines of the religious life.

My tutors' comfortable, peaceful rooms increasingly seemed a haven. As I walked around Oxford, I realized that the world had undergone radical change while I had been inside. I had begun my Postulantship in 1962, just before the sexual, social and political upheavals of the 1960s. In the 50s, when I had grown up, young people had looked like miniature versions of their parents. Boys wore flannel trousers and ties; and girls were clad in demure twinsets and prim pearl necklaces. We were kept under fairly strict surveillance. I had been only seventeen years old when I had left this world, a product of convent schooling with an ingrained fear of sexuality. The dangers of premarital sex had been burned into my soul. And, indeed, before the contraceptive pill, it was a risky enterprise for girls. But all that had clearly changed. Girls and boys walked with their arms casually slung around one another, in ways that might or might not be sexual. Some embraced languorously in public places. They certainly did not subscribe to the old shibboleths, though I knew that my Catholic friends still agonized about how far they could go without falling into mortal sin. But the demeanour of these young people was even more startling. They had long flowing hair instead of the tidy repressed bobs of my youth. The neat sweaters and ties had been thrown out. Their attire was careless, ragged and often eccentric – flowered or ruffled shirts for the men, evening dress worn with jaunty insouciance in the middle of the day; the girls wore skirts that barely covered their thighs or long, flowing, vaguely eastern robes.

Above all, they were confident. I had just come from an institution in which young people were required to be absolutely obedient and submissive. We were never supposed to call attention to ourselves, never to question or criticize established custom, and, if you were invited to address your elders, you did so with deference and courtesy that bordered on the obsequious. We knelt down when we spoke to our superiors to remind ourselves that they stood in the place of God. These young people, however, seemed openly and unashamedly rebellious. They protested, noisily and vociferously. They even took part in events called 'demonstrations', where they publicly aired their grievances, a concept that could not have been more alien to me. What on earth were they trying to demonstrate? What had they got to be so angry about?

This was the spring of 1969, and I now realize that, on the international stage, the weeks that had elapsed since my departure from the convent had been momentous. Richard Nixon had been inaugurated as President of the United States, Yasser Arafat had been elected chairman of the Palestine Liberation Organization, and a military coup had taken place in Pakistan. Palestinian terrorists had attacked an Israeli airliner at Zurich airport; Nixon had authorized the secret bombing of Cambodia, and Soviet and Chinese forces had clashed on the Manchurian border. I knew nothing of this. I had never heard of either Nixon or Arafat, and would have had difficulty in locating either Cambodia or Manchuria on the map. In the convent, we had not kept abreast of current events. In the novitiate, indeed, we did not even see newspapers. We were told of the Cuban missile crisis, which occurred a few weeks after I entered, but our superiors forgot to tell us that the conflict had been resolved, so we spent three whole weeks in terror, hourly expecting the outbreak of World War Three. Mother Walter also told us about the shocking assassination of John F. Kennedy, the Catholic president. Later, this strict embargo on the news was mitigated somewhat, but in general political interest was frowned upon. As a result, I entered the secular world completely ignorant of the problems of our time, and because I lacked basic information, could not make head or tail of the newspapers. What I needed was a crash course in the current political scene, but this was not available, and I felt so ashamed of my ignorance that I did not dare to ask questions that would have revealed its abysmal depths.

As it happened, there were students at my college who would have been delighted to take my education in hand, because St Anne's was probably the most politically-minded of all the five women's colleges. This was, of course, the great period of student unrest. In January, while I was preparing to leave my convent, the Czech student Jan Palach had publicly burned himself to death to protest Soviet occupation, and in Spain student disturbances had led to the imposition of martial law. In April, left-wing students at Cornell University in New York State staged a three-day 'sit-in' to draw attention to their outdated curriculum, while at Harvard, three hundred students occupied the campus administration building, and were forcibly removed by the police. Oxford was also aflame with revolutionary enthusiasm. But the ringleaders looked absolutely terrifying to me – unapproachable in their righteous rage. I would as soon have approached a charging bull, as expose my political *naïveté* to them

Almost every Saturday afternoon, I watched in bewilderment as crowds of students gathered on the college lawn, carrying placards emblazoned with slogans directed against the government, the university authorities, the syllabus, and something mysteriously called 'The System'. They seemed furious about everything. I heard astonishing reports of violent meetings in the English Faculty Library, where undergraduates screamed abuse at the dons. They demanded that the formidable linguistic requirements of the course be scrapped, that the syllabus include contemporary literature (it currently stopped at 1900), and that the study of Anglo-Saxon be abolished. To me, who had fallen passionately in love with Old English literature, this rage was incomprehensible. When I heard some of my fellow-students at St Anne's inveighing against the 'tyranny' of the dons, I gazed at them nonplussed. After the draconian atmosphere of the convent, the mildly liberal, laissez-faire atmosphere of St Anne's seemed like paradise to me. These kids didn't know what tyranny was! But then I remembered my last painful year in the convent, when *I* had been the rebel, and had argued relentlessly with my superior about the Rule. I had also been full of rage, constantly frustrated by the convent 'Establishment', and passionately eager for change. Perhaps I was not so different from my contemporaries, after all. We had just been fighting in different wars.

29

Willy-nilly, I found myself drawn into the climate of protest. Somewhat to my astonishment, I had been approached the previous term, while still a nun, and asked if I would let my name go forward as a candidate in the forthcoming elections for the Junior Common Room committee. I had been reluctant – a humiliating defeat seemed inevitable – but my supporters were insistent and it seemed churlish to refuse. For a couple of weeks I slunk past the noticeboard, wincing at the sight of my photograph, complete with veil and crucifix, beside those of my wild-haired rivals. What student in her right mind would vote for me? I looked like a creature from another planet. I scarcely dared to approach the noticeboard on the morning after the election, but, amazed, I saw the same photograph prominently displayed, informing the college that I was now the secretary of the Common Room.

So now I found that, whether I liked it or not, I was being drawn into student politics. I had to attend protest meetings in the JCR, and take part in intense committee discussions about how to bring St Anne's into line with the 60s. The most pressing issue was cohabitation in the colleges. Until the early twentieth century, women had not been permitted to attend the universities of Oxford and Cambridge. It was assumed that the effort of studying to the same level as men would blow their inferior little brains to smithereens. But some women had refused to accept this exclusion, had set up colleges of their own, and the university had eventually accepted them. The five women's colleges of Oxford had been a Trojan Horse, smuggling the weaker sex into the male preserve of academia, but now, some believed, their day was over. All the colleges should be open to both sexes. Men should be allowed to come to St Anne's and women should be admitted to the prestigious male colleges of Magdalene or Balliol.

The present arrangements did not penalize women educationally. All students attended exactly the same lectures and took the same examinations. Men and women competed against one another on equal terms. The college could arrange for us to study with any tutor of our choice. Fellows of St John's and Merton had taught me, for example, and the St Anne's Fellows, especially in the English department, which had an exceptional reputation, tutored male students. In fact, the women's colleges often had a higher rate of academic success: because there were fewer places for women, the standard of those selected at the entrance examinations tended to be higher. During my years at Oxford, St Anne's regularly came top of the Norrington Scale, the league tables which charted the performance of undergraduates in the final examinations. By the 1960s, therefore, women had proved that they were quite capable of holding their own in the university.

So to many, mixed-sex colleges seemed the next logical step. But that might take time. Women, for example, would require better bathroom facilities than the gruesome arrangements in the men's colleges. But as a preliminary, students all over the university were demanding that the 'Gate Hours' be abolished. We all had to be in college by midnight, and visitors were obliged to write their names in a book at the Porter's Lodge, and sign out before the gates were closed. Of course, people disregarded these 'Gate Hours'. There were several places where it was very easy to climb over the college wall; everybody knew this and most turned a blind eye. If somebody were caught, he or she would suffer a mild reprimand and pay a small fine. But in these heady days of revolution, these rules seemed absurd to the more radical and, in my new official capacity, I had to attend heated meetings in which students and dons argued about them. As far as I was concerned, the question was wholly academic. There was no man clamouring to spend the night in my small college room, and the possibility of my climbing over the college wall after a love tryst was about as remote as my scaling the Great Wall of China. Moreover, until a few weeks before, I had been a very visible representative of an institution that condemned all sex outside marriage as gravely sinful.

But those days were over. I still regarded myself as a Catholic, but I was aware that its traditional teachings on sexual matters had become extremely controversial within the Church itself. Some of the nuns had been devastated the previous summer when Pope Paul VI's encyclical *Humanae Vitae* had outlawed the practice of artificial contraception. In one of our convents, I had heard, one of the more adventurous nuns had caused a minor sensation, on the morning after the papal ruling, by putting a pill (a mere aspirin, of course) on each of the sisters' breakfast plates. Nuns naturally had no personal stake in the Pope's decision, but the encyclical had become symbolic of the authoritarian government of the Church: by ignoring the advice of married couples, doctors and psychologists in order to reassert the Church's traditional position, Paul VI seemed to be withdrawing from the new spirit of the Vatican Council, retreating yet again from the laity, and turning his back on the plight of those married couples who were loyal Catholics but who wanted to limit their families responsibly. The Catholic Church was undergoing its own sexual revolution, but most of those who campaigned against *Humanae Vitae* would not have condoned the use of the contraceptive pill by unmarried people and many of them would have expected me to take a strong line on the 'Gate Hours' issue and speak up for good Catholic values. A few weeks earlier, I would probably have done this without hesitation.

Now, though, I was no longer an official representative of the

Catholic Church, and while I listened to the arguments from the Common Room floor, I found, somewhat to my surprise, that I felt no desire to support those students who fought against the abolition of the 'Gate Hours' on Christian grounds. My indifference was in part the result of an anxious preoccupation with my own personal drama. I was drained and exhausted by the events of the past few weeks, and had little energy to spare for this battle. But there was more to it than that. When I thought about the issue, I found only a question mark where the old conviction should have been. I had experienced this time and again recently; it seemed as though I had discarded a good deal of my old religious self when I had taken off my habit. Beliefs and principles that I had taken so completely for granted that they seemed part of my very being now appeared strangely abstract and remote. In fact, I reflected uneasily, I did not seem to think or feel anything very strongly any more.

I had now been studying at Oxford for nearly eighteen months, and for two years before that I had been preparing for the rigorous entrance examinations to the university. Academia had its own disciplines that were as exacting in their own way as those of the convent. One of these was already ingrained in my heart and mind: do not pronounce on subjects that you know nothing about. I had now acquired a healthy respect for the limits of my own knowledge and expertise. One of the chief effects of my education so far had been an acute consciousness of everything that I did *not* know. What did I know about sex? I asked myself during the explosive Common Room debates. What did I know about men, relationships or love? What did I know about the brave new world of the 60s? I knew nothing at all, and was not, therefore, entitled to an opinion. And, remembering my own protests against an outworn system only a few months earlier, I felt that I should listen carefully to those who demanded change. In the meantime, there seemed no need for me to contribute.

I was not allowed to remain on the sidelines, however. The college had appointed a new Dean of Discipline. For years Dorothy Bednarowska, my literature tutor, whose approach had been liberal and relaxed, had filled this post. The new Dean was Emily Franklin, a large, bovine woman who, I learned with some astonishment, was only a few years older than I. Her pupils told me that she was a fine teacher, if a trifle dull. But despite her relative youth, Miss Franklin had no time for student protest, and had decreed that not only would there be no change in the current 'Gate Hours', but that the gates would be locked an hour earlier. Furthermore, she had increased the fines for offenders, and, as her *pièce de résistance*, a barbed-wire hedge had appeared, without warning, underneath the favourite climbing-in spot. The college was in an uproar.

'Of course, this is quite absurd', Mrs Bednarowska said, drawing me aside one day in the corridor. 'The silly woman is out of her mind. The Virgin Vote will be delighted, but it won't wash.'

'The Virgin Vote?' I asked.

'Oh – the conservative wing on the college governing body,' Mrs Bednarowska replied. '*You* know who they are! They're not all virgins, of course, but they might as well be. Anyway, the point *is*, my dear, what is the Common Room going to do about this?'

'We're sending a deputation to the Dean, asking her to reconsider,' I said, a little dazed by my tutor's assumption that I would take the liberal line.

Mrs Bednarowska gave her characteristic yelp of laughter. '*That* won't work – though it's very correct, of course,' she opined, as she strode off with her curiously splay-footed gait to her rooms.

What I had not realized was that, as Secretary, I was expected to go with the president of the JCR to put our views to Miss Franklin. Maureen Mackintosh, a clever girl with masses of long red hair, was one of the most politically radical students in college, and I found her distinctly alarming. I always expected her to treat me with disdain, and dreaded lest she strike up a conversation about Vietnam and Cambodia in which I would certainly not be able to hold my own. And what on earth was an ex-nun doing campaigning for students to spend illicit nights together? To my relief, however, Maureen seemed untroubled by my presence as we set off for Miss Franklin's apartment. We sat together, side by side, on a sofa in the Dean's room, drinking tiny glasses of sherry in an atmosphere that was distinctly chilly, while the champion of the Virgin Vote sat with her back to the window, her cat Smokey purring noisily on her knee.

'No more concessions!' she replied, when we formally requested that the new measures be withdrawn and the wire fence removed. She repeated the phrase like a mantra at intervals during the ensuing discussion, almost chanting it in a strangely expressionless falsetto. 'No more concessions!'

This irritated me. 'You can't call these "concessions",' I pointed out. 'You've taken away rights that have already been given to us. We're simply asking for a return to the *status quo*. Not for concessions.'

I might as well have kept my mouth shut. 'No more concessions,' Miss Franklin repeated.

'The Common Room won't accept this, Miss Franklin,' Maureen replied sternly. 'If you don't at least restore the old "Gate Hours", we shall have to take action. And that barbed wire is extremely dangerous. You didn't warn us. Somebody could have been seriously injured.'

'Then she – or he – would only have themselves to blame,' Miss Franklin retorted smoothly. 'You are here to be educated, not to indulge in unlicensed sex at all hours. Nor to organize childish demonstrations, at the expense of your studies.'

Maureen sighed, and again I felt indignant. The remark was entirely uncalled for. Maureen's political activities certainly did not interfere with her work. She had recently won one of the highly coveted and prestigious Kennedy Scholarships for post-graduate study in the United States, and was going to Berkeley, which, I gathered, was the new Mecca for 60s revolutionaries. 'I can only repeat,' she persisted, with admirable self-control, 'that the Common Room will have to take action.'

'No more concessions!' Miss Franklin sang implacably, turning away from us to give her attention to Smokey, and crooning endearments in his ear as he tried to climb over her ample bosom to the windowsill. I studied her with perplexity. All my life I had accepted the fact that some opinions were right and others wrong. And yet how deeply unattractive such a stance could be. Nothing we could say would cause Miss Franklin a moment's doubt. Her mind was closed to any other possibility. She reminded me of those virginal saints in the Catholic legends who were utterly impermeable: wild beasts fell back from them in terror; swords could not pierce their invulnerable flesh; even when they were thrust into brothels, they proved impenetrable. They seemed to be surrounded by an invisible shield, a barricade that preserved them in a world of their own. In the convent we had sung hymns to the Virgin Mary, which compared her to a 'garden enclosed' or 'a well sealed up'. I had been proud to take my vow of chastity, but I knew that right now I was no longer on the same side as the Virgin Vote.

I turned to Maureen inquiringly. She nodded and rose to her

feet. 'I don't think we have anything more to say to one another,' she said.

That night, under cover of darkness, I accompanied Maureen and a group of other students to the college wall. Each of us carried a pair of wire-clippers. Grimly and methodically we demolished the barbed-wire fence, and deposited it in a heap of ten-inch fragments on the lawn outside Miss Franklin's window. I seemed to have thrown in my lot with the sexual revolution.

But a few days later, when I went to my first party, I was not quite so sure. Yet again, when I walked into the murky, smoke-filled room, the noise almost knocked me sideways. The parties I had attended before the convent had been sedate, elderly affairs. Under the benign but hawk-like gaze of our elders, we had lurched around the room in pairs, trying to match our faltering steps to the polite strains of waltzes and quicksteps. Bored, I had to admit, almost to stupefaction. But nobody seemed bored here, I noted, as I groped my way uncertainly to a corner where I had spotted Jane with her boyfriend Mark and accepted a glass of wine. I sipped it gratefully, hoping it might have some anaesthetic effect, as I stared, dazed, at the scene before me. The room was as dark as an underground cavern, the gloom relieved periodically by flickering lights that transformed us all into granite-hued hags. Jane's skin looked blanched, her lips black. On the other side of the room, I could see Pat and Fiona, their pretty, fresh faces also drained of colour, their animated expressions curiously at variance with their corpse-like pallor.

'You look stunned.' Mark, a tall, solemn young man with the regular good looks of a male model, bent towards me solicitously. He had to shout above the din of a jangled crashing that I was trying to identify as music. Amplified male voices screamed, guitars thrummed, cymbals clashed and, beneath it all, a drum beat a primitive, disturbing pulse.

'No. No, not at all,' I yelled back, politely. It would have been so much easier, I now realize, if I had admitted how strange this new world appeared to me, had shared my confusion and dismay and let people in. But I seemed quite unable to do this. In my own way, I was quite as impenetrable as Miss Franklin or any Virgin Martyr. I wanted people to believe that I was taking it all in my stride and that leaving a convent was as easy as falling off a log. I didn't want to be the object of pity or curiosity, and the convent habit of reticence was now almost reflexive. I tried to take an intelligent interest. 'Who are the singers?'

With a unanimity that was almost comical, Jane and Mark both did a double-take. 'The Beatles, of course!' Jane exclaimed. And then, as I continued to look blank, she added, a little more tentatively: 'You have heard of the Beatles, haven't you?'

I had. Just. My sister had mentioned the group to me on one of her visits, and the name had cropped up occasionally in the conversation of my fellow-students. But even though it was now 1969, I had no idea who the Beatles really were, no notion of their extraordinary impact on British society during the 60s, had never encountered Beatlemania, and had certainly never knowingly heard a note of their music. Jane and Mark tried to explain to me what the Beatles meant for their generation, but I took little in. I could see that they were slightly alarmed by my ignorance. Jane was looking at me thoughtfully, though I made her laugh when I asked, in some perplexity, why the band was named after those rather unpleasant black insects. On my other side, Mark was reciting the lyrics, which shocked me by their unabashed expression of naked need: 'Love, Love Me Do!', 'I Wanna Hold Your Hand!', 'Please, Please Me!' I could not even have admitted to myself that I had such needs, let alone shouted my yearnings aloud in such wild abandonment. Yet the words touched some raw place within me, making me aware of my loneliness in this crowded room. All around me I noticed feet tapping, heads nodding, lips mouthing the words of the songs, glances exchanged as though a phrase had a special private significance. The Beatles were a current that united everybody at the party; a thread that bound the room together. They were the spokesmen of their generation, but even though they must have been about my own age, they could not speak for me. I was present at the party, but only as an outsider. The ease and confidence with which the Beatles simply said what they wanted appalled me, and yet I longed to be able to do the same. Even today, more than thirty years later, when I have come to appreciate their real genius, I find their songs almost unbearably poignant. Those desires had been schooled out of me, and yet the painfully direct appeal of the lyrics made me realize that I wished that I had them. I felt my throat swell with unshed tears: 'All You Need Is Love'.

But love in *this* context? I stared bemused at the dancers. These new acquaintances of mine had obviously never heard of the quickstep. Instead, they were leaping, twisting, gyrating together in pairs. Some even danced singly, and no one followed any predetermined pattern. They shot into the air, waved their arms, swung out legs at odd angles. Doing what came naturally. But it was not natural for me. For a second I felt a pang of pure envy. I would love to be able to do that, I thought, and to be so wild, uninhibited and free. These students were living fully and intensely, in a way that I could not. When Mark, kindly, asked me if I would like to dance, I shook my head. I could no more fling myself around like that than fly.

For years, I had been trained in absolute physical restraint.

Nuns had to walk smoothly, at a moderate pace. Unless there was some dire emergency, they must never run. At first all this had been difficult. Most of us were young and it was hard to quench the impulse to run upstairs, two steps at a time, or to hurry to a class when late. But gradually I had learned to keep myself in check. I had, however, never fully mastered these rules of 'religious modesty' which were supposed to regulate a nun's demeanour. I was, and am, clumsy and badly coordinated. I never quite achieved the noiseless, gliding carriage of some of my fellow-novices, and I was always hopeless at 'custody of the eyes', the quaintly named monastic habit of keeping one's gaze fixed on the ground. I like to know what is happening, and if I heard an unusual noise or somebody entering the room, I found it almost impossible not to check it out. I was often reprimanded for staring boldly at my superiors, instead of casting my eyes down humbly. I did not mean to be disrespectful, but I had been brought up to look people directly in the eye when I spoke to them. Yet for all these failings, some of this convent discipline had rubbed off on me, and to this day I have never been able to dance. I have often fantasized about being a disco-girl, imagining an alternative Karen, able to leap about, let go, and disappear into the music. It must be a marvellous feeling. But it has never been possible. At a very impressionable age, my body was schooled in quite other rhythms and it has, for better or worse, taken the print.

As I watched the dancers, I felt completely out of my element. I could see that this kind of dancing was unabashedly sexual. It reminded me of the ceremonial dances performed by Africans that I had seen occasionally on documentaries or newsreels. It was interesting, but had nothing to do with me. I tried to look nonchalant and at ease, but felt miserably that I must look as out of place as the Queen, in her suburban, matronly clothes, carrying her ubiquitous handbag like a shield, staring with a glazed smile at the ritual dances performed in her honour during a tour of the Commonwealth. I had found, to my considerable sorrow, that even though I no longer belonged in the convent, I didn't belong out here either.

Looking back, I can see that, during those first few months, I was experiencing something akin to the culture shock of those who, for one reason or another, have been forced to leave homes in Pakistan, Palestine or Zimbabwe, and migrate to a Western country. The violent upheavals of the twentieth century have made millions of people homeless in one traumatic uprooting after another. Exile is, of course, not simply a change of address. It is also a spiritual dislocation. Anthropologists and psychologists tell us that displaced people feel lost in a universe that has suddenly become alien. Once the fixed point of 'home' is gone, there is a fundamental lack of orientation that makes everything seem relative and aimless. Cut off from the roots of their culture and identity, migrants and refugees can feel that they are somehow withering away, and becoming insubstantial. Their 'world' – inextricably linked with their unique place in the cosmos – has literally come to an end.

Now I was sharing something of this twentieth-century experience. True, I had left my 'home' in the convent of my own free will, and was not languishing in a camp, but I did feel in exile from everything that made sense. Because I could take nothing for granted, and did not know how to interpret the 60s' world that had come into being during my absence, I too felt that the world had no meaning. Because I had lost my fundamental orientation, I felt spiritually dizzy, lacking all sense of direction, not knowing where to turn. I could see the same kind of stunned

41

bewilderment in the eyes of the old Bangladeshi lady who served in the corner shop near St Anne's, where we bought newspapers and sweets.

I saw it again in the eyes of Sister Mary Sylvia, a nun in my college. She had recently come from India to take a degree in English literature, and was living in my old convent at Cherwell Edge. In India, apparently, she had earned a first-class degree, had run schools, and held high office in her order. But the move from India seemed to have unhinged her completely. She was quite unable to write a coherent essay, complete the simple procedures that enabled her to take books out of the college library, or remember the times of lectures and seminars. I knew about this all too well, because – as one familiar with the arcane ways of nuns – I was constantly called to the rescue. When I tried to help Sister Mary Sylvia with her essays, I noticed that she simply could not take in what I was trying to tell her. One day when she failed to turn up to the philology class that, as usual, was being held in the small seminar room, I found her sitting all alone in the dining hall with her notebook, smiling benignly, while puzzled college servants tried to work around her, waxing the floor and laying the tables for dinner. She was clearly in shock, could make no sense of her surroundings, and had entirely lost her bearings. I was in better shape, but I sensed something of what she was going through. Deprived of the familiar, I too seemed to have lost my way in a world that meant nothing to me. When later that year, I watched my namesake Neil Armstrong make his 'giant leap for mankind', and jump on to the pitted surface of the moon, the utterly bleak, dark and eerily empty lunar landscape epitomized exactly what Planet Earth had become for me.

*　　*　　*

It was little better when I returned home during the vacation. My family gave me a wonderful welcome, but they were expecting the daughter and sister who had left home seven years earlier. My parents were tremulously eager to resume normal family life, but they seemed almost strangers to me. They had been allowed to visit at six-monthly intervals and I had been permitted to write to them only once every four weeks. These communications had, to put it mildly, been unsatisfactory. Visits to the convent parlour were starchy and artificial. Nuns were not allowed to eat with 'seculars', so my parents had some appalling meals surrounded by a bevy of nuns pouring out tea and making polite conversation, while I went off to eat with the community in the convent refectory. My sister Lindsey, who was three years younger than I, had hated these visits. As she watched us process into the chapel, genuflecting before the altar with near military precision, and kneeling motionless in the pews, the underlying tension, the humourless rigidity, and the fear that somebody might ruin this perfection by making a mistake so petrified her that, to the amusement of some members of the community, she often passed out, and had to be carried outside, even though she never fainted anywhere else. My letters were little better. We were never allowed to speak of what happened inside the convent, and since for years I scarcely left the enclosure, I had to confine my remarks to anodyne descriptions of the countryside or reverential accounts of church services.

My parents, therefore, had no idea what my life had been like for the last seven years. At a deeper and more worrying level, I found that I simply could not respond to their affection. I shied away from any intimacy, could not bear to be touched or embraced, and could speak to my family only in the rather formal, distant way of nuns. Naturally my parents were hurt, I felt bad about hurting them, and there was an impasse. The training seemed to have worked, after all. My capacity for affection had either atrophied or been so badly damaged that it could not function normally. I felt frozen and could see what people meant when they said that their heart had turned to stone. I could almost feel this new hardness within, like a cold, heavy weight. I had become a person who could not love and who seemed incapable of reaching out to others. Whether I liked it or not, I was now a garden enclosed, a well sealed up.

Leaving the religious life in those days was not like changing your job or moving house. Our novitiate had not simply provided us with new professional skills, and left our deepest selves untouched. It was a conditioning. For about three years, we were wholly isolated from the outside world, and also from the rest of the community. The door of the Noviceship was kept permanently locked, and we spoke to the other nuns only on very special feast-days. This meant that the novitiate became our whole world; no other existed for us, and the whims and moods of our Mistress acquired monumental importance. When we were punished, it seemed a cosmic event; when we were lonely or miserable, there was no possibility of comfort. The atmosphere was frigid, and sometimes even frightening. At night in our long dormitory, we often heard one another weeping, but knew that we must never ask what was wrong. We lived together in community, cheek by jowl, but were so lonely that we might as well have been living in solitary confinement. We became entirely dependent upon our Superior's every move, and accepted her worldview and her opinion of ourselves as gospel truth. I was so young that I could draw upon no experience to counter this regime. So the world receded, and the tiny dramas and cold values of Noviceship life filled my entire horizon.

This type of isolation is central to the rituals of initiation, practised in the ancient world and in many indigenous societies today. On reaching puberty, boys are taken away from their mothers, separated from their tribe and subjected to a series of frightening ordeals that change them irrevocably. It is a process of death and resurrection: initiates die to their childhood and rise again to an entirely different life as mature human beings. They are often told that they are about to suffer a horrible death; they are forced to lie alone in a cave or a tomb; they are buried alive, experience intense physical pain (the boys are often circumcised or tattooed), and undergo terrifying rituals. The idea is that in these extreme circumstances, the young discover inner resources that will enable them to serve their people as fully functioning adults. The purpose of these rites of passage is thus to transform dependent children into responsible, self-reliant adults, who are ready to risk their lives as hunters and warriors, and, if necessary, to die in order to protect their people

Our training had been an initiation. We too had been segregated from the world, deprived of normal affection, and subjected to trials that were designed to test our resolve. We too were to be warriors of sorts – soldiers of God, who practised the military obedience devised by St Ignatius Loyola, the founder of the Jesuits, whose Rule we followed. The training was designed to make us wholly self-reliant, so that we no longer needed human love or approval. We too were told that we were to die to our old selves, and to our worldly, secular way of looking at things. Of course, we were not buried alive in a tomb or anything of that sort, but we were constantly undermined, belittled, publicly castigated, or ordered to do things that were patently absurd. As Ignatius's Rule put it, we were to become utterly pliable to the will of God, as expressed through our superiors, in the same way as 'a dead body allows itself to be treated in any manner whatever, or as an old man's stick serves him who holds it in every place and for every use alike'. Dead to ourselves, we would live a fuller, enhanced existence, as Jesus had promised in a text that we liked to quote: 'Unless the grain of wheat falls into the ground and dies, it will remain nothing but a grain of wheat. But if it dies, it will bear much fruit.' On our profession day, while the choir sang the Litany of the Saints, we lay under a funeral pall, symbolically dead to the world, and to our greedy, needy, selves that clung, infant-like, to ordinary, worthless consolations.

Now, it seemed to me that I had indeed died, but I was certainly not bringing forth much fruit. I felt as though I had entered a twilight zone between life and death, and that instead of being transfigured, as I had hoped, I had got the worst of both worlds. Instead of being full of courage, fearless, active and protective of others, like the initiate of a tribal rite of passage, I was scared stiff. Unable to love or to accept love, I had become less than human. I had wanted to be transformed and enriched; instead I was diminished. Instead of becoming strong, I was simply hard. The coldness and frequent unkindness, designed to 'toughen us up', had left me feeling merely impaired, like a piece of tough steak. The training was designed to make us transcend ourselves, and go beyond the egotism and selfishness that hold us back from God. But now I seemed stuck inside myself, unable either to escape, or to reach out to others. An initiation prepares you for life in the community; I had left the community that I was supposed to serve, and was inhabiting a world that I had been trained, at a profound level, to reject.

One of the most difficult things about returning to the family home was that at every turn I kept meeting my former self – the undamaged, seventeen-year-old Karen, who had been vital and full of hope. In my bedroom, I remembered how I had sat in this very chair, and lain on that very bed, full of excitement about the great adventure I was about to begin. When I took down a book from my shelves, I remembered my wonder and delight when I had first read this novel, or come across that poem. There were boxes of letters and postcards to friends, full of affection and an easy intimacy that I could no longer imagine. That person had gone; she had indeed died under the funeral pall. I felt bereaved – full of grief as though for a dead friend. This, I knew, was entirely my own fault. My superiors had not intended this to happen to me; they had not meant to push me into this limbo. I had not responded properly to the training. I had been too feeble to go all the way, to let myself truly die. I had kept on hankering for love and affection, and wept because I was too weak to endure these robust austerities. I had attempted something that was beyond my capacities, and been injured by my presumption – like a little girl who, in her impatience to become a ballerina, insists on going *en pointe* too early, before her feet are properly mature, and hobbles herself for ever.

Love was beyond me; even friendship was difficult. But at least I had my work. I knew that I was good at academic study. Despite the upheaval of leaving the religious life, I had done very well at Oxford so far and was expected to get a first-class degree. With that under my belt, I could become an academic, engaged in full-time study and teaching the subject I loved. So I returned to Oxford for the summer, full of renewed determination to do even better and make this prospect a reality. If I had lost one cloister, I could immure myself in my studies and find another.

To my dismay, I found a new obstacle. This term I was sent out to study with a young tutor at one of the men's colleges. My tutorial partner was Charlotte, an immensely gifted girl who had her own troubles. Her mother had died during our first year and Charlotte had become anorexic. Even though she seemed over the worst, she was still thin and wary of food. We had often eyed each other knowingly, wryly acknowledging that we were both struggling, so it was good to be spending more time together. Charlotte wanted to be a novelist. 'She can really write,' Dorothy Bednarowska had told me, and she had already introduced Charlotte to a literary agent. But Charlotte found the academic study of literature difficult. Her work was brilliant and original but, 'Studying literature so critically and technically is bad for my writing,' she told me. Fearing that it would cramp her own style, she refused to study the novel at all. As was customary at Oxford, we had to read our essays aloud to our tutor during the weekly tutorial, and Charlotte was obviously perplexed, even repelled by mine. 'I don't know how you churn out all this stuff,' she had said to me once. 'It's beautiful in a way. Your essays are like Gothic cathedrals, with all the right scholars and theories slotted together and built into a massive structure of conformity.' I wasn't sure that I liked the sound of that. I enjoyed reading the literary criticism that Charlotte hated. I found it fun to weigh one scholar against another and make a pattern of my own out of other people's thoughts. But I was uneasily aware that not much of myself was going into my work, and that what I was presenting, week after week, was other people's ideas rather than my own.

That would not be allowed this term, however. Our new tutor was a rather affected but reputedly very clever young don at one of the more modern colleges. We sat in his bright, book-lined room overlooking the forecourt, watching some students teasing the goldfish in the moat. Dr Brentwood Smyth sprawled elegantly in a large leather armchair, leaping up occasionally to consult a text. 'You got a Violet Vaughan Morgan prize, didn't you?' he asked me. 'Impressive. You must be very good at exams.' I could tell that he did not think much of this accomplishment. He seemed more interested in Charlotte, whose original, thoughtful response to his questions clearly intrigued him.

'Oh, don't let's have a fixed time!' he cried impatiently when I asked him when we should come for tutorials. 'That's the trouble with the women's colleges! They're organized like high schools. Just ring me up when your essay is done.'

'What should we write about?' I asked him.

'Oh, anything you like! I'm not going to set you one of those dreary exam questions. I'm sure you get quite enough of those at St Anne's. No. Just write me something on one poem. Take "Frost at Midnight". Coleridge. Don't read any literary criticism. Just live with the poem for a week and then tell me what it means to *you*. Not to anybody else. When you're ready, give me a call.'

This was music to Charlotte's ears, but worrying for me. I could see that it was a good idea and, indeed in later years when I came to teach literature myself, I would often set my students a similar task. But the problem back then was that I just couldn't do it. I needed to escape into other people's books and minds because, when left entirely to my own devices, I found that I had nothing to say. It wasn't exactly that the poem did not speak to me. It was clearly an extraordinary work. I could have made it the basis for a fascinating essay on the English Romantic movement. But what did the poem say to *me*? That was what Dr Brentwood Smyth wanted to know and I didn't know what I was going to tell him. I found myself thinking of some other lines by Coleridge, written in a period of deep depression, when he looked out at the evening sky 'with its peculiar tint of yellow-green', at the thin clouds, the moon and the stars:

I see them all so excellently fair,
I see, not feel, how beautiful they are!

I should have been pierced by the poem, and then have leapt out to meet it. I used to be like that. I remembered how deeply poetry had touched me while I was at school. But yet again, as with my relations with people, there was only deadness, nothingness. I was now impervious even to the literature that I thought I had loved.

An initiation is supposed to make you self-reliant, but mine had made me dependent. As I struggled to fill the requisite number of pages for my essay, I had to face the grim fact that I no longer had ideas of my own. Indeed, I had been carefully trained *not* to have them. There had been a moment early in the Postulantship, when I had heard a warning bell. We were doing a little course in Apologetics, which explained the rational grounds for faith. I was set an essay: 'Assess the historical evidence for the Resurrection.' I had read the requisite textbooks, could see what was required, and duly produced a discussion of the events of the first Easter Sunday that made Jesus' rising from the tomb as uncontroversial and unproblematic historically as the Battle of Waterloo. This was nonsense, of course, but that did not seem to matter in Apologetics.

'Yes, Sister, very nice.' Mother Greta, the pale, delicate nun who was supervising our studies, smiled at me as she handed back my essay. 'This is a very good piece of work.'

'But, Mother,' I suddenly found myself saying. 'It isn't true, is it?'

Mother Greta sighed, pushing her hand under her tightly-fitting cap and rubbing her forehead as if to erase unwelcome thoughts. 'No, Sister,' she said wearily. 'It isn't true. But please don't tell the others.'

This did not mean that Mother Greta did not believe in the resurrection of Jesus, or that she had lost her faith. But she had studied at the prestigious Catholic University of Louvain in Belgium and knew that the kind of essay I had written was no longer regarded as a respectable intellectual exercise. A careful study of the resurrection stories in the gospels, which consistently contradict each other, shows that these were not factual accounts that could ever satisfy a modern historian, but mythical attempts to describe the religious convictions of the early Christians, who had experienced the risen Jesus as a dynamic presence in their own lives and had made a similar spiritual passage from death to life. As I stared wordlessly back at Mother Greta I knew that, if it had been up to her, she would have scrapped this course in Apologetics and introduced us to a more fruitful study of the New Testament. But, like any nun, she was bound by the orders of her superiors. What I had written was not true, because the insights of faith are not amenable to rational or historical analysis. Even at this early stage, in a confused, incoherent way, I knew this, and Mother Greta knew that I knew it.

It was a sobering moment, and when I look back now on that scene in the Postulantship, with the autumn sun coming through the window, the older nun mentally tired and demoralized, while the postulant gazed at her blankly, both of us deliberately turning our minds away from the light, I wonder what on earth we all thought we were doing. I had been set a quite pointless task. For a week, while preparing my essay, writing it and learning how to dispose of the obvious problems with various mental sleights of hand, I had been doing something perverse. I had been telling an elaborate lie. I had deflected the natural healthy bias of my mind from a truth that was staring me in the face and forced it to deny what should have been as clear as day. Years later, while I was having my breakdown, I learned that Mother Greta had been very anxious indeed about the way we were being trained, had voiced her disapproval, and had been overruled. What had our superiors been about, and why did I not tear up that dishonest piece of work, or at least argue with Mother Greta? I had simply gone along with the whole unholy muddle.

But I was only eighteen years old and this had not been an isolated incident. On the very first day of our Postulantship, Mother Albert, our Mistress, explained that during the first years of our religious lives we would constantly be told things that seemed incredible or irrational. But they only seemed this way because we were lacking in spiritual maturity. We were learning to inhabit a different element from the rest of the world, to breathe another atmosphere. We were still fresh from 'the world' and its taints; we still thought and responded like secular people, but now we had to enter into God's perspective. Had God not told Isaiah:

For my thoughts are not your thoughts,
My ways are not your ways,
For as high as the heavens are above the earth
So are my thoughts above your thoughts, my ways above your
    ways.

So when we were tempted to question the ideas, principles and customs of the order, we must remember that as yet we were simply not in a position to understand. We were like babies, learning an entirely new language. One day, in the not too distant future, when we had developed spiritually, we would see all these matters quite differently. Until then, we just had to wait patiently, in what the mystics had called the cloud of unknowing, and all would be revealed. So my lying little essay on the Resurrection was part of this larger programme.

So was the fact that I had once, during my Postulantship, spent hours treadling a sewing machine that had no needle. To be fair, this was the result of a misunderstanding, but the underlying principle still applied. I was finding all needlework very difficult indeed, and had just put the good sewing machine in our community room out of action. Furious, Mother Albert told me to practise on an older machine in the adjoining room for half an hour a day. But it had no needle. My mistake was to point this out. Mother Albert had been meaning to replace that needle for some time, but it had completely slipped her mind. She was already angry with me, however, and I was not supposed to answer back in this way. 'How dare you!' she said, her voice cold with rage. 'Don't you know that a nun must never correct her superior in such a pert manner. "There's no needle in that machine!"' she cried, tossing her head in supposed imitation of my defensive manner. 'You will go to that machine next door, Sister, and work on it every day, needle or no needle, until I give you permission to stop.'

So I did, treadling away at the empty machine, telling myself that because I was acting under obedience, however pointless this exercise might seem to a profane eye, this was the best possible way of spending my time. It was God's way. I had almost succeeded in quelling the objections that stubbornly erupted in my mind from time to time, when Mother Albert walked into the room two weeks later and stared at me as though I had lost my wits. But this time, when she cried in outraged astonishment, 'What on earth do you think you are doing?' I was ready for her.

'Practising machining, Mother,' I replied demurely.

'But there's no needle in that . . .'

Even as she spoke, I saw light dawning and realized that she had completely forgotten about the whole thing. She clapped her hand to the back of her head, and turned away abruptly, lips twitching with suppressed mirth. After recovering herself, she gave me a searing lecture on my pride and disobedience. No nun should ever correct her superior, as I had done that day, even if convinced that she was wrong. As far as I was concerned, my superior was right, because she stood in the place of God. It was my wretched intellectual pride that blocked my spiritual advancement, and I would make no progress as long as I refused to regard things from a supernatural point of view.

Yet could you behave like that indefinitely, without inflicting real and lasting damage on your mind? I remembered the moment, a year or so later, when I had realized that my mind no longer worked freely. It was the recreation hour in the Noviceship. We all sat around the long table in the community room with our needlework, Mother Walter, our Novice Mistress, presiding. That night we were talking about the liturgical changes that were being introduced by the Second Vatican Council: the mass was being said in English instead of Latin, for example, and that morning the children in the adjacent boarding school had played guitars to accompany a song they had composed themselves. Mother Walter had not enjoyed that song. She was devoted to the Gregorian chant and had taught us to love it too. Even though she once told me that I had a voice like a broken knife-grinder, I had to sing in the choir and, though I could never hit the higher notes and was ruefully aware of the tunelessness of my efforts, I was beginning to appreciate the spiritual quality of plainsong – the way the music circled meditatively around the words and drew attention to a phrase or obscure preposition that could easily have passed unnoticed, but which proved to have rich meaning. Now it looked as if the days of the chant were numbered and though Mother Walter would have cut out her tongue rather than criticize the Vatican, she was convinced that this would be an irreparable loss. 'Of course the Council is inspired by the Holy Spirit,' she was saying, 'but it is hard to see how we can replace a musical tradition that goes back hundreds of years. Just think: St Bernard would have sung the same chant as we do. So would Thomas Aquinas and Francis of Assisi. And now we have to listen to those silly children playing guitars.' For a moment, the measured calm of her voice faltered and her face darkened in a way we had learned to dread.

'But, Mother,' Sister Mary Jonathan, a novice who was a year ahead of me and who had been my 'guardian angel' when I had begun my novitiate, spoke up eagerly. 'Surely the changes needn't necessarily be a disaster? After all, there's nothing intrinsically wrong with playing a guitar at mass, is there?'

Mother frowned. 'I should have thought,' she replied coldly, 'that this is a matter we need not discuss.' We all bent our heads obediently over our needlework, distancing ourselves. The topic had been closed. No one would dream of taking it any further, against the expressed wish of our superior.

'But some people,' Sister Mary Jonathan continued, to my astonishment, 'might go to church initially to enjoy the guitar because they like that kind of music. *We've* learned to love the chant, but lots of people can't understand the Latin, and the music is so different from anything they are used to that they can't make anything of it.'

Mother Walter laughed shortly. It came out as an angry bark. 'Anyone who needs a guitar to get them to mass must have a pretty feeble faith!' Her eyes had hardened and her lower lip protruded in a scowl. The tension in the room was almost palpable. Nobody ever answered back like that and the rest of us were sewing as though our lives depended upon it. But I found myself looking hopefully at Sister Mary Jonathan, willing her to go on. I used to be able to do that, I thought wonderingly. I used to like exploring different points of view, building up an argument step by step, sharpening an idea against somebody else's mind. But I could no more do that now than run naked down the cloister. Not only would I never have dared to cross Mother Walter – and, indeed, I hastily reminded myself, Sister Mary Jonathan was breaking several rules at once – but I wouldn't be able to think like that any more. I no longer had it in me. But Sister Mary Jonathan did.

'The guitar might give God a chance,' she countered brightly. 'People might come to listen and then find something more . . .'

'Really, Sister!' Mother's voice was thunderous. 'I would have thought that you of all people would understand.' Sister Mary Jonathan was very musical. 'Do you think God needs a *guitar*,' she uttered the word as though it were an obscenity, 'to give him a chance?'

Sister was undeterred. 'But surely Jesus would have used a guitar, if he'd been alive today?'

'Nonsense, Sister! I've never heard such rubbish! He would have done no such thing!'

I had to bend my head quickly over the stocking that I was darning to hide an involuntary smile. I had a sudden mental picture of Jesus standing on a hill in Galilee, surrounded by his Jewish audience, singing plainsong. He looked pretty silly.

Mother Walter had spotted me. 'I am glad that you find this amusing, Sister,' she said with heavy sarcasm. 'I find it extremely sad. Sister Mary Jonathan has committed a serious fault against obedience and against charity, by spoiling recreation for everybody!'

That had been the end of the matter; though, when Mother wasn't looking, Sister Mary Jonathan had winked at me and pulled a face. With hindsight, that complicity had been prophetic. She had left the order shortly before I had. She had fallen in love with a young Jesuit, with whom she was studying at London University. Somehow she had held on to herself better than I had. I was quite sure that she would not find it difficult to tell anybody what she thought. My problem, as I wrestled with my highly unsatisfactory essay for Dr Brentwood Smyth, was that I had no thoughts of my own at all. Every time the frail shoots of a potentially subversive idea had broken ground, I had stamped on them so firmly that they tended not to come any more. True, at the very end of my religious life I had argued with Mother Praeterita, my Oxford superior, but the ideas I used against her had not been mine. I was simply parroting books and articles that I had read. It seemed that I could no longer operate as an intellectual free agent. You can probably abuse your mind and do it irrevocable harm, just as you can damage your body by feeding it the wrong kind of food, depriving it of exercise or forcing your limbs into a constricting straitjacket. My brain had been bound as tightly as the feet of a Chinese woman; I had read that when the bandages were taken off, the pain was excruciating. The restraints had been removed too late, and she would never walk normally again.

I knew that a good nun must be ready to give up everything and count the world well lost for God. But what had happened to God? My life had been turned upside down, but God should still be the same. It seemed that, without realizing it, I had indeed become like St Ignatius's dead body or the old man's stick. My heart and my mind both seemed numb and etiolated, but God seemed to have gone too. In the place that he had occupied in my mind, there was now a curious blank.

Or perhaps it was only now that I could admit to this God-shaped gap in my consciousness. One of the most painful failures of my convent life had been my inability to pray. Our whole existence had God as its pivot. The silence of our days had been designed to enable us to listen to him. But he had never spoken to me.

Every morning at six o'clock, we had knelt in the convent church for an hour of meditation, according to the method that St Ignatius had designed for his Jesuits in the *Spiritual Exercises*. This had been a highly structured discipline. As a preliminary step, we prepared the topic the night before. Each of us spent fifteen minutes selecting a passage from scripture or a devotional book, and making a note of the topics that we intended to consider in the morning. Ignatius's meditation was based on a three-part programme: See, Judge and Act. First we all stood in silence for a few minutes, reciting to ourselves a prayer that reminded us that we were in the presence of God, and then we knelt down, took out our books and notes, and began with 'See'. This meant that we had to use our imaginations to picture the gospel scene we had chosen, and even if the subject of our meditation was more abstract, we had to give it a local habitation and 'place' it in some concrete way. Ignatius had thought it very important that all the faculties be engaged, so that the whole man (Ignatius had a poor opinion of women) was brought into the divine ambience. This 'composition of place', as it was called, was also meant to ward off distraction. If you were busily picturing the road from Jericho to Jerusalem, evoking a sense of the Middle Eastern heat, looking at the sand dunes, listening to the braying donkeys and so forth, your imagination was less likely to stray to profane topics. At least, that was the theory.

Next came 'Judge', when the intellect was brought into play.

This was the point when you were supposed to reflect on the topics you had listed the night before. Finally you proceeded to 'Act' which, for Ignatius, was the real moment of prayer. As a result of your deliberations, you made an act of will, applying the lessons you had learned to the day that lay ahead. There had to be a specific resolution. It was no good vaguely vowing to live a better life from that day forward. You had to settle for something concrete: to try harder with your sewing, for example, or to make a special effort not to think uncharitable thoughts about a sister who irritated you beyond endurance. Prayer, Ignatius taught, was an act of will. It had nothing to do with pious thoughts or feelings; these were simply a preparation for the moment of decision. Ignatian spirituality was never an end in itself but was directed towards action and efficiency. He wanted his Jesuits to be effective in the world and their daily meditation ensured that their activities would proceed from God.

But this did not work for me. Every morning I resolved that this time I would crack it. This time there would be no distractions. I would kneel as intent upon God as my sisters, none of whom seemed to have my difficulties. I had never before had any problems of concentration. I had always been able to immerse myself in my studies for hours at a time. But to my intense distress, I found that I could not keep my mind on God for two minutes. The whole point of the careful preparation was to prevent this. It was acknowledged that at 6.00 a.m. we were likely to be less than fully alert and would need help in focusing our thoughts. But as soon as I sank to my knees, my mind either went off at a tangent or scuttled through a maze of pointless worries, fears or fantasies, or else I was engulfed by the torpor of physical malaise. Like most adolescents, I craved sleep and experienced the 5.30 a.m. call as a violent assault. I often felt queasy with hunger and fatigue, and clung dizzily to the pew in front of me. At 6.30, the clock in the cloister chimed and we could sit down. But this sweet relief gave way to another trial, as I battled against sleep, and was comforted to see that even some of the older nuns listed and slumped in such a way that it was clear that they had succumbed. The minutes crawled by until the sacristan appeared to light the candles on the altar as a welcome signal that mass was about to begin.

At breakfast, an hour later, we were supposed to examine our meditation, going through a ten-point questionnaire. Had I made myself fully conscious of the Presence of God? No. Had I made sufficient effort in the 'composition of place'? No. Had all my senses been fully engaged? No. And so on. I didn't need the fifteen minutes we were supposed to devote to this self-appraisal. I didn't have to spend any time grading my performance on a scale of one to ten. I was just a Big Zero.

Meditation was only the first spiritual exercise of the day. Four times daily we chanted our version of the divine office in choir. Twice a day, for fifteen minutes, we examined our consciences, according to Ignatius's five-point plan: this involved marking off one's faults and achievements in a little book, and counting the number of times we had failed to perform the special task for this week (in Ignatian terminology this was called the 'particular examen'): there was half an hour's spiritual reading, a community exercise during which one of us read aloud and the rest continued our everlasting needlework; half an hour's silent 'adoration' in the chapel in the early evening; and the private recitation of the rosary. Yet again, I flunked. Throughout my seven years, I hugged to myself the shameful secret that, unlike the other sisters, I could not pray. And, we were told, without prayer our religious lives were a complete sham. For several hours a day on every single day of the year, I had to confront and experience my abject failure. In other ways, my mind was capable and even gifted, but it seemed allergic to God. This disgrace festered corrosively at the very heart of my life and spilled over into everything, poisoning each activity. How could I possibly be a nun if, when it came right down to it, I seemed completely uninterested in God and God appeared quite indifferent to me?

I don't know quite what I thought *should* be happening. Certainly I didn't expect visions and voices. These, we were told, were only for the greatest saints and could be delusions, sent by the devil to make us proud. But all the books that I read about prayer spoke of moments of 'consolation' that punctuated the inevitable periods of dryness. Periodically God would comfort the soul, make it feel that he was near and enable it to experience the warmth of his presence and love. God would, as it were, woo the soul, offering this periodic breakthrough as a carrot, until the soul outgrew this need and could progress to the next stage of its journey. Gradually the soul would be drawn into the higher states of prayer, into further reaches of silence, and into a mysterious state that lay beyond the reach of thoughts and feeling.

That was the theory. But far from progressing to these more advanced states, I never left base-camp. Of course there were moments when I felt moved by the beauty of the music or uplifted by a rousing sermon, but in my view this did not count. It was simply an aesthetic response, something that even an atheist could experience at a concert or when she was exposed to skilful rhetoric. I never had what seemed to be an encounter with anything supernatural, with a being that existed outside myself. I never felt caught up in something greater, never felt personally transfigured by a presence that I encountered in the depths of my being. I never experienced Somebody Else. And how could I possibly hope to have such an encounter when my mind was unable to wait upon God? Prayer, we were always told, was simply a way of quieting the soul, enabling it to apprehend the divine. You had to gather up your dissipated faculties, bring them together and present yourself, whole and entire, to God, so that every single part of your mind and heart could honestly say with the prophet Samuel: 'Speak, Lord, for your servant is listening.' But my mind, heart and faculties remained scattered. Try as I would, I could not re-collect them, so there was no way that God could get through to me.

I tried to discuss this with my superiors, of course. On several occasions, I explained that I never had any 'consolation' and could not keep my mind on my meditation. But they seemed frankly incredulous. 'You're always so extreme, Sister!' Mother Frances, the Mistress of Scholastics, had said with irritation. 'You're always exaggerating. *Everybody* has consolation at some time or another. Are you seriously telling me that in all the six years of your religious life you have never *once* experienced consolation?' I had nodded. She had looked baffled. 'Well, I really don't know what to say to you,' she had said, clearly at a loss. 'That's most unusual. I don't know how anybody could go on without some consolation. But I'm sure that things aren't really as bad as you say,' she had gone on briskly. 'You probably just feel a bit down at the moment, that's all, and being you, you have to make a major drama out of the whole business.' This was not reassuring. I must be a particularly hard case, I thought miserably. As for my confession that I could never keep my mind on my prayers, this was also airily waved to one side. 'Everybody has their off-days, Sister!' Nobody would believe that I would love to have had some off-days, because it would have meant that some of my days were 'on'.

So even in the convent, God had been conspicuous by his absence from my life. And that, I became convinced, must be *my* fault. My case seemed to be so peculiar that it could not be a mere failure of the system. If only I had tried a little harder, concentrated just that little bit more, or found more interesting topics for meditation. The quality of a nun's commitment was reflected in the quality of her prayer. And how could I hope to sense God's presence when I continually broke the silence, frequently had uncharitable thoughts, and, above all, constantly yearned for human affection, and wept when reprimanded? It was, of course, a vicious circle. The more empty my prayers, the more I sought consolation in mundane things and in people. Round and round. Then there were my secret doubts. Even though I tried to tiptoe gingerly around difficult articles of faith, I could not stop wondering whether the Virgin Mary really *had* been conceived without Original Sin and been taken up body and soul into heaven after her death. How did anybody *know* that Jesus was God? And was there even a God out there at all? Was that why I never encountered him in prayer? As I knelt in the chapel, watching my sisters kneeling quietly with their heads bowed contemplatively in their hands, I would sometimes wonder whether it wasn't a bit like the Emperor's New Clothes. Nobody ever experienced God but nobody dared to admit it. And then I would mentally shake myself. How could God reveal himself to a nun who harboured these shocking doubts?

And so came the morning when, just a few days after I had been dispensed from my vows, my alarm rang at six o'clock and instead of getting up and walking down the road to St Aloysius's Church for early mass, I simply switched it off and went back to sleep. For seven years, each day had begun with prayer and Eucharist, but now there seemed no point in any of that. I would still go to mass on Sundays, of course, because this was obligatory, binding upon all Catholics. Leaving the Church as well as the convent was at present a step too far. But the very idea of kneeling silently in a darkened church – yet again – filled me with immense fatigue. I cannot do that any more, I told myself wearily that morning; I simply cannot do it. The accumulated failure had left me feeling not merely exhausted but also slightly sick.

I *had* tried, I told myself, as I turned over and faced the white-washed brick wall of my cheerful college room. I had not been the best nun in the world, but I had honestly done my best, and my superiors had all tried to help me. But it was just no good. If God did exist, he clearly wanted nothing to do with me, and, right now, I couldn't blame him. There was something in me that was proof against religion, closed to the divine. Let it go, I told myself sleepily. Don't beat yourself up any longer. Just live simply as a secular, and give up these inappropriate spiritual ambitions. You're in the world now. Make friends with it. One day at a time.

But soon even that would become impossible.

∾ 2 ∾

THE DEVIL OF THE STAIRS

It began with the smell. It was a sweet but sulphury aroma, reminiscent of bad eggs and giving off an aura of imminent menace. Like any odour, it was also intensely evocative. I recognized it immediately. This was how it always started. In the convent, I had several times been assailed by this strange smell, had looked around for a cause and found the world splintering around me. The sunlight, the flickering candles of the altar and the electric light seemed to oscillate crazily; there would be a moment of pure nausea, and then nothing: a long, long fall into emptiness.

These fainting attacks had occurred four or five times, to the intense irritation of my superiors. Once it had happened on the day before Easter, and although afterwards I felt reasonably well, Mother Frances had sent me to bed in disgrace and I was forbidden to attend the midnight Vigil. The next day I had to go to mass at Our Lady of Victories in Kensington High Street, escorted as if under penal guard, and was subjected to a merciless scolding on my return. 'Emotional indulgence. Exhibitionism . . . weakness of will' – I knew the list almost by heart. Nuns were not supposed to faint like wilting Victorian ladies; we were meant to be strong women, in control of our lives, exercising an iron constraint over our emotions and bodily functions. Ignatius had wanted his Jesuits to be soldiers of Christ, and we were to cultivate the same virile spirit. Whoever heard of a soldier fainting on the parade ground, crumpling helplessly into a heap as he stood to attention before his commanding officer? And so these blackouts of mine had been greeted with cold disapproval. 'You must pull yourself together, Sister,' Mother Frances had concluded, tight-lipped.

But how was I supposed to do this? Whatever my superiors thought, I did not plan these bouts of unconsciousness. They terrified me. When I felt one coming on, I fought it to the last. And there seemed to be no reason for them. My superiors assumed that they were caused by my unruly emotions, but they rarely happened when I was upset. On that Holy Saturday night, for example, I had been feeling positively light-hearted. We were coming to the end of the penitential season of Lent and were all looking forward to the magical liturgy that evening: the lighting of the new fire, the strange unearthly chant of the Exsultet (the great theological hymn of the Easter mystery), the blessing of the baptismal waters, and the triumphant mass at midnight. The ritual re-enacted the passage from darkness to light, from death to life. There were also the simple earthly joys of Easter Sunday to look forward to: we had boiled eggs for breakfast, could talk all day long, and read our Easter mail. When the attack happened, I was feeling nothing but pleasurable anticipation. Where had it all come from: the smell, the fractured light, the sickness and the slide into unconsciousness?

Nobody ever thought that I should see a doctor. Fainting meant only one thing: hysteria. It had been the same at my school. When girls had fainted, they were subjected to a hostile inquisition and told in no uncertain terms to stop showing off. I had once watched my headmistress, Mother Katherine, grab a girl who had fainted during a seemingly interminable church service, seize her under the armpits, haul the inert body down the polished aisle, and dump it outside the chapel door, returning immediately, stony-faced. Over the years, I had imbibed this ethos, and though I could not account for these attacks, I assumed that even though I might not be feeling especially upset, I was displaying some subconscious need for notice, love or intimacy. The blackouts, I concluded, must be a bid for attention. And yet, I reflected wryly, my unconscious mind must be very slow on the uptake. You would think that by now it would have learned that, far from eliciting the tender concern I craved, the fainting simply inspired anger and disdain.

So my fainting, we all agreed, was emotional self-indulgence. And in my last year in the order, my body did indeed seem to be staging a rebellion all of its own. I wept uncontrollably, convulsed more by anger than grief; I found it impossible to keep my food down; suffered such severe nose bleeds that I had to have a vein cauterized, and ... I fainted. It was as though my whole physical self had risen in protest and demanded that I take notice, telling me that, however much I might want to stay in the convent, something was badly wrong. Finally in the refectory of our convent in Harrogate, where I had been sent for the Long Vacation, I had given up the battle and succumbed to a break-down. It was only logical to assume that there had been unconscious tension all along, which had finally and irrevocably surfaced and taken me out of the religious life. And now I was out in the world. I was no longer struggling to conform to a way of life to which I was not suited. I was free, fortunate, privileged to be attending one of the finest universities in the world, and even though I was having some trouble adjusting, I was now on the mend. Wasn't I?

So why were the symptoms recurring, as though my body had not been informed that the battle was over? Why was it behaving in the same old way? I was not kneeling in a convent chapel this time, but sitting in a pleasant library in Merton College. The room was full but not unduly crowded; it was not stuffy, even on this warm summer day. The tall leaded windows were open and a light, fragrant breeze wafted into the room, gently lifting the threadbare curtains. I was listening to John Jones's lectures on nineteenth-century England, enjoying the slightly eccentric cast of his mind and his delightful command of the language, when the familiar stench choked me, the voice of the lecturer became a confused babble of meaningless sound, the light in the room looked suddenly uncanny, there was a moment of pure terror, and then I felt myself falling down that familiar narrow shaft.

When I opened my eyes, I was conscious of a hard band of pain across my forehead. The brown blur in front of me composed itself into the grain of a polished wood floor, and I groaned and rolled over on to my stomach to try to blot out the world for a few more minutes.

'I think she's coming round now.' The voice was male and familiar. Slowly, as from a deep well, the memories came back to me. The lecture . . . John Jones . . . 'Keep back and let her get some air.' To my right I could see a large scuffed brogue and an expanse of worn corduroy trouser. I knew that in a few moments I would feel embarrassed, but right now the world had shattered into separate, meaningless shapes, none of which seemed related to anything else.

'Look, I think we'd better call it a day,' Mr Jones was saying.

I tried to raise my head, but it was pushed firmly down again. 'I don't think any of us feels like carrying on with the lecture. Does anybody know who this poor lady is?'

'Yes, I do – she's at my college. I can take her home. Karen, it's Jane.' I peered up at her and tried to smile. She looked strange from this unfamiliar angle and I realized that she was alarmed. Gradually I began to be aware of the disruption I had caused.

'I am . . . so sorry,' I muttered, as I always did after one of these attacks. 'So sorry.'

'For heaven's sake,' Mr Jones sounded genuinely astonished, and when I looked round at him, his large kind face was creased with concern. 'You didn't do it on purpose. We're just sad for you.' That was a bit of a change. I blinked uncertainly. 'You still don't look too good to me. How are you feeling? That was quite a long faint. Better get her to a doctor?' That last, clearly, was addressed to Jane.

'Definitely.' Jane sounded uncharacteristically subdued. 'Do you think we could phone for a taxi?' I closed my eyes, mentally shaking my head. Sympathy, doctors, taxis – I could not take it all in. I must have tried to protest feebly, but nobody took any notice and I lay there gratefully, thankful that it was over, but feeling hugely tired.

As we drove up the Banbury Road towards St Anne's and climbed the short flight of stairs to my room in the Gatehouse, Jane kept up a determined flow of chatter. The fright that I had seen in her eyes had gone and she was now recasting the whole event in her usual ebullient manner.

'I always longed to faint at school,' she said cheerfully, as she opened the large window overlooking the college lawn. We could see students hurrying past in ones and twos, going about the business of a normal Tuesday morning. 'I always thought it would be a sign of such sensitivity and refinement. I tried everything. Put blotting paper in my shoes, held my breath. Nothing happened. Not a hope. I'm just too horribly healthy.'

I smiled as Jane glared at herself in the mirror and threw back her long blonde hair. It was indeed difficult to imagine her wilting feebly; she was built on too large a scale, was too confident for that. 'Have you ever fainted before?' she asked, suddenly serious.

I nodded. 'It used to happen quite a lot in the convent. It's all emotional – all in the mind. At least, that's what the nuns said.'

'Don't tell me! I was at a convent school, remember? And I suppose you *have* been under a strain, giving up that lovely peaceful life.' I grimaced slightly, amazed as I always was that even people who knew nuns at first hand had such an unrealistically idyllic image of convent life. 'Tell me,' Jane said abruptly, 'do you feel guilty?'

I thought hard for a moment. People often asked me this, because they seemed to associate Catholicism with guilt. 'No,' I said at last. 'I don't feel at all guilty. Guilt is not the word.' One of the good things that I had learned from my superiors was that guilt could be pure self-indulgence, a wallowing in the ego. Guilt, I was told, usually sprang from misplaced pride; it might simply be chagrin that you were not as wonderful as you hoped. 'I feel sad,' I went on, 'a failure, in some ways. But not guilty exactly.'

'God, you are lucky!' Jane flung herself down in my armchair. 'I feel endlessly, endlessly guilty about sleeping with Mark. It means that I can't go to mass, communion or confession, because I don't have a "firm purpose of amendment", as they say. I'm not going to stop doing it, so I haven't truly repented. So now I'm that dreadful thing called a lapsed Catholic.'

'Do you miss it?' I asked, and then surprised myself by adding, 'Do you care?' I noticed how far I had moved in the last few months. This time last year, I could not have imagined living outside the Catholic Church, but now I wasn't so sure. Did God really care so much about Jane's sexual life? Was sleeping with her fiancé as bad as telling lies or being unkind, sins which didn't debar anybody from the sacraments?

Jane sat quite still for a moment and then shrugged. 'In some ways, no – of course, I don't care. I can't believe that God – if there *is* a God, I must say I do wonder sometimes – is really a narrow-minded prude. And I know that lots of people right here in college just carry on going to communion, no matter what they do. But I can't manage that. It seems dishonest . . .' she tailed off.

'But do you miss it?' I probed. Jane seemed so much at ease with the world and so bracingly positive, that it was hard to imagine her style cramped by a disapproving Church.

'Oh, heavens, yes!' she breathed. 'I used to love the liturgy at school. Last Christmas, Mark and I were in Paris and went to Midnight Mass in Notre Dame. You can imagine . . . Mark couldn't believe that I had been able to give all that up. "You're a heroine," he said. Though I can't say I believe in much of it any more, frankly.'

I wondered how much of a Catholic I really was. No one would ever have admitted to doubts in the convent, and it was somehow liberating to have Jane do it for me. 'But that's enough about me!' Jane got up and reached for her books. 'I'm going to get the college nurse to have a look at you . . . I know, I know, she really is perfectly awful, but I promised Mr Jones. And it *is* sensible, you must admit, even if it is all due to stress. Mr Jones was right. That really was a very long faint.'

Before she left, Jane looked around the room. A typically modern box: shiny cork flooring, matching orange curtains and bedspread, desk and dressing-table combined. 'You ought to try to put your own stamp on this,' she said appraisingly. 'It looks anonymous. Have some of your own things around. Whoops!' she laughed. 'You probably haven't *got* any things. Well, you'd better acquire some. You're not a nun now. No more holy poverty for you. What about a record player? You like music and you won the Violet Vaughan Morgan last year. You must have some of that prize money stashed away in the bank. Go on, treat yourself.'

'Yes,' I replied thoughtfully. 'Perhaps I will.'

The college nurse was brisk and matter-of-fact. Yes, the fainting was almost certainly due to stress. I had had a confusing time and it was bound to take its toll. But worse things happened at sea. Mustn't give in or feel sorry for yourself. Get back into the swing of things. Put your best foot forward. I listened to this string of clichés with mounting irritation. It was easy to be brisk and bracing about other people's difficulties. I was quite aware that leaving a convent must rank very low on the scale of human suffering. Certainly, a bad divorce or bereavement must be even more painful, but, after all, it was not a competition. 'Do make an appointment with your GP, however,' the nurse concluded. 'Always wise to get these things checked out, especially if it's happened before.'

I promised that I would. It did seem a sensible precaution, and I was grateful for the concern that was so different from the icy response of my superiors. News of the faint travelled fast. People I scarcely knew stopped me in the corridor and asked how I was feeling. Pat and Fiona gave me a bunch of flowers and Rosemary had thoughtfully provided a little vase, realizing that I probably didn't have one. Charlotte asked me quite a lot about the incident and we again silently sized each other up as fellow-neurotics.

Charlotte and I were no longer tutorial partners. Dr Brentwood Smyth had got rid of me fairly rapidly and passed me on to one of his graduate students. The college had responded indignantly. I was being groomed for a first-class degree and should not have been relegated to what they regarded as the scrap heap in this way. Now I was back with Mrs Bednarowska, who was quite happy with my intricate gothic essays and everybody seemed pleased with me. But I had not forgotten the emptiness I had encountered when I had had to rely on my own thoughts, and felt that Dr Brentwood Smyth had seen through my polished intellectual exterior to the vacuum at the core, as had Charlotte, though she knew too much about the numbing effects of shock to dismiss me as contemptuously as our tutor.

So some good had come out of that faint. I had become closer to Jane, let down my guard a little and allowed people to see that all was not well. And I decided to take Jane's advice and buy myself a record player. As the new spirit of Vatican II slowly percolated through the convent, we had been encouraged to listen to music. A record player had appeared in the community room of the Scholasticate, and we were allowed to use it during the afternoon recreation hour. I discovered a new world. I remember walking into the room one day after doing the washing-up and being almost shocked by the beauty of the slow movement of Beethoven's Emperor Concerto. Now thanks to my simple little player, for which I paid the princely sum of twenty-five pounds, I could have this sublime treat any time I wanted. Jane introduced me to the late quartets of Beethoven and I would play these almost nightly. This, I was aware, was probably the kind of experience I had sought in religion. While I listened, I felt my spirit knitting together. Things began to make sense.

But one night, the world broke apart again. It was early evening and I was tired, having stayed up most of the previous night to write my essay. This weekly 'essay crisis', as we called it, was a feature of Oxford life. Throughout the college, lights burned all night as students scribbled earnestly, trying to get their piece finished in time. Since leaving the convent, I had fallen into this weekly ritual and in a perverse way quite enjoyed it. There was something rather magical about sitting alone in the lamplight, surrounded by darkness and absolute stillness. Occasionally there would be a gentle scratching on the door, and Rosemary or Charlotte, whose essay night coincided with my own, would peer cautiously round the door and we would have a midnight coffee-break before returning to our books. The next day I felt hollow and depleted, but triumphant, and I used to revel in the post-tutorial euphoria: essay done, duly praised, and a lovely fresh assignment beckoning me invitingly into the next week.

But on this particular occasion, my eyes prickled with fatigue. Suddenly I found myself invaded by the familiar stench, but this time it was different. My brain felt as though a cosmic potato masher was pounding it, reducing it to long worms of sensation like spaghetti, but spaghetti that was alive. I could hear a bell ringing mournfully in the distance and I was convinced that some-body was standing beside me. I could almost glimpse his face out of the corner of my eye. An aged, senile mask, with empty eyes. Some part of me knew that there was nobody there, and that if I reached out to touch him my hand would encounter empty air. And yet I could not connect this knowledge with the spectre because it had its own reality, its own absolutely commanding presence. I had no leisure to think about this, because I was gripped suddenly by a quite overwhelming fear. When I looked around me, the room was wholly unfamiliar, as though I had never seen any of these objects before. The world had become uncanny and horrifying. I did not know who, what or where I was, but was aware only of my extreme terror, a cold sickening dread that made everything around me seem brown, rotten and repulsive, because it had no meaning.

And yet, of course, it wasn't like that at all. I am trying to describe an experience that has nothing whatever to do with words or ideas and is not amenable to the logic of grammar and neat sentences that put things into an order that makes sense. Maybe I could explain it better if I were a poet. But I am sure that this is the kind of horror that Hieronymus Bosch tried to convey in his paintings. It is as though a comforting veil of illusion has been ripped away and you see the world without form, without significance, purposeless, blind, trivial, spiteful and ugly to the core. T. S. Eliot describes something similar in the third poem of *Ash-Wednesday*. He is climbing a spiral staircase, a mythical image of the 'ascent' of the mind and heart to spiritual enlightenment. But 'At the first turning of the second stair' he sees a shape twisted into the banister, surrounded by vaporous, foetid air, and he is forced to struggle with 'the devil of the stairs'. He leaves these convoluted forms behind, and at the next turning finds only darkness: 'Damp, jaggèd, like an old man's mouth drivelling, beyond repair, Or the toothed gullet of an agèd shark', the underbelly of consciousness that lurks in the basement of all our minds.

When the horror recedes, and the world resumes its normal shape, you cannot forget it. You have seen what is 'really' there, the empty horror that exists when the consoling illusion of our mundane experience is stripped away, so you can never re-spond to the world in quite the same way again. The revelation remains embedded in your soul and affects everything you feel and everything you see. But when you try to express this vision in words, you inevitably distort it, and find yourself writing purple, melodramatic prose. Better to be as simple as Coleridge, when he describes the recurrent terror of the ancient mariner after his ordeal, which makes him feel:

> Like one that on a lonesome road
> Doth walk in fear and dread,
> And having once turned round walks on,
> And turns no more his head;
> Because he knows, a frightful fiend,
> Doth close behind him tread.

The words are flat, and the image of the 'frightful fiend' deliberately banal, but the simple description of a fear that is constantly beside you but just out of reach captures the sensation exactly.

This was not an isolated experience. Some weeks later, while I was shopping in Cornmarket, the world seemed to have lost all connection with the fundamental laws that give it meaning and coherence. It took on the grotesque aspect of a cartoon. The women ahead of me in the queue at Marks and Spencer looked as though they belonged in a primitive painting by Beryl Cook; their features became coarse and alien. Again there was that paralysing fear. I had no idea where I was or what I was doing. When I reached the till, the woman sitting behind it seemed to be shouting at me, pointing to my purse. I stared back at her blankly, unable to understand what she was saying or what she wanted me to do. Somebody took my purse from me, and opened it, but I could make nothing of the round metal discs inside. Dazed, I put down my wire basket and wandered out into the street. I don't know how long it was before I found myself sitting outside Brasenose College in Radcliffe Square, contemplating the perfect dome of the Camera, an image of wholeness and harmony.

It was one of my favourite haunts, a place where I loved to come and study. It had been raining. I was wet and chilled, but back in my skin on a planet that had returned to normal.

I never imagined for one moment that these were supernatural visitations. I knew at once that I must be ill and assumed that, like my fainting attacks, these 'visions' were symptoms of strain. This seemed oddly appropriate. The world that I had rejected had turned on me and exacted a revenge, in which my surroundings periodically took on a nightmarish unfamiliarity. But as these strange interludes became more frequent, I became frightened, and took myself off to the doctor. How was I going to live with a horror that descended upon me without warning and made it impossible for me to function? It seemed as though the world and I had become chronically incompatible; that I would never be able to live in it. And what if one day I remained trapped on the other side of the looking glass?

The doctor dismissed these worries as excessive but agreed that I was not very well. He talked sagely about 'anxiety attacks', told me that these things happened, were fairly common and could easily be dealt with. After all, I had been under a strain; I was probably working too hard. In my final year now, was I? Exams next summer? Yes, people often got het up about these things. But in view of my . . . er . . . history, it might be a good idea to go and see a specialist. He knew a very good chap at the Littlemore Hospital. Somebody would write to me in due course to set up an appointment. Good idea to talk things over, perhaps take some medication – only temporarily, of course – to get rid of these bouts of panic, and then I'd soon be on my feet.

The Littlemore. One of Oxford's two psychiatric hospitals. My heart sank. I had seen it coming, but now that the process had been set in motion, it felt like a real defeat. Psychiatry had certainly not been part of the convent ethos. The very idea of 'talking things over' with anyone was anathema. But I could see no alternative. The way both the doctor and the college nurse had taken refuge immediately in cliché when confronted with my predicament indicated that they felt out of their depth. I needed expert help, but I still shrank from exposing the mess of my life to a stranger, who would examine it clinically and make his own appraisal, and I hated the prospect of being known to be mentally ill.

It was partly to prevent this, I suppose, that I started to become more reclusive and reserved. I was afraid of experiencing one of these uncanny episodes when I was with other people. I had lost confidence. Where previously I had felt only shy and socially inhibited, I could now place no trust in either my body or my mind. I no longer took it for granted that I could get through a party or a quiet evening with friends without succumbing to this malady, and, indeed, I had noticed that the flickering lighting to which people seemed so strangely addicted these days made me feel very odd indeed. And so, just as I had started to put out feelers to the world, I began to withdraw again.

There was another, deeper reason for this. These frightening incidents were changing me. I now knew that at any second, the pleasant, innocent-seeming surface of normality could split apart, and this knowledge infected everything. I knew that other people had been to this dark place. I could see it in Van Gogh's tormented, writhing olive trees and swirling starry skies. It was in the infernal visions of Bosch; it was the heart of darkness evoked by Joseph Conrad. It didn't matter how often I told myself that these experiences had no substantive reality. However you accounted for them, this was a region of the human mind. And because I had visited it, I felt set apart. I was surrounded by girls whose existence was beginning to blossom. Most of them were hopeful, cheerful and excited by their unfolding lives, but I could no longer share this instinctive optimism. I was now doubly out of place among my fellow-students, as though I were the wicked fairy in the story, brooding balefully over the party.

Increasingly I felt as though I were witnessing everything at one remove. As time went on, solid physical objects appeared ephemeral, and people seemed like ghosts, with no clearly defined identity. When your surroundings can so suddenly take on a frightening aspect, you start to experience them as fluid, unreliable and without inherent integrity. Things seemed to flow into one another; a kind face could rapidly become menacing, a pleasant landscape take on a malign aspect. Sometimes I felt as though I were looking at reality through a sheet of glass. If I put my hand out to touch an object. I often expected to feel this barrier; sounds seemed faint and dim. This happened so gradually and became so habitual that, after a time, I ceased to remark upon it. It became the norm, the element in which I lived. I was rather like the little fish in the Sufi parable, who asks his mother about this stuff called water that he hears everybody discussing but which he has never seen. It is not until the condition lifts that you realize that it was abnormal. At the time, it simply seemed that the world from which I had retreated had now begun to recede from me.

This made it even more difficult to relate to other people. When you feel that you are talking to somebody through a plate-glass window, it is hard to make real contact. I also found it impossible to feel strongly about current events, which seemed somehow vague and remote. During the spring of 1970, when I read about the fighting between Israelis and Syrians on the Golan Heights, looked at a newspaper photograph of a despairing child in Biafra, or watched television footage of the Viet Cong offensive in Laos, I could not feel anything at all. In May, the anti-Vietnam War rally in Washington DC, which delighted so many of my fellow-students at St Anne's, seemed like something you might see in a surrealist dream, weird and insubstantial. I viewed these distant crises as through the wrong end of a telescope. They might as well be taking place on another planet that I would never visit.

Yet again, work became my refuge, because it made me feel relatively normal. If I could write good, competent essays about Chaucer or Shakespeare, my mind might not be irretrievably damaged. I could still think logically and coherently, if not originally. The more I read and studied, the more competent work I produced, the easier it was to believe that I was not completely mad and that one day I might be able to make my way in the world as an ordinary person. If I could stay for ever in the nice secure realm of scholarship, doing a little teaching, or writing the occasional article on Emily Brontë or Wordsworth, I might be able to keep my demons at bay.

Besides turning me into a solitary, these attacks of fear dealt yet another blow to my already wavering faith. No, I did not imagine that I had seen Satan during these visitations and knew very well that the evil I sensed had no metaphysical existence but was simply the product of my own mind. But these 'visions' got me thinking. In an age that was less scientific than our own, it would surely have been natural to conclude that the ghostly, senile presence that I sensed with hallucinatory intensity was a real diabolic personality. Poets and mystics had often spoken of the foul stench of hell. Almost certainly, hell was simply the creation of infirm minds like my own. There was no objective evidence to support such a belief. That was a wonderful and liberating thought, but what if God was also a mental aberration? The ecstatic, celestial visions of the saints could be just as fantastic as my own infernal sensations. What we called God could also be a disease, the invention of a mind that had momentarily lost its bearings. I was slightly dismayed to find that this idea did not trouble me overmuch. If there were no God, then much of my life had been nonsense, and I should, surely, have felt more upset. But then, God had never been a real presence to me. He had been so consistently absent that he might just as well not exist. Perhaps I should just leave the Church and have done with it.

Father Geoffrey Preston, a benign Dominican at Blackfriars in St Giles urged me not to make too hasty a decision. I had started to attend mass at Blackfriars at the suggestion of one of my tutors, who was also recovering from an unhappy Catholic past, and sometimes looked as though she had barely survived the struggle. She had recommended the family mass on Sunday mornings, and I found that it was indeed a cheerful, imaginative liturgy, geared to the needs of children who could crawl or run around the church freely and, within reason, make as much noise as they liked. My tutor also advised me to talk to Geoffrey.

He was clearly a kind man, but seemed faintly ill at ease, and I suspected that, like many priests, he had ambivalent feelings about nuns. 'I hope you're not feeling guilty about all this.' He shifted his massive girth uncomfortably around on the formal parlour chair. 'I know nuns tend to trade on guilt. I expect you had to count up your faults on a special string of beads and write them down in a little book,' he chuckled, inviting me to share what he clearly assumed was a joke.

'Yes, we did, actually,' I said.

Geoffrey's head snapped to attention, his eyes startled. 'You're not serious, are you?' I nodded. 'Good God.' He gazed, lost for words for a moment, at the ceiling. 'We always thought that was a silly fantasy – one of the absurd stories that people tell about nuns. I had no idea that they actually *did* it.'

'You've had a sheltered life, Geoffrey.' I stood up and started putting on my coat. 'If you're not careful, I'll tell you the whole story one day.'

'I'm not sure that I could take it.' Geoffrey was smiling but I could sense his real distaste. 'I suppose that's women for you,' he said reflectively as we walked down the cloister. 'We always said in the army that they were no good at community life. They seem to get bogged down in petty rules and regulations – can't see the wood for the trees.'

Perhaps, I thought, as I headed back to college. But I also knew enough about the Church to know that it was men who had made the rules in the first place.

I had mixed feelings as the train thrust its way through the lush Sussex countryside. In one sense, I was going home, going back to the convent where I had spent the first three years of my religious life. I had received a letter from Sister Rebecca, asking me if I could come to see her. This in itself was surprising. Visitors were generally discouraged and I could scarcely be considered a suitable companion for Rebecca. Things had obviously changed during the fourteen months that I had been away. But I had some misgivings about my own reactions. I had no idea how it would feel to be in a convent atmosphere once more.

Sister Rebecca had been two years ahead of me. When I had been a postulant, she had been a second-year novice, and we had all seen her as the perfect young nun. She had the serene face of a Botticelli Madonna, her habit was never creased, her eyes were modestly cast down, and she spoke always in a quiet, dispassionate tone, just above a whisper. Most of us forgot how to be nuns from time to time. We would run upstairs, burst into loud laughter or answer back when reprimanded, but not Sister Rebecca. She was always controlled, composed and peaceful. When I had arrived at Oxford in the autumn of 1967, she was in her final year at St Anne's, reading French and Italian, and because we were the only two student nuns in the community, we were thrown much together. We went to the convent chapel together after lunch every afternoon to perform all our spiritual duties, one after the other, in a soulless marathon of examination of conscience, rosary, spiritual reading and thirty minutes of mental prayer. The idea was that we should get these 'out of the way', so that we could spend the evening studying. When we had finished praying, we took a forty-five minute walk. And we talked.

Although we were not supposed to form friendships, Rebecca and I were so isolated from the other students and from the rest of the community that inevitably a relationship developed. We both loved our work but had nobody else to discuss it with. I would tell her all about Milton, and she would impart to me her latest discoveries about Dante or Proust. But the conversation did not always remain on such an exalted level. I was beginning to rebel. The Oxford community was not an easy one. Most of the nuns there were adamantly opposed to the reforms, about which both Rebecca and I were excited. The evening recreation would often consist of long communal lamentations about the abolition of the old ways, and Rebecca and I would exchange sardonic looks. I discovered that beneath her apparently perfect exterior, Rebecca had quite a sharp tongue and a salty turn of phrase, though she was unfailingly sweet to the older nuns and never showed her irritation, as I so frequently did.

During our walks, Rebecca had listened to my growing saga of frustration with the religious life. She had been a lifeline in that last difficult year, but she had not shared my disenchantment. Why had she summoned me? I wondered, as we pulled into the station. Was she in trouble? We had arranged that she would meet my train with the convent car, but I did not see her on the platform; nor was she in the entrance hall after I had handed in my ticket. Then, suddenly, I caught sight of a nun standing beneath the old-fashioned wall-clock, wearing one of those modern habits that gave her the appearance of an Edwardian nurse. There was something familiar about her but she was far, far too thin. That could not be Rebecca. I looked around again, but found my gaze drawn back to that modest figure, whose eyes were meekly cast down on the tiled floor. The nun looked up, and her face brightened with delighted recognition, as she gave me a small, discreet wave. And for a moment, my heart stopped.

Gone was the serene Madonna. This nun looked as though she had just been released from a concentration camp or was in the final stages of cancer. Her face had shrunk, so that she looked all eyes, which now seemed huge and protuberant. There were cavernous hollows beneath her sharply-etched cheekbones. As she crossed the hall towards me, I was appalled to see how skeletal her legs were. She was about five foot ten inches, and could not have weighed more than eighty pounds. But when she spoke, her voice was the same and I had to face it. This was indeed Rebecca, but dreadfully, frighteningly altered. Quickly, I pulled my own face into what I hoped was an answering smile. 'I didn't recognize you for a moment in your new habit,' I murmured, as we exchanged the nun-like kiss, pressing each other's cheeks smartly, one after the other. I kept smiling. 'It's lovely to see you.'

'And so good of you to come.' Together we crossed the station forecourt and got into the car.

'This is a first,' I said, in what I hoped was a cheery tone of voice. 'How long have you been allowed to drive? We could have done with this car in Oxford. Think of the lovely trips we could have taken!'

'To the Cotswolds . . . Blenheim . . . how is it all? I do miss it.' Rebecca inched through the traffic and we started the forty-minute drive to the convent.

'Oh, it's all much the same,' I replied. 'Though, of course, it isn't the same being "outside".'

'You sound as though you've just got out of prison!' We laughed uneasily, our eyes firmly fixed on the road ahead. 'But it's all so different "inside" these days,' she continued. 'The car, the habit – those are the most obvious changes, and we have more baths, more talking. We can make our cells into bed-sitting-rooms and give each other cups of Nescafé. It's probably a bit like St Anne's – lots of girlish laughter; intense discussions and pop psychology. We all sit around talking about how damaged we are.'

There we were; we had arrived at the heart of what was uppermost in both our minds. There was silence, and then Rebecca said quietly: 'Karen, *thank* you for not saying anything.'

'About your weight.' It was not a question. I forced myself to turn and look directly at her. 'When did it happen?'

'Very quickly.' Rebecca sighed. 'In London, while I was doing the Certificate of Education. I hated it, hated teaching – and I just got thinner and thinner.'

'But what is it?'

'*Anorexia nervosa*, the eating disease.' I nodded. Besides Charlotte, a number of other girls in college had it. 'At first the doctors thought that I might just have an over-active thyroid. Everybody was very keen on that – anything so long as I wasn't suffering from a mental illness, an *emotional* disorder. Some of the community still refuse to accept it.' Again I nodded wordlessly. I could imagine that all too well.

'But what are they going to *do* about it?' I demanded. An eating disorder required hospitalization, special programmes and expert help. It could, in extreme cases, even be fatal.

'Nothing,' Rebecca said flatly.

'But you need a doctor!' I persisted. 'You can't teach looking like that.'

'Oh yes, I can,' Rebecca spoke grimly, and I was beginning to sense that underneath the studied calm she was very, very angry. 'I'm teaching French in the school here, and Reverend Mother Provincial says that she cannot find a replacement at the moment. And then,' her voice took on a real edge, 'in a few years, I am to be the next headmistress.'

I was shocked into silence. This was not the ideal solution for somebody who hated teaching, and was becoming dangerously ill. It could kill her. 'Are you eating?' I said at last.

'I'm eating all right,' Rebecca explained, as we drove slowly up the village street that led to the imposing convent gatehouse. 'Apparently I've got an extreme form of the disease. I'm just not absorbing the food.'

I began to feel really frightened. 'You know,' Rebecca went on, 'I put it down to that Oxford regime. Remember? We'd get in from our lectures, too late to go to the first table sitting for lunch and wait outside the Refectory until the community finished their meal. Then we'd have to rush in and gulp down two full courses in ten minutes, to make sure that we were kneeling in our places in church to do our prayers on the dot of one forty-five.'

I realized that the disease must have a deeper root cause than this, but this ridiculous arrangement could have focused Rebecca's attention on food, making it a symbol of a deeper discontent. 'Supper was no better,' I recalled. 'I had to read to the community for fifteen minutes and bolt down my food in ten; you were up and down serving throughout the entire meal. They meant it kindly, I suppose. They wanted us to be free to go to Compline with them after dinner.'

Rebecca might joke about it, but the religious life *had* damaged her, as, in a different way, it had me. She took the car into the long drive, and through the avenue of cedars towards the fourteenth-century chapel. It all looked so peaceful: the sunlit lawns, the nineteenth-century school buildings; the old tower; the novitiate. We came to a halt before the front door. 'How does it feel to be back?' Rebecca asked me.

I shook my head. 'I don't know,' I said.

But in fact, even after the disturbing revelations in the car, as soon as I stepped inside, something within me relaxed. In a strange way, it did feel like home. I could smell the polish, which we had made ourselves out of melted candle stubs. I could see the gleaming rust and gold tiles stretching ahead across the large courtyard near the front door, which I must have swept a hundred times. I looked at the huge crucifix on the wall. A bell clanged in the distance, a special signal to summon one of the nuns. Instinctively I counted the strokes: three clangs, then a pause, and then two further beats. Not 'my' bell then. But, I remembered, I didn't have a 'bell' any more, because I didn't belong. At the far end of the courtyard was the heavy enclosure door. If I opened it, I knew exactly what I would see: the cloister reaching far into the distance, the deep window embrasures, the double doors of the Refectory and, at the corner, the *pietà*, a life-sized statue of Mary holding the dead Christ. But, of course, I was a secular, and the enclosure was barred to me now.

Time and again during the next twenty-four hours, I felt caught up in a world that was so familiar that I responded automatically, as though I were still a member of the community strolling with

Rebecca down the country lanes, where we had walked almost every day for three years, frightening courting couples out of their wits when they saw this weird crocodile of nuns bearing down upon them; waking at night to hear the clock of the nearby Anglican church chime every quarter; laying down my book or coffee cup at the first sound of the bell that called the nuns to prayer. I felt drawn towards the old routine. And it was all so restful. The confusions of the outside world receded, and I felt strangely at peace.

And yet in other ways the convent was simply not the same. The old hushed silence had gone. Nuns stood in groups, chatting and laughing – sometimes quite loudly. They wore short utilitarian skirts and flighty little veils. Doors closed noisily and the younger nuns often swung their arms as they walked with defiant casualness. Even in church there was a new restlessness. In the old habit you had to kneel perfectly still, or the veil fell over your shoulders like a tent, and your legs tangled and twisted the voluminous skirts. I had no romantic regrets about the old habit. It was hot, inconvenient and unhygienic. But the modern dress gave the nuns greater freedom of movement, and I noticed that some of them fidgeted in their pews, as though the imposed stillness had become more of a strain. Or – and this was an arresting thought – perhaps I had not been the only one who had had difficulties with prayer.

The next morning, I knelt with a few other seculars in the chapel for Mass, which was now said facing the people, in accordance with the directives of the Vatican Council. When the nuns processed up the aisle to receive communion, I glanced at Rebecca, and felt the shock as acutely as though I were seeing her emaciated frame for the first time. The whole decorous structure of the convent suddenly seemed a sham. The nuns who gathered together around the altar seemed an image of prayerful community, and yet they were allowing one of their number to waste away before their very eyes. They might have comfortable chairs in the community room and take more frequent baths, but the old attitudes were still in place. How could women, who had spent thirty or forty years in the religious life and been even more indelibly shaped by the old system than I, change overnight?

No, I told myself, as I watched them file back to their seats, their eyes cast down and their gaze directed inwards, it was no good looking back with nostalgia. When the world outside seemed baffling, I sometimes felt homesick for a way of life that, with all its shortcomings, was at least familiar, just as I had instinctively relaxed when I had walked into the convent yesterday. I could only move forwards, however difficult that might seem.

'Karen, my dear, how very nice to see you.' I looked up from my breakfast, which I was enjoying in the elegant parlour. How odd it was to be waited on in this way, as I had so often waited on visitors, bringing in coffee, toast and eggs, while, a few hundred yards away, the community were eating cornflakes, bread and margarine. There were some advantages to secular life, I reflected, helping myself to more marmalade, but hastily suppressing my involuntary smile of enjoyment when Mother Frances came into the room. She looked somewhat less imposing in her new habit, but she had recently been promoted to become one of the Provincial Councillors.

'But I'm interrupting your breakfast,' Mother Frances gestured towards the hot buttered toast.

'Not at all, Reverend Mother.' Instantly I became the young nun again, unable to swallow a single mouthful while my former superior stood waiting to speak to me.

'Well, you're looking very well,' she went on, settling herself in one of the oak carvers at the head of the table. 'Are you well?'

'Not really, Reverend Mother.' I knew that I was supposed to say that everything was fine, but I suddenly pictured Rebecca's stricken face. 'I'm finding it very hard – almost impossible – to adapt. And it seems to be making me ill.' I briefly gave her the headlines: the fainting, the panic attacks and the psychiatrist.

'Oh, really, Sister – Karen, I mean,' she corrected herself, laughing lightly but without amusement. 'I really had hoped that you would grow out of all that nonsense! It's high time, surely. You must be twenty-five? Twenty-six?'

'Twenty-five,' I replied, though I couldn't really see what my age had to do with it.

'Well, there you are then. Far too old for these childish displays.'

'But how *do* I adjust?' Perhaps she should understand the problem so that she could advise other nuns who were thinking of leaving. 'I trained to become a nun for five solid years: you know what it was like. You call it "formation" now, I believe, and that's what it is. It's a training that shapes you at a very deep level. And I just can't *stop* being a nun. I need a new training – one that is equally intensive – to turn me into a secular. Undoing habits and attitudes, which are now ingrained. I don't know how to do this. You and Mother Walter made me a nun, but how do I reverse that? I don't have anybody to help me deprogramme myself and I don't think I can do it alone.'

'Still as dramatic as ever, I see.' Mother Frances sounded bored, as she often did when, I suspected, she felt on uncertain ground. 'It's bound to be difficult at first. Of course it is.' She smiled brightly and, in an effort, perhaps, to avoid my eye, she started to brush away the crumbs scattered on the gleaming tabletop. 'But I'm sure it's only a matter of time.' There was finality in her tone. Subject closed. I felt pushed back into myself, locked into my perplexity. I could almost hear her turn the key. 'So, tell me about your plans,' she went on briskly. 'You have your final exams soon. This term, isn't it?'

'Six weeks away,' I nodded. I had been accepted to do post-graduate work, provided that I obtained a first-class degree and secured the state scholarship that would give me funding for a further three years' study.

'Well, we'll just have to keep our fingers crossed,' Mother Frances pronounced. 'You seem to be able to do your work all right. I don't think there can be much the matter with you, do you.' It was not a question.

Have it your own way, I thought wearily. I could see that she didn't *want* to admit that there might be a real difficulty; if I had been somehow disabled by the regime, this would raise some very hard questions. As if she were reading my thoughts, Mother Frances's eyes narrowed slightly as she looked at me again. 'And how do you find Sister Rebecca?'

'Dreadful, Reverend Mother. She needs to see a doctor. At once.'

'She has seen a doctor. As you know.' There was a new coldness and more than a hint of reproof. 'I'm still hoping that we'll find that it's all due to an over-active thyroid. This other possibility –' she broke off rather than name the disease. 'Well, that would be quite unacceptable.'

'Unacceptable?' I stared at her. 'But it's entirely irrelevant whether you accept it or not. It's just a fact. She'll die, if this goes on.'

'For heaven's sake, Karen,' Mother Frances laughed that dismissive laugh again, her eyes wary. She got up to go and looked quizzically at me, her hands resting on the table. 'There you go again. All this extremity! It's so unnecessary!' With an air of exasperation, she got up and kissed me on both cheeks in a way that felt more like a slap than a salutation, and sighed, her hands still on my shoulders, shaking me slightly, clearly mentally reviewing the tears, fainting, vomiting and bleeding that had punctuated my religious career. 'I don't think anyone ever died of *nerves*, Karen,' she said finally and made for the door, looking back at me one last time.

'You and Sister Rebecca.' She shook her head yet again. 'You are a pair!'

I found myself thinking about Mother Frances's parting shot when, a few days later, now back in Oxford, I boarded the No. 1 bus in the High Street to go to my first meeting with the psychiatrist to whom I had been assigned. Maybe Rebecca and I had taken the rules and strictures too seriously? I remembered Mother Frances saying to me once in exasperation, 'You really are a literal-minded blockhead!' after I had pointed out some inconsistency or other in our training. Or maybe it was just because we had thought too much about it all and tried to make sense of an essentially senseless system.

I had already seen the consultant psychiatrist at the Littlemore, a Basque doctor with an excellent reputation, and I was feeling hopeful. Every couple of weeks I would see one of his registrars. In fact, I saw a string of registrars, and was passed from one to the other, but, to avoid confusion, let us create a composite figure to stand for them all, and call him Dr Piet. The consultant had not seemed unduly perturbed about my plight. All these anxiety attacks were, perhaps, understandable in the circumstances. And he had said one thing that had made an impression upon me. 'You seem to me to be stalled in some way. Life is hurtling on, like a giant merry-go-round; you are watching, but you can't get on. You want to join in, but you can't – for reasons that we shall have to discover.' His remark had gone home and I had recognized that it was true. I could see myself confronted with the carnival of 60s Oxford: the other young people with their long hair, confident gestures and eager voices all understood instinctively how to make something of their lives. I cast my mind back to that party, when I had heard my first Beatles record, and felt alone and out of place, unable to dance or participate in any way. Maybe Dr Piet would help me.

So when I faced him in his small functional office, I had hopes that together we could find a solution. He asked me about the fainting and the panic, and I described the strange smell, the mounting fear, those moments when the world became unrecognizable, the hallucinatory glimpses of something horrifying, the senile old man, his cavernous head nodding on a frail stalk-like neck.

'Have you ever seen him – or anyone like him – in real life?' Dr Piet wanted to know.

'Yes.' In fact, this interested me. I had dropped into the Junior Common Room one evening and joined a group who were watching an adaptation of a D. H. Lawrence short story on the television. It had been about a young woman in flight from her sexuality. The play had ended with the disturbing shot of the rich old man she eventually married, who was rather like my visitant. As I explained this connection, I saw Dr Piet brighten and scribble something on the pad in front of him. My heart sank. You didn't have to be a genius to see how he would interpret this information. And sure enough:

'Did you find yourself relating to the heroine in that play?' he asked. 'Did you feel that she was like you?'

As a matter of fact, I did not. She had been very flighty, beautiful, uneducated, had lots of money and not enough to fill her day. No, not very much like me. But then what did I know? I probably was in flight from my sexuality, though as no man ever displayed the slightest interest in me, I did not see what I could do about this. Dr Piet smiled rather smugly when I said this, as though he knew better. Perhaps he did. In the interests of my own recovery, I ought to give him the benefit of the doubt.

'I'm interested that it is only the old man's *head* that you see.' I raised my eyebrows. 'Well, your life seems to revolve around the intellect. You seem fixated on heads and brains,' Dr Piet continued. 'You never see any of the other parts of his body.' I reflected, wryly, that perhaps I ought to be thankful for small mercies. If Dr Piet meant what I thought he meant, these visions could be a whole lot worse.

'I think we're going to look at your relations with your parents,' Dr Piet continued, leaning back in his chair and looking at me in a pleased kind of way, as though I were a promising child who had come out with all the right answers. 'You see, these panic attacks seem to me to relate to your early childhood. To some shock or deprivation that occurred while you were growing up. They are rather classic images.' Again, the nod of professional pleasure. 'And then, of course, we have to find out why you went into a convent in the first place. That's hardly a normal decision for a teenage girl. Until we get to the root of that – find out what had gone so wrong in your life that you decided to leave the world – *and*,' he added pointedly, '*to leave your family*,' he paused significantly, 'we cannot really get to the root of your problem.'

And so it began. I embarked on years of psychiatric sessions during which we raked over the memories of my unexceptional childhood. No doubt this conformed to the orthodoxy of the day, and in many cases I am sure that this is an effective way to treat the problems of adult life. But in my case, it simply did not work. The anxiety attacks, the terror and the occasional loss of consciousness continued, and each hallucinatory episode pushed me further away from the rest of the world, making it even more impossible for me to get on to that merry-go-round.

When I wrote *Beginning the World*, I used the conversations with Dr Piet as a narrative device to explain what I thought was happening to me psychologically. But the truth is that I remember very little about them. I desperately wanted the treatment to work and cooperated as fully as I could, but Freud, I believe, once said that if you are suffering from toothache, you cannot engage in any productive analysis. You cannot even fall in love. Against the background of these strange, periodic attacks, which Dr Piet dismissed as mere symptoms of a deeper malaise, these psychiatric sessions felt as though we were conducting an esoteric discussion of medieval history while the house was on fire.

I wish that Dr Piet had allowed me to discuss my experiences in the convent. If I could have talked to him about the novitiate, the loneliness, the strain of the last few years of religious life, or my ambivalent feelings about it all, then maybe I could have begun to process the experience. But Dr Piet usually deflected any such discussion. He saw it as a distraction, a smokescreen that enabled me to hide from my real problems.

'You see, in the convent, you were safe,' he would tell me earnestly. 'You were not challenged in any way. It was a secure, quiet existence – far from the madding crowd, if you like. You didn't have to face up to emotional or sexual issues. You were in abeyance. You had, as it were, crawled back to the womb.'

I would listen, bemused by this fantasy. For Dr Piet, the religious life was like the secret gardens or lost domains of literature. He saw serene processions of beautiful nuns gliding down sunlit cloisters, and imagined the convent as an enclave of sisterly peace and concord. Seductive as the religious life had undoubtedly been, he would tell me sternly, I had been running away from my true problems and responsibilities. Indeed, he clung to this idyllic vision so persistently when I tried to interject a little reality into the discussion, that I sometimes wondered what psychological significance this fiction held for *him*. True, we had been shielded from some of the uncomfortable realities of the outside world, but anybody who entered a convent simply to escape unpleasant- ness would not have lasted a month, let alone seven years. Further- more, it was not really accurate to say that I had been running away. The core of most of our problems is our own self, and in the religious life I was forced to confront this self for twenty-four hours a day, three hundred and sixty-five days a year. You have far more opportunities to escape from self-knowledge in secular life. It is very easy to change the subject, pick up the telephone, turn on the television or pour a stiff drink. None of these options was available in the convent, and as a result we very quickly came to a most uncomfortable perception of our own limitations.

But Dr Piet was my only chance. Without him, I could be condemned to a lifetime of these uncanny eruptions of horror, each one of which made the darkness encroach a little more. I felt as though I were standing on a beach, with my back to a cliff, watching the tide creep up the shore a little closer ... and then a little closer still. So I went back to Dr Piet, telling myself that I couldn't expect a miracle overnight. What did I know about psychiatry and the mystery of the human mind? If I persevered I might well find that everything suddenly fell into place. But then, I would be overtaken by a queasy sense of *déjà vu*. This was exactly the sort of reasoning that I had used in the convent, and look where it had got me.

*   *   *

It was a hot, sticky day in July 1970. The room in the Examination Schools that had been set aside for the viva voce examination seemed to echo to our footsteps, as the four of us trooped in and sat in a miserable little huddle against the wall. I looked hopelessly at the members of the board of examiners who were sitting around three sides of a large table in the big bay window – sixteen dons in full academic dress, gazing at us expressionlessly. Opposite them was a lonely chair for the candidate, and the ten question papers of the final examinations that we had sat some six weeks earlier.

I was pleased and relieved to be summoned to a viva. In the English Faculty, only those who were borderline cases between classes, or who were being considered for a first-class degree had to undergo an oral examination. No viva, therefore, no first. For the umpteenth time, I mentally reviewed my papers. A viva, I knew, could last for hours. But when I looked again at the examiners, I felt my hopes plummet. I cannot do this, I thought bleakly. All my written answers had been carefully contrived. During the long weeks of revision, I had prepared essays that could be adapted to meet almost any contingency. They were my usual 'gothic cathedral' creations, intricate edifices of other people's thoughts. But now I knew that there was no chance that I would be able to think on my feet, in the way that would be expected of me. I still sat tongue-tied in class, marvelling at the way the others could play confidently with ideas, get fresh insights in the course of a discussion, and produce arguments to support their case at a moment's notice. I was especially impressed by the ease with which other people could say, 'I think'. I had no notion what 'I' thought. When I scoured my brain, I still encountered the old blank. There was no way that I could talk freely and impressively to the board.

Miserably I listened as the chairman of the examiners read out the list of our names, telling each of us (all of whose names began with the letter A) what time we should present ourselves. He didn't mention me and, for a moment compounded of both disappointment and wild relief, I thought it had all been a mistake. I had got a safe 'second' and wouldn't have to face the examiners after all. Then the chairman nodded at me, with the same courteous little smile that he had given to the others. 'And, Miss Armstrong, would you stay here now, please.'

I stood up slowly, adjusting my gown, while the others filed out of the room. 'Come over here.' The chairman gestured towards the chair and I began the interminable journey across the carpet.

It took a while before I recognized the sudden explosion of sound that stopped me in my tracks. It was clapping. I looked up to find that the examiners had risen to their feet and were applauding. The men had doffed their mortarboards. All were smiling broadly. And I remembered the old tradition.

'Miss Armstrong,' the chairman said when the decorous clapping had petered out. 'We wish to congratulate you on your papers, which were all quite excellent.'

I felt a huge smile break my face in two and a wave of pure delight. I had done it. I had somehow managed to achieve what they called a 'Congratulatory First'. If I could do that, with all the distractions that I had had, I could do anything. I would survive. For a moment, the path ahead seemed clear and secure.

∿ 3 ∿

I RENOUNCE THE BLESSÈD FACE

Looking around my new room, I smiled with relief and delight. Yes, I would be able to work here. This would be the place where I would write my doctoral thesis. The walls had been painted a long time ago in a pale green, which had now faded into a pallid, dreamy wash. There were two pretty leaded windows, surrounded by a leafy creeper, which gave the low-ceilinged room a cottage-like air. A washbasin, a divan against the wall, two wicker arm-chairs, and a desk – there was everything I needed.

'Is it all right?' Jenifer Hart, my new landlady, sounded nervous. She was the tutor in modern history at St Anne's, and I had often seen her in college, striding around in flamboyant clothes which never quite matched and which seemed to make a defiant state-ment against age and convention. She must have been in her mid-fifties, but her straight, shoulder-length hair, which she wore pushed behind her ears, was still golden red, though, like so many things in her house, it was beginning to fade. Her tanned face was lined – she wore little make-up – and she gave off a rather fierce, uncompromising aura. Yet now she looked anxious and even vulnerable. I had approached her about the room with some trepidation. Word had gone round that she was offering free lodging in return for rather unusual babysitting. This was attractive, since my state grant, though adequate, was not princely. The location was perfect: the large, white house in Manor Place was just minutes away from the English Faculty Library. Mrs Hart was somewhat alarming; her pupils told fearsome tales of her low boredom threshold and her impatience with anything that she regarded as stupidity. She was also famously left-wing, and one of the most radical of the dons. When I had met her in her college suite, I had felt boring, conventional – and religious, something I sensed immediately would be incomprehensible to her. But to my surprise, she had responded eagerly to my inquiries about the room and had been very keen, even desperate, that I should join the household. Had I been of a more suspicious nature, I might have smelled a rat. My own tutors' reactions to the plan had been less than reassuring. 'Lodging with Jenifer Hart? Oh, Lord!' Miss Griffiths had cried in obvious dismay. Dorothy Bednarowska had been more restrained, but even she had been unable to suppress the characteristic rictus of the facial muscles that she made involuntarily when confronted with something alarming. 'Well, I don't suppose it will do you any harm,' she had said reluctantly. 'For a while, anyway.'

So I went to view the room with some misgivings and when Mrs Hart opened her front door, I was greeted by rather a startling spectacle. The hall was painted scarlet, the dining room a violent purple, and the kitchen a brilliant turquoise – this at a time when white was almost *de rigueur* in interior decor. But it was clear that housekeeping was not one of my prospective landlady's priorities. The walls had not seen a lick of paint for years, and were scuffed, scarred and slightly grubby. Dust coated every object and had accumulated on shelves and skirting boards in peaceful, undisturbed drifts. There was clutter everywhere. As I walked into the hall and followed Mrs Hart into the drawing room, I almost tripped over a duffle-coat which lay spread-eagled across the floor. There were some perfectly serviceable hooks just inside the front door, but they seemed to be supporting a grime-laden conglomeration of tennis-racquets, umbrellas and walking sticks wedged tightly together against the wall. There were piles of books and papers on almost every shelf, interspersed with mugs, in which, I later learned, lurked fossilized dregs of Nescafé. When we went upstairs to view the room, it became apparent that something had happened to the banister, because a thick rope was slung along the wall instead, and at the top of the stairs we both had to step over a large pile of dirty sheets and underwear, which uninhibitedly blocked our path. The loud unconventional colours and the mess did not repel me, however. After the militant tidiness of the convent, and the tasteful but impersonal decor of St Anne's, there was something liberating about this cheerful disregard for appearances. I was, however, beginning to be concerned about what my own room was like, and relieved to see that it was a little haven of order in the surrounding chaos.

'Is it all right?' Mrs Hart asked again, even more anxiously. I realized suddenly that a great deal of effort had gone into the reclamation of this room.

'Thank you, Mrs Hart, it's very nice.'

She visibly relaxed, and again I felt a flicker of unease about her obvious anxiety to secure me as a babysitter. 'You'll need a bookcase, of course.' Her words almost fell over one another in her eagerness to please. 'I've got one, actually, in my other sons' bedroom. We could go and get it now, if you like.' I followed her back down the corridor. As we passed the pile of laundry, she gave it an absent-minded kick, and a pair of underpants, thus dislodged, fluttered down the stairwell.

'Here we are . . . Ghastly, isn't it?' She sighed, and, lost for words, I could only smile weakly. The large room was completely papered in sheets of newspaper, now stiff and yellow with age. The light-fittings had been torn out, leaving gaping holes, and the words FUCK OFF! had been painted across the ceiling in thick, dark blue letters. 'One day I'll have to strip this.' She scrabbled in a defeated way at the newspaper. 'But, you see, it's layers thick. It'll take weeks – and bring off most of the plaster, probably. The boys insisted on doing it.'

'Are they living here now?' I tried to sound calm about the prospect.

'Oh no! They're finished with university and living in communes, learning to be hippies and bricklayers.' Her face looked suddenly sad in the bleak light. 'They don't come home very often.' Abruptly she turned to a tall, white-painted bookcase, crammed with old paperbacks. 'This should do for now, and I've got another small one downstairs that you can have.'

'What should I do with these books, Mrs Hart?' I asked.

'Oh, for heaven's sake, call me Jenifer.' She sounded impatient, but she was clearly trying to be friendly. She looked helplessly around the room, full to overflowing with old guitars, obsolete gramophones and, in the dark recess of one corner, I could just make out a superannuated bicycle. 'We'll just pile them on this bed for now,' she sighed.

Twenty minutes later, we went back to the drawing room which opened directly into Jenifer's study. This last was almost entirely occupied by a massive desk, piled high with papers and heavily laden bookshelves, but the room where we were sitting was pleasant with two small-paned French windows that looked out on to an immaculate garden, glimmering green and silent in the early evening light. Jenifer handed me some sherry in a tiny silver goblet as if to fortify me for what was to come. 'Well, now it's time to talk about Jacob,' she said.

She had told me a little about Jacob when I first applied for the room, as he was the reason for my presence in the house. He was her eight-year-old mentally handicapped son. When she spoke of him, her rather gruff voice took on a range of different inflections expressing anxiety and a disarming eagerness to present him in an attractive light. Jacob had been an afterthought, born when the other three children were almost grown-up. The birth had been precipitous and Jacob had emerged with the umbilical cord wound around his neck. Deprived of oxygen, his brain had been irretrievably damaged, and he was now diagnosed officially as autistic. Recently, he had also started to have epileptic seizures. I had assumed that autistic children were silent and withdrawn, but apparently Jacob never stopped talking and loved language. He lived in a fantasy world, however, unable, because of his malfunctioning brain, to see his surroundings in the same way as other people. He had, Jenifer told me, terrible fears. He could be driven into frenzy by a loud noise or a thunderstorm, because, however carefully these alarming events were explained to him, they always retained the force of the unknown and the inexplicable. These terrors could often result in temper-tantrums, during which he would lie on the floor and kick and scream, quite beside himself. At such moments it was impossible to do anything with him. 'I seem to have a particularly bad effect on him,' Jenifer had smiled ruefully. 'But then I never seemed to have much control over my other children either.' The Harts had a nanny who had lived with the family for almost thirty years, ever since their oldest child

Joanna had been born. 'Nanny is a treasure,' Jenifer had told me sternly. 'It's vital that you get on with Nanny.' And Jacob was able to attend a special school for educationally disadvantaged children, which wasn't really right for him, as, in some ways, he was apparently very bright. He had, I was told, an extraordinary vocabulary for his age, and could read fluently.

'The doctors told me that he would never be able to read,' Jenifer said. 'I think they thought that because we are academics, we were obsessed with literacy. They kept telling us not to push it. But, you know, it happened quite naturally – by accident, really. When he was little, he used to sit next to me at breakfast while I read the paper, so to keep him quiet and give him something to do, I taught him to pick out all the Os and then the As and so on, and then, all of a sudden, he started reading all by himself.'

My job would be to look after Jacob while Nanny was off-duty. That meant that I would take care of him after supper on Wednesday evenings, when Nanny went off to visit a friend, and Jenifer and I would share him on Saturday, which was Nanny's half-day. Jenifer would take him during the afternoon and give him his supper, and then I would take him to my room until it was time for bed. Because of his epilepsy, I would have to sit with him while he went off to sleep until Jenifer came to bed at about 10.30 p.m. I was startled to hear that for years she had shared a large attic room at the top of the house with Jacob, who was absolutely terrified of the dark and could not sleep alone because of his night terrors and seizures. Herbert, Jenifer's husband, slept in his study next to the drawing room, a small chronically disordered lair that was almost entirely filled with a massive home-made stereo system, constructed out of large wooden crates by Alan Ryan, the Harts' former son-in-law who was about to take up a Fellowship at New College. Even though he was now divorced from Joanna, I was told that Alan was still very much a part of the family – an idea that I found intriguing. In my Catholic family, divorce was a cataclysm that led to permanent estrangement.

'And,' Jenifer continued, 'I wonder if you would mind relieving Nanny, who usually sits with him, when I am especially late – out at a dinner or something. Only if you're free, of course,' she added hastily. 'You can read up there. Jacob will go to sleep with the bedside light on, and you can sit on my bed until I come up.'

It had sounded quite manageable when Jenifer had run through the job description in her peaceful college rooms. Now that I was about to meet Jacob, I was not so sure.

'I hope you're not worried about all this,' Jenifer said, clearly anxious herself, as she settled opposite me on the white sofa with her own goblet of sherry. 'There's no need to be. In fact, it's very important that you don't show any nervousness, because he'll pick it up in a second, and then it really will be impossible.' I smiled with what I hoped looked like confidence, but I was afraid that I might be instinctively repelled by Jacob. Would he look dull and drooling? I had never done anything like this and had no idea how I would cope. How would I occupy a brain-damaged child for hours at a time, week after week? As if reading my thoughts, Jenifer only increased my anxiety as she gave me some last-minute advice.

'You'll have to find your own way,' she explained. 'Find your own special thing to do with him. He tends to put us all into watertight compartments, and won't let anyone *ever* encroach on somebody else's territory. I believe this kind of ritual behaviour is quite common with autistic children. Nanny is the only one who is allowed to read to him; he and I play backgammon – or try to,' she gave a short bark of a laugh. 'He usually loses his temper. And he'll help me in the garden or we'll go for a walk.

Just now, he's out with my husband, who takes him for long drives. Though that's not ideal really,' she added. 'Herbert is not the world's best driver. Anyway,' she brightened, 'I'm sure you'll find something. It's really not difficult – not as hard as it sounds. He's basically very open and loving. He generally adores grown-ups. He'll be very eager to be your friend.'

I hoped so. 'What about other children?' I asked. 'Does he have friends at school, for instance?'

Jenifer shook her head. 'No. Children worry him. Jacob is very tall for his age, you see, and he gets alarmed when little people scurry about. They're too noisy. And I suppose they're a bit frightened of him, and he senses that.' She stretched out her thin brown legs and contemplated her feet, clad in clumsy men's sandals. 'That's one of the reasons why we've never sent him away. To a home or hospital.' She frowned, and her tone darkened. 'Lots of people said that we should do that, but it's ludicrous!' She seemed to be rehearsing an argument that she had had many times before. 'We manage very well. With Nanny, and now that you're coming it will be even better. We can't just send him away. That seems terribly irresponsible. And in his own way, he's happy here – as happy as he can be. He adores Nanny and he has lots of special adult friends. We've got a house in Cornwall, where we spend the Easter and summer vacs, and that's marvellous for him. It's a huge house, right on a cliff, and he feels free there. You must come down. We have interesting people to stay.'

A key rattled in the front door and I looked up apprehensively. 'He'll be very shy at first,' Jenifer warned me. 'He might even throw a tantrum. Just take no notice.' I swallowed hard, and assumed what I hoped was a nonchalant expression.

'Mummy!' There was a peremptory cry from the hall, a jumble of footsteps, and then Jacob exploded into the room. I was quite unprepared for him, and the artificial smile I had carefully put on turned involuntarily to one of genuine pleasure. Jacob was beautiful. Tall and slim, his skin delicately tanned, an elegantly structured face, and tousled blond curls. But also formidable: he slammed the door and looked warily around him.

'Who is that?' He spoke quietly, separating each word with care.

'This is Karen, Jacob. She's going to come and live here and help to look after you. Won't that be nice?' Her tone turned the question into a plea. Jacob stared at me with hostility.

'Hello, Jacob.' Even I could hear the anxiety in my voice. Jacob turned away in apparent disdain, and walked to the far end of the room. His gait was the only thing that indicated that there might be something wrong. He shuffled rather clumsily, his long arms swinging at his side, as though they didn't quite belong to his body. 'Go away!' he roared suddenly, and flung himself face down on the floor. Jenifer crossed the room and knelt beside him.

'Karen's such a nice girl. She's going to sleep in the room next to your playroom. When she brings her luggage over from college, you could help her unpack.'

I tried – I feared unsuccessfully – to look delighted at the prospect. From the next room, the serene strains of a Mozart piano concerto filled the air.

'Be quiet!' Jacob ordered. 'Or I shall become very, very angry.'

Jenifer gave up and returned to the sofa. 'Herbert!' she shouted. 'Come and meet Karen.' The Mozart stopped abruptly, there was another confusion of footsteps, and the door of the drawing room was flung open after much fumbling with the handle, and crashed against the wooden arm of one of the chairs. Herbert Hart, former Professor of Jurisprudence, at Oxford, now retired, made his way towards me, with an absent but charming smile, uncombed hair, clever Jewish face, and with clothes somewhat haphazardly put together. As he stumbled erratically across the room, missing the coffee table more by accident than design, I realized that Jacob's deportment was not the result of his disability but was hereditary.

'How do you do?' He was, I noticed, a shy person. 'How very nice to have you with us.'

'This is Karen Armstrong.' Jenifer started to make the introductions. 'Karen, this is my husband, Herbert –'

'The Royal Arms!' The words were spoken with emphasis. We all turned, puzzled, to Jacob beside the french doors. 'The Royal Arms!' he intoned again, still lying face down on the floor.

We looked at one another, and Herbert shrugged elaborately as he hurled himself perilously into a chair. 'A pub, I suppose,' he muttered. 'I don't think I've taken him to one called the Royal Arms. He probably saw the sign during our drive. Jacob, tell Mummy and . . . er . . . Karen where we went this afternoon.'

'The Royal Arms!' Jacob scrambled into a sitting position and beamed happily at us. We smiled back, grateful but mystified.

'No, we didn't go to the Royal Arms, darling,' Herbert's rather husky voice was patient. 'We went to –? Can you remember?'

'No!' Jacob flapped his hands about, as it to dismiss his father's irrelevant questioning. He shuffled over and stood directly in front of me, looked at me carefully, and nodded, as though making a careful assessment. He then said, quietly and deliberately: 'It's the Royal Arms.'

'Oh!' I suddenly understood. 'It's my name. *Arm*strong.'

Jacob beamed again, entranced with his pun, and looked at me with his head bent inquiringly to one side. 'It's the Royal –' he waited.

'Arms!' I capped, and we laughed together. We had established a connection and his parents visibly relaxed.

'That's a good joke, Jacob,' Jenifer said happily, and, in order to capitalize on this unexpected harmony, added: 'What about helping Karen and me to carry that little bookcase up to her room?'

'Yes!' Jacob roared with enthusiasm, bounding into Jenifer's study, grabbing books from shelves, and hurling them around the room with joyous abandon, ignoring his mother's timid requests to proceed more quietly. I recovered the books as they fell and started to pile them up by the door. 'Karen.' Jacob was now on his knees, peering intently into the crevice between the bookcase and the wall. 'Karen,' he said again (like his father, he could not pronounce his Rs), 'come and have a look at this.'

To humour him, Jenifer and I went to look, only to have our superior smiles wiped from our faces. 'How ludicrous,' Jenifer breathed. 'It's fantastic. Herbert, come and see.'

A small rose bush had somehow forced its way up from the foundations, broken through the floorboards, and grown, thin and spindly, to a height of eighteen inches.

'It's a tree!' Jacob danced ecstatically. 'Growing in the drawing room!'

'Nature reasserts itself against the thin veneer of human civilization. If you can call this civilized,' Herbert mused. 'Isn't there a poem about that?' He looked at me interrogatively. 'Something about "laughing Ceres"?'

'Pope. *The Epistle to Burlington*,' I replied. 'He's making fun of that awful country house. "Deep harvests bury all his pride has planned –"'

'"And laughing Ceres reassume the land".' Rose tree and all else forgotten, Herbert went back to the living room and started rummaging in a bookcase for a copy of Pope's collected works.

'You should keep that rose tree,' I said to Jenifer, as we

manoeuvred the bookcase with some difficulty out of the drawing room. Herbert glanced up benignly from the sofa, spectacles askew, clutching the book in a somewhat awkward grasp. 'Marvellous poem!' he beamed, watching our efforts absently.

And so, yet again, a new life began.

Within a few weeks, I had managed to impose a shape on my day. I had a gas ring in my room, but was allowed to use the Harts' kitchen whenever I wished. Not that I ever attempted any elaborate cooking: it was simply a question of scrambling eggs and heating cans of soup. But even if I had been more ambitious, it would not have mattered. There was never any hint that I was in the way or interrupting family life. There was no family life, as such. This was a household of separate individuals, who shared a house cooperatively. Nanny was not the starchy Gorgon I had feared, but a sweet-faced, ageing woman, who battled bravely with the mounting chaos of the house. She and Jacob usually ate breakfast together, while Herbert, Jenifer and I queued up politely for cooker or kettle, preparing our own meals. During the day, Herbert and Jenifer lunched and often dined in their respective colleges. If she was at home, Jenifer's suppers were as perfunctory as my own, whereas Herbert enjoyed preparing experimental little messes for himself.

The day would begin with a great deal of coming and going. Herbert would plunge back and forth in his dressing-gown between the kitchen and his study/bedroom with mugs of coffee, which he tended to park and forget. Nanny would retrieve some of them later in the day. Jenifer would sit in the dining room, looking gaunt and weary in a brown camel-hair dressing-gown that had seen better days, black National Health spectacles on her nose, studying the newspapers. Jacob chattered ceaselessly, snatching pages from his mother and reading out phrases at the top of his voice, which sounded surreal when isolated in this way. 'Crisis Looms!' he would announce portentously. 'Mummy – The Trend Persists! Persists! Karen – Ministers Gather! At nine o'clock. Nine o'clock sharp,' he would add thoughtfully. 'If they don't arrive sharply, there'll be trouble. They might arrive bluntly. Mummy, what will happen if they don't arrive sharply?'

'Oh, I expect they will.'

'But if they *don't*? If they *don't*?' he persisted. 'Will the Prime Minister be very angry? Will he say: "You're bad, bad ministers"? Recession Imminent! Mummy, what *is* recession?' Jenifer and I would look at one another helplessly. Jacob would not be fobbed off with anything less than an adequate answer, unless another phrase caught his fancy.

'Moon Rises!' he would invariably shout as soon as I arrived downstairs to make my breakfast. 'Karen – moon rises! Twelve forty-five a.m.!'

'What *is* he talking about?' I had asked Nanny on my first morning.

'It's in the paper. The time the moon rises each day. It's the first thing he looks for every morning.' Nanny smiled into the saucepan of porridge. 'It's one of his little games. You'll soon get used to us, Karen.'

And so I did. I got used to a house where rose trees grew in the drawing room, where walls were covered in newspaper and where the day began with a stentorian announcement of moonrise. When I returned from the library in the evening, and climbed the stairs to my room, I learned to expect Jacob's unfailing greeting. 'The Royal –' he would shout from Nanny's room, where he was watching television.

'Arms!' I would yell back as a matter of course, checking in.

Soon I felt at home in a house which seemed odd enough to absorb my own strangeness.

It was good to have this focus, because Oxford had become a ghost city. Life as a graduate student was very different. True, I had not made many close friends during the last eighteen months, but the crowded, cheerful life of St Anne's had given an illusion of sociability. There had always been somebody to have coffee with after dinner; there were tea parties almost every day, and there was usually somebody around in the Junior Common Room. But when the Michaelmas Term began in October 1970, Oxford, though crowded with students, seemed deserted. Nearly all my former classmates had scattered to begin new professional lives in publishing, teaching, the Civil Service or business. Very few had stayed to do graduate work. The college was now full of a new generation of undergraduates, who were complete strangers. The dons were always reminding us that we were only birds of passage in Oxford. Soon our turn would be over and we would have to leave this artificially constructed existence for the unpredictable, challenging world outside. I never wanted to hear this. I had had my fill of leaving things, places and people and longed for some stability. Yet one day, I, too, would have to face the larger world, which lurked threateningly beyond the groves of academe: unknown, dangerous and indifferent.

But right now I had another three years at Oxford, and perhaps I need never leave the academic world. I seemed to be good at scholarship, and if I did well enough, maybe I could remain in this intellectual haven. I had decided to write my doctoral thesis on Tennyson's poetic style. Most people thought that this was a good idea, since Tennyson had been much neglected. For decades, students had been taught to dismiss his poetry as sentimental. To deride one of the chief spokesmen of the Victorian era had been a way of exorcising the influence of this crucial but conflicted period. In the 1960s, however, the tide had turned, and scholars started to rediscover the extraordinary beauty and power of some of Tennyson's verse. I had been drawn to it at once. Writing years before Darwin had published his *Origin of Species*, Tennyson had been one of the first people to realize the impact that modern biology and geology would have on religion, and his great poem *In Memoriam* plangently explored the ambiguities of doubt and faith, in a way that reflected my own perplexities.

At a deeper level, there was a mood in Tennyson's poetry that I immediately recognized. So many of his characters seemed walled up in an invincible but menacing solitude, as I was. They too seemed to see the world at one remove, as if from a great distance. Mariana was trapped in her lonely moated grange, where old faces glimmered at the windows and mice shrieked in the wainscot. The Lady of Shalott was imprisoned in a tower; confined there by some unexplained curse, because she could not confront external, objective reality. When she finally did fall in love and ventured into the outside world, it killed her immediately. All this resonated with the hallucinatory visitations that kept me imprisoned in my own inner world. Like so many of Tennyson's people, I longed to join in the vibrant life that was going on all around me, but found myself compelled to withdraw by forces that I did not understand. Like me, Tennyson seemed sucked into a horror of his own. When he contemplates the yew tree beside the grave of Arthur Hallam, he imagines its roots wrapping themselves around his friend's bones and skull. Mesmerized and, as I so often was, unable to break away from the grotesque vision of horror that he has spun from his own brain, he tells the corpse-rooted tree: 'I seem to fail from out my blood, and grow incorporate into thee.'

113

Still more reminiscent of my own plight were those odd passages from *The Princess*, where the hero describes the 'weird seizures' which periodically descended upon him and which drained his surroundings of reality:

> On a sudden in the midst of men and day,
> And while I walk'd and talk'd as heretofore,
> I seemed to move amongst a world of ghosts,
> And feel myself the shadow of a dream.

When I read Tennyson, it seemed that I had found a friend. Our circumstances could not have been more different, but it was as though we inhabited the same unpredictable world, in which 'All things were and were not'. I felt closer to him than to almost any of my living contemporaries. Because, despite Dr Piet's confident predictions, my anxiety states were becoming more frequent. Increasingly, I found myself unable to sleep because of this sense of encroaching dread, and the more exhausted I became, the more I was assailed by this hallucinatory fear. So every night, I swallowed huge, evil-looking sleeping pills, prescribed by Dr Piet, and during the day I took a sedative called Largactil, which encased me in a mental fog, made the ground seem curiously far away and caused my hands to shake. But none of this formidable medication made the slightest difference to the fear that continued to erupt and transform my environment into a 'world of ghosts'. Dr Piet could, if he wished, dismiss these attacks as a mere symptom, but for me, they were the problem, and Tennyson seemed to have a clearer understanding of what they were like than my psychiatrist.

An added difficulty was that I was becoming very lonely. The Oxford D.Phil. programme was, in those days, rather different from that of other universities. There was no course work and, after the first two terms, there were no classes. The student had one task: to write a thesis of about one hundred thousand words with the help of a supervisor. I saw mine about once a term, and that was it. There wasn't even a graduate centre, as there was in Cambridge, where we could congregate for coffee or a drink.

Fortunately, Jane had also stayed on to do a doctorate. Her thesis was to be on the political beliefs of W. B. Yeats. She lived quite close to the Harts' house in the modern wing of Holywell Manor and became a lifeline. We would often sit in her sleek, contemporary room to have coffee or a glass of sherry. During the first two terms, while we were studying for the qualifying examinations, we had two classes that were obligatory for all D.Phil. students: on bibliography and paleography. Both were mind-bogglingly boring. 'God, what a dreary crew!' she would mutter, far too audibly, as she sank into the seat beside me, and I had to agree that our fellow-students were not an inspiring bunch. Many of them seemed besotted with the intricacies of bibliographical science and were producing definitive editions of minor works by little-known writers in lieu of a thesis. Some of them looked as though they had been born in a library. Jane held aloof from all this, and made a point in class of asking the most intelligent and witty questions that she could think of, and I followed suit.

To hide my mental distress, I was developing a hard, intellectual manner that, I thought, provided me with some protection. I felt that I was a soft, mollusc-like, hopelessly vulnerable creature who needed a thick shell in order to survive, and I was learning to use words to create this carapace. I did not want to appear before the world as pathetic, depressed and psychologically ill, so I erected a barricade of words and wit around myself, so that nobody could see how needy I really was. Some of my remarks were so scathing that even Jane was surprised. 'My God, Karen, I would really hate to incur your enmity!' she exclaimed one day, after a particularly biting riposte. This surprised me, as I tended to underestimate the power of my tongue. In the convent, I had grown accustomed to extremely abrasive treatment, and I thought that my own retorts were mild in comparison to the rebukes of some of my superiors, which I now reproduced in a secular context. Like many frightened people, I tended to lash out like a wounded animal, and very rarely said anything nice about anybody.

Charlotte had also stayed in Oxford, but was not doing graduate work. She had begun to write seriously and now lived in a tiny room in the Iffley Road, and to pay the rent was working as a clerk in the local tax office. There was just enough space for a bed and a desk. When we sat there together, drinking coffee or a bottle of cheap wine, I felt full of admiration. I could not imagine how anybody had the courage to be a writer, but, undeterred by her grim surroundings, Charlotte was steadily amassing a pile of typewritten sheets. Yet in some ways, Charlotte seemed as ill-equipped for the world as I. She too seemed to be imprisoned in her own Shalott. She was in love, and Mike, whom none of us was allowed to meet, dropped in on her sporadically whenever it suited him. Charlotte could never go to visit him or even call him, because she was not permitted to know his address or telephone number. Meanwhile, Mike roamed the countryside in his van, eschewing the trap of security and a regular job. It seemed imperative to his masculinity that he retain the initiative in his dealings with Charlotte. I had scarcely heard of feminism, but I found it outrageous that brave, talented Charlotte should live as a virtual prisoner, because this useless drifter needed to be 'free'. She was reluctant to leave her room in case Mike deigned to drop by while she was out. So she could never come and visit me at the Harts' and we could never meet in a pub or some more cheerful venue. Whenever Charlotte jumped up at the sound of the communal phone or because a car door slammed in the street below, I vowed that if I ever fell in love, I would never allow myself to be so enslaved.

Charlotte was not so far gone, though, that she could not see that her situation was absurd. Something had to be done, and we had a project. Her uncle had just visited Paris for the first time and had been completely intoxicated by the experience. He had sent Charlotte a cheque for fifty pounds and told her to take herself there for a weekend. Charlotte wanted me to go with her. There was no reason why I should not go. I was living at the Harts' rent-free and so was much better off than most graduate students. And yet every time we mentioned Paris I felt a strong internal veto, and I could see that Charlotte felt the same. It was partly due to a fear of spending a significant amount of money after all those years of holy poverty. But it was more than that. Paris represented life, sensuality, freedom and fun. And that some-how made it impossible. I had no business in such a place, because I belonged to the shadows. In our very different ways, Charlotte and I both dwelt on the periphery. We were stuck there for the present. But that was just for now. One day, we told each other firmly, we would really do it. We would buy our tickets and make our reservations. But not yet. Not just yet.

Jacob sat at my desk, his head clasped in his hands, rocking backwards and forwards. It was Wednesday night, Nanny's night off, and so he was spending the evening with me. He always came to my room willingly enough, but it was hard work to keep him occupied until his bedtime. We would play cards or dominoes sometimes, but Jacob soon lost interest and frankly I did not enjoy these games much either. We would listen to the radio or play word games but I still had not found my 'special' thing to do with him. Yet tonight was different. Jacob was clearly upset, and I couldn't reach him. His dressing-gown had come undone and his legs in their striped pyjamas wound tightly around my chair.

'What is it, Jacob?' I asked, as persuasively as I could. 'Look at me, and tell me what's wrong, or I can't help you.'

He turned his face away, as he always did when asked a direct question. It was one of the clear signs of his autism. He simply could not bear any attempt, however well intentioned, to penetrate his inner life. Chin pressed down hard on his chest, he muttered quietly to himself in the third person: 'Karen wanted to know what was wrong, but Jacob absolutely refused to answer. The question was impossible.'

I knew what the trouble was. When Nanny had brought him to my room, she had whispered that he had got it into his head that there was going to be a storm. 'It was those dark clouds we had earlier. I've *told* him that there won't be a storm. But . . .' she sighed and shook her head. He had never managed to get used to thunderstorms. Jenifer explained that these irrational terrors were almost certainly related to his epilepsy; and were due to a syndrome called *jamais vu*, when an electrical discharge in the brain made everything so unfamiliar that it was as though he had never seen any of it before.

'Look.' I took his hand, but he instantly snatched it away and clamped it over his ear. 'There isn't going to *be* a storm. If you like, we'll listen to the weather forecast.' Even as I spoke, I knew that this would be useless. When Jacob was in one of these states, nothing logical could reassure him.

'I've got a record with a lovely thunderstorm on it.' I don't know what put this idea into my head. 'You can hear the thunder and the lightning clearly, but it's all been made into wonderful music by a man called Beethoven.' Jacob lifted his head and stared at the wall, but I could tell that he was listening. 'And then,' I went on, 'suddenly it's all over, and you can hear the thunder going further and further away over the hills, just as it does when there is a real storm. And everything is peaceful, and the music becomes so free and happy.'

Jacob swivelled round in the chair and studied my washbasin.

'Would you like to listen to it?' Why not? Jacob loved ritual, which seemed to make the terror of his life recede and gave his chronically unpredictable world some kind of pattern. Perhaps this was the point of any ritual, religious or otherwise. The music might formalize the storm for him in some way, give it a beginning, middle and end, and thus make it manageable.

'The Royal –?' Jacob spoke softly.

'Arms!' I replied on cue. He giggled, momentarily distracted.

'Would you like to listen to it?' I asked again.

Jacob got up and sat in the cane chair, gathering his dressing-gown around him. 'Put it on!' he ordered, looking at me slyly out of the corner of his eye.

'I beg your pardon?' I demanded, feigning disapproval.

'You're not angry?' Jacob's face was alight with glee. My insistence on good manners was another of our games. In Manor Place, where there was such principled informality, this was a novelty instead of a tedious and ubiquitous adult requirement.

'I most certainly shall be angry.' I frowned theatrically, making Jacob squirm with delight. 'Put it on *what*?'

'Please. Put it on *please*.' He came and stooped over me, his face angelic, while he stroked my arm. 'Please. Dear Karen.'

'All right. You can plug in the record player. That's right. Look

119

at the cover, and all those people playing in the country. Now. Listen. You'll hear the thunder very quietly at first, building up and up and *up*. Then you'll hear it go away, as it always does . . .'

'Karen says the thunder always goes gradually away,' Jacob informed the gas fire *sotto voce*, as we listened to the first chords of the storm sequence in the Pastoral Symphony.

At first, I acted as the commentator. 'Here are the raindrops. Now – the first rumble of the thunder.'

'Rumble!' Jacob echoed, but after a few moments he indicated imperiously that he wanted me to be quiet, and for once I did not insist on a 'please'. He began to sway thoughtfully to the music, keeping perfect time. 'Whoosh! There goes the lightning! Brroom! That's the thunder!' and, as the storm died out, he sank back with a histrionic sigh of relief. As the final notes of the symphony died away, Jacob demanded that we play the other side.

'All right. This time you'll hear a cuckoo and some people dancing.'

By the end of the evening, I was as enthusiastic as Jacob. We had also got through the whole of the Elgar Cello Concerto, which was another hit. He immediately called the cello the 'deep violin', and when I introduced him later to the Dvorak concerto, he dubbed it the 'new deep violin record'. His comments showed astonishing sensitivity. 'Listen, Karen, the violins are asking a question', or, 'Oh dear, this is so sad. Somebody's crying!' But mostly he just listened quietly.

A little after nine, as we got up to go to his bedroom, he stood at the door and bowed solemnly. 'Thank you, Karen,' he said formally, obviously imitating one of his parents' dinner guests. 'I enjoyed this evening very much indeed.' He almost clicked his bare heels together. 'In fact, it was our best evening yet, don't you agree.' I nodded. 'So can we listen to your records next time I come to your room? *Please?*'

'Of course. Next time we'll hear something different.'

'Something different *and* the thunderstorm again. Please.' He grinned and became a child again. 'And now – *off* to the lavatory!' he yelled, and then, forestalling me, 'And don't forget to pull the chain!'

'Is that all you are having for dinner? It's quite ludicrous! You must eat more than that.' Jenifer was standing at the top of the stairs, poised as if for flight and clearly uneasy. It was against her principles to proffer unwanted advice to the young. We looked at my supper tray: a boiled egg, two slices of crispbread, and a tub of plain yogurt. It seemed more than enough to me.

I had now narrowed down my expenditure dramatically, so that I spent only about two pounds a week on food. I bought one small carton of eggs, which had to last six days. I was also learning to make my own yogurt in a thermos flask, which was a great deal cheaper but an uncertain process. Hence the tub I had permitted myself tonight. For lunch I consumed two pieces of crispbread covered with cottage cheese (again, one carton had to last the week). So I never actually stopped eating. I just cut it back, and the results were gratifying: I had really started to lose weight.

This had begun quite deliberately. I knew that I was not anorexic like Rebecca, because that was an illness that was beyond one's conscious control. I, however, was choosing of my own free will not to eat. I was often ravenously hungry, and would sometimes allow myself a piece of real toast and butter, which, if I had been truly anorexic, I told myself, would have been quite impossible. And I was not driven by any ulterior or unconscious motive. My purpose was, I believed, simple and pragmatic: I wanted to save money.

Money had become a major issue. I had never handled money much before. In the convent, we had owned nothing but everything had been provided, and the same had been true while I had lived in St Anne's as an undergraduate. At the beginning of each term, when we had received our grant cheques from the government, we paid a fixed sum to the college for bed and board. Our rooms were cleaned for us and meals were served three times a day. But now I had to buy my own food and manage my own budget, and I found this obscurely frightening. I had started to panic about the future. Academic jobs were notoriously hard to get and my present scholarship would last only for three years. What would happen then? If I couldn't get a post as a university teacher, whatever would become of me? I was trained for nothing else, and, at twenty-six, I was really too old to start again. There was school teaching, of course, but I knew that I did not want to do that. There was one precaution that I could take, however. I could save money. If I built up a reserve fund, I could perhaps hang on for a few years until I finished my doctorate and was eligible for the coveted academic post. Then I would be set up for life and could eat and spend whatever I wanted.

I made it sound rational, at least to myself, but this was a crazy scheme and a telling indication of the state I was in. Compared with most students, I was well off. My grant more than covered my needs and I also had five hundred pounds on deposit, a not inconsiderable sum in those days. The order had given me a hundred pounds on my departure, my grandmother had left me a small legacy, and I had won an academic prize worth another hundred guineas. But saving and hoarding had become an obsession, so much so that when I came to buy my first apartment in 1976, I had squirrelled away enough money to put down a deposit and furnish the entire flat. I can still see the astonishment on the face of the building society representative, when I told him that I had saved this money from my student grant; he agreed to allow me a mortgage without further demur.

Money is not a neutral factor, but is highly symbolic. I had convinced myself that I was not going to be able to earn my own living, and I simply could not make myself believe that this was a ridiculous assumption. What I was really saying was that I did not have a future. I was just not making it out here as a secular. I could not, as that perceptive Basque consultant had noted, attach myself to anything. How could I engage with life, when my heart was dead? How could I become an academic, when I was no longer able to respond spontaneously to literature? How could I function, when I was increasingly subject to 'weird seizures'? When I looked ahead, the only possible future I could see for myself was a locked ward or a padded cell. My years as a nun had somehow made me unfit for the world, had broken something within me, and now I seemed unable to put myself together again.

And I did not want to nourish myself. What was the point of feeding my body, when my mind and heart had been irreparably broken? And yet, in a way, I also felt that by starving myself I was reaching out to the world. I was asking for help. People kept telling me that I was fine and congratulating me on how well I was doing. But I was not fine and I wanted people to know this. As the pounds fell off, as people like Jenifer started to notice my growing emaciation, I felt a perverse gratification. Look, I was saying, this is what I really feel like. Please notice – and help me.

'Well . . .' Jenifer tailed off. Her heart was just not in this. 'Don't let your egg get cold. By the way,' she added, as if in an afterthought. 'I've been thinking that it might be nice if you could join us for Sunday lunch. It's the only meal that we all eat together, and you are part of the household now. I really mean it,' she went on, less embarrassed now that she felt on firmer ground. 'You've fitted in so well. It seems wrong that you should be upstairs on your own on Sundays. You should be with the rest of us.'

'Thank you, Jenifer.' I felt immensely moved. This was not a casually issued invitation. The Harts fulfilled most of their social obligations by inviting people to their Cornwall house, or taking them to guest nights in their respective colleges. They rarely had friends to dine in Manor Place. It didn't matter that Jenifer was transparently trying to ensure that I ate at least one decent meal a week. It was kindly meant, and kindness was something that I had learned to value. 'Thank you,' I said again. 'I should like that very much indeed.'

Sunday lunch, I was not surprised to learn, was neither a decorous nor an elegant occasion.

'Mummy! I'm going to tip the water jug right over!' Jacob tilted the jug at a perilous angle, his eyes fixed on Jenifer.

'No, Jacob, don't do that,' she replied somewhat ineffectually, while she briskly carved slices of roast lamb and tried to continue a civilized conversation. 'Where do you go to mass, Karen?' she inquired politely. The Harts were mildly intrigued by my Catholicism. My years in the convent were so remote from anything in their experience that I might just as well have spent seven years living with a peculiarly exotic tribe in New Guinea. In fact, they would probably have found that a good deal easier to understand.

Both Herbert and Jenifer were committed atheists. Herbert found the whole structure of religion utterly incomprehensible and to Jenifer any form of religion was 'ludicrous'. Like many intellectuals of her generation, she had been a member of the Communist Party; there were occasional wild and inaccurate speculations in the media that she had been the 'Fifth Man' in the Burgess–MacLean spy circle, a charge she vehemently denied. She had long been disillusioned with the Party, but her disdain for religion remained intact. Both she and Herbert regarded Christianity in general and Catholicism in particular, as 'monstrous'.

Yet today, for some reason, Jenifer seemed unusually interested in my church-going. I told her briefly about Blackfriars, thinking that she could not possibly be interested, but she persisted: 'So it doesn't matter if the children at this family mass are noisy or make a scene?'

'No. But actually because they feel relaxed, they tend to behave fairly well,' I replied. 'They seem to enjoy it.'

'What is the sermon like?' Herbert asked. 'There are some intelligent men there, I believe.'

'Don't talk about these boring things, Karen!' Jacob yelled, bringing his fork splat down on his plate and causing a brief volcanic eruption of gravy and cabbage.

'Ssh ... It's interesting what Karen is saying, Jacob,' Jenifer protested, wiping gravy from her check.

'It is interesting, up to a point,' Herbert conceded. 'Remarkable that reasonably educated people can go on believing in the Virgin Birth or the Trinity. Might as well believe in the Olympian pantheon. I mean, why Jehovah rather than Apollo? Frankly, I think Apollo might be the more appealing option.'

I could see his point. Jehovah had done little enough for me. Perhaps I should give Apollo a try.

'Catholicism doesn't seem to have made you very happy,' Jenifer remarked, echoing my own thoughts and ducking as Jacob hurled a potato across the room. It splattered steamily on the large mirror, and there were exclamations of protest. 'Jacob, eat up now!'

'How could the Catholic Church possibly make anybody happy?' Herbert grinned at me. He enjoyed baiting me about the notorious abuses of history. 'Centuries of oppression and fear. The Inquisition, the sale of indulgences . . .'

'The immorality of the Popes,' I threw in.

'Book-burning. Pogroms.'

'Jesuits and Equivocation!'

'This conversation has been going on for too long! Talk about something else,' Jacob demanded at the top of his voice. 'We don't want to hear about churches and popes and all that stuff!'

'All right.' Jenifer turned to him. 'You start a conversation.'

'Let's talk about Bonfire Night.' Jacob relaxed now that the conversation was within his range. The fifth of November was one of the landmarks of Jacob's year. He started looking forward to it months in advance. At first he had been terrified by the noise of the fireworks and the lurid effigies of Guy Fawkes but Nanny and his parents had managed to coax him out of his fears by making a little festival of it.

'Daddy, tell about how it will get dark and you will light the bonfire.'

'And the flames will start to crackle in the twigs,' Herbert obliged.

'Snap, crackle and pop!'

'And you will be so excited, Jacob,' Jenifer put in, 'when the fireworks start.'

'Whoosh! But Karen, *you* may be a little bit frightened. Just at first. But I'll say to you: "Don't worry. There's nothing to be scared of."'

'Thank you, Jacob.'

'Daddy! Who was Guy Fawkes?'

'He was a Catholic!' Herbert shouted in glee, pushing his chair back from the table, while the meal ended in laughter.

*   *   *

I followed the nurse down the corridor, inhaling that inimitable hospital smell, catching glimpses of other people's dramas. Blue bedspreads, a trolley, a wheelchair. 'Straight down to the end,' the nurse told me cheerily, 'and your friend is in the small ward on your left.'

'Karen!' Rebecca's voice was unchanged. It was still soft, controlled and peaceful, despite the violence that she had done to herself. 'Thank you for coming! And so quickly too!' I had thought she had looked bad the last time I saw her, but now it seemed astonishing that she was still alive. Her face was already a death's head. I said nothing, however, and if Rebecca noticed my own weight-loss, she also kept a tactful silence. We stared at each other bleakly.

That morning I had received a postcard, written in Rebecca's characteristically spiky script. She had been moved from Sussex to the London convent, had been sent into Oxford Street on an errand, had collapsed and been brought to the intensive care department of the West Middlesex Hospital. She was not yet quite out of danger.

'How are you?' It seemed a stupid question. I sat beside the bed, trying not to flinch from the horror of her profile and the shallowness of her chest. Her skin now had a bluish pallor, and her eyes protruded even more starkly than before.

'Much better. Really much better now.' That was difficult to believe, and I felt a sudden rush of pure rage. How could the community have sat back and watched her waste away like this, day after day? What on earth had they been about? Had they wanted to kill her?

'I'm sorry,' I said, turning my gaze with relief from Rebecca to the tray of food in front of her. 'I seem to have interrupted your lunch.' It was three o'clock in the afternoon – an odd time to be eating lunch but, obedient and docile as ever, Rebecca plunged her fork into a steaming, smelly mess of sausage, baked beans and chips.

She shook her head, swallowed a mouthful and loaded her fork again. I blenched. 'No, I'm being given something to eat every hour. They won't let me out of here until I've reached at least ninety pounds and I have a long way to go. I'm *still* not putting on weight,' she reflected calmly, 'even though I'm eating all this, but at least I'm not losing any.'

'Oh, let's look on the bright side, by all means,' I said drily, as a nurse bustled into the room and deposited a fruit yogurt on the tray. 'Are you getting any other help?'

'Yes. I'm seeing a psychiatrist twice a week. He's a Catholic. That should help.'

Again we looked at each another. I recalled Mother Frances's words: 'You and Rebecca!' We both seemed bent on a destructive course. I watched Rebecca spoon up the pink, sugary yogurt, which her body refused to absorb. Like me, she seemed to be losing her hold on life, seemed unable to move forward into the future. We no longer knew how to live. We had somehow lost the knack.

'Have you seen him yet, the psychiatrist?' I recalled Mother Frances's distaste for the very idea of such an expedient. But she had been wrong. It seemed, as I looked at Rebecca, that you could die of 'nerves' after all.

Rebecca nodded. 'We've talked about my childhood mostly.' She smiled – a terrible corpse-like smile. 'It's interesting. I'd quite forgotten. I was a rather passionate, violent child. Always losing my temper. I used to lock myself up in cupboards and refuse to come out until I had made my point.'

'You? Violent?' I was astonished. Where had all that fury gone?

That, of course, was another silly question. Whoever heard of a passionate or rebellious nun? And yet, I asked myself suddenly, why not? 'Why couldn't they just work with what we were?' I was thinking aloud, really. 'Why try to change us so drastically? With you it was fury and passion; I was always "too sensitive". "What are we going to do about your sensitivity, Sister?"' I mimicked the assistant Novice Mistress's exasperated, faintly disgusted tone. 'But what's wrong with passion? What's wrong with sensitivity? Jesus was a passionate man, wasn't he? You couldn't call him insensitive, either. Hardly an example of the stiff-upper-lip.'

'I know.' Rebecca sounded defeated. 'But, you know, I wanted to change,' she continued dispassionately, as though her former self had no connection with her at all. 'I wanted to be another kind of person.'

'We wanted to be transformed.' I noted that I, too, spoke abstractly, as though about somebody else. As though I had already passed away. 'But that's different, surely?' I thought of Jesus on Mount Tabor when, the gospels tell us, his disciples had seen him transfigured: light streamed from his face, his garments had shone white as snow. He had not been diminished but enhanced. His personality and body had remained intact but, transfused with divine power, he had perfected his humanity. 'They didn't have to get rid of us; they could have perfected what we were.'

But that hadn't happened. There was, literally, almost nothing left of Rebecca. A nurse came in with a wheelchair. 'Time for your X-ray, Sister.'

'Can't you walk?' I asked in dismay, as Rebecca pulled on her dressing-gown and settled herself uncertainly in the chair.

'She's got to conserve her energy,' the nurse explained matter-of-factly. 'We can't have her burning up all those lovely calories by running up and down stairs, now, can we? Every little helps.'

I hoped it did, but it seemed unlikely. In every sense of the word, Rebecca was wasted: all that energy and intensity had been quashed and, like me, she was broken, unable to function or even to move freely.

'I'll come again soon,' I promised, as the nurse wheeled her away.

'But of course you have the same illness as Rebecca.' Dr Piet pushed back his chair from the desk and looked at me, eyebrows raised. This was one of our better sessions, and the panic of my response showed that he had scored a bulls-eye.

'No, we're different!' I protested vehemently. 'It's my mind, not my body that's the problem.'

Dr Piet shook his head dismissively, as he usually did when I referred to my panic attacks. 'Same difference,' he said. 'Those hallucinations, those eruptions of fear are simply the symptoms of a repression, similar to Rebecca's suppression of the passionate little girl she once was. The feelings have got to come out some-how. It's the only way you can allow yourself to feel anything at all.'

'But Rebecca's starving herself to death!'

'It's just a matter of degree.' Dr Piet doodled on his blotter. 'True, you're not as physically ill as your friend. You weigh – what is it? – ninety pounds to her seventy? But you have an eating disorder, all the same. You and Rebecca are both anorexics.'

'But it's different. I feel it's different,' I said again, stubbornly. My refusal to eat was a cry for help, surely, rather than anorexia proper. The refusal of food and the weight loss was – surely? – the result of conscious choice and never a compulsion that I could not control.

'Well, neither of you is doing much living at the moment,' Dr

Piet continued. 'You have that in common. You stay alone in your room, afraid to go out in case you have an anxiety attack; you've never been in love; you don't want to look like a woman, so you are deliberately getting rid of your breasts, your shape, your periods, and becoming an androgynous figure. You're still to an extent living in a convent, one of your own making. Both you and Rebecca are using all these repressed emotions to punish yourselves.'

'But what can I *do* about it?' I wailed. 'I don't want to be like this.'

'We've got to get to the root of all that pent-up emotion,' Dr Piet replied calmly. 'Until we do that, you'll remain stuck in that ivory tower you've built round yourself as a kind of prison. It's time now, Karen. It's time to come out.'

But this was easier said than done. I was still locked inside my own head, in rather the same way as Charlotte was imprisoned in her bedsitting-room and Rebecca in her hospital bed. I couldn't be like Jane, who seemed instinctively to know how to reach out and have a good time. She and Mark would often invite me to join them for a drive and lunch in the country, or she would descend upon me in the library and sweep me off to the pub. Jane knew how things worked and was at home in the world in a way I feared I would never be. And (I was becoming aware) she was obviously going to succeed professionally and (it seemed increasingly clear) I was not.

Jane and I had both sailed through the qualifying examinations for the doctoral programme with distinction. But now our paths were dividing. Jane had won a junior Research Fellowship at St Anne's; I had been advised not to apply. My tutors told me repeatedly that I had no future in academia: I should think

131

about travelling, perhaps. I could get a job in a liberal arts college in the United States, a place most of them regarded with ill-concealed disdain. Or I should seriously consider school teaching. That, Dorothy Bednarowska claimed, would be much more my *métier*. I could not agree. A school, with its bells, rules and authority figures, was far too like the convent. I wanted to be a scholar.

Somehow, it was made clear to me, my face did not fit. This was nothing to do with class, nor was anybody concerned about my mental instability. Nobody took my psychiatric troubles very seriously. Those who knew that I was seeing Dr Piet simply thought that I was making rather heavy weather about leaving the convent, and would soon come to my senses. Besides, Oxford dons are not the most stable group of people in the world. No, their opposition to my academic career seemed more deeply rooted. 'They were really determined to get rid of you,' Jane agreed, years after it had ceased to matter. 'They wanted me and they didn't want you.' But why? My work was considered good. Jane was obviously more 'normal' than I, but when had Oxford ever been interested in the norm? There was something about me that my tutors and mentors felt instinctively to be 'wrong'; their recoil was similar, perhaps, to the way a patient will reject a transplanted heart as alien, something that her body cannot assimilate. I doubt they could have put it into words, and now, with hindsight, I think they were right. I was not really suited to the life of a university teacher, nor to the type of scholarship that was currently in vogue at Oxford. I had different talents, but none of us could have known that in 1971, when, in some ways, I seemed a model student.

Whatever the reason, my sudden fall from grace was a great blow. The possibility of a future in scholarship had been the one hopeful thing in my life. Now, yet again, it seemed that I was to be prised away from a familiar world.

Jacob slept peacefully, turned on his side away from me. I took out my book and started to read by the small circle of pale light that came from Jenifer's bedside lamp. I was on the late shift, sitting with Jacob until his mother, who was at a college dinner, returned home. Lying on Jenifer's bed in the long attic room, I felt peacefully away from things. An owl hooted outside and I looked anxiously at Jacob, who was a light sleeper and, once woken, was likely to remain restless all night. But he slept on, while the alarm clock on the cluttered bedside table ticked loudly in the silence.

Suddenly, Jacob reared up and gazed ahead, his eyes fixed and frightened and yet also, I sensed, unseeing. He began to make a strange keening sound in his throat and for a moment I felt pure panic. This was it: he was about to have an epileptic seizure.

Snatching the rubber teething ring that Jenifer kept by her bed, I carefully inserted it into Jacob's mouth, as instructed, and pushed him gently back on his side. Then we both waited. I was frightened: I had no idea what I would see or how I would cope. Jacob was a big child, taller and probably stronger than I. How could I prevent him from hurting himself? And what if he did not stop convulsing? If he had not regained consciousness within ten minutes, this would be a medical emergency. *Status epilepticus*, I had been told, could be fatal. But I was alone in the house and the nearest telephone was downstairs.

Suddenly Jacob stopped breathing for what seemed like minutes but was probably only a few seconds. His face became distorted, and his eyes brutish and angry. The colour drained from his skin, until it took on the mottled hue of a dirty stone. Then, after what seemed another long interval, his teeth locked on the teething ring and his body started to jerk convulsively. Please, let this stop, I prayed to nobody in particular, while it went on and on.

Then, just as suddenly, the convulsions ceased and Jacob relaxed. The teething ring fell from his mouth, and he fell into a heavy comatose sleep, his breathing rasping and ugly. The colour gradually seeped back into his face. It was over.

But I knew that there was always the danger of another seizure. If that happened, I must send for an ambulance immediately. Gradually, however, Jacob's breathing returned to normal and he slid into a peaceful sleep.

It seemed so unfair. Jacob had only recently started to have seizures. Did he not have enough to deal with? I wanted to blame somebody and God was the obvious target, but somehow I could not get into this. Did I really believe that there was a Being up there somehow responsible for everything that happened on earth, including Jacob's disabilities? No, I did not. Not only did it seem highly unlikely that there was an overseeing deity, supervising earthly events, apportioning trials and rewards according to some inscrutable programme of his own, but the idea was also grotesque. If there was a loving providence, it bore no relation to any kind of love that I could conceive. I did not believe that this God existed, and, as I sat that night beside Jacob in the semi-darkness, I wondered if I ever really had.

I heard movement below, and realized that Jenifer was climbing cautiously up the wrought-iron staircase leading to the attic. Her lean, athletic frame appeared behind the frosted glass, and I watched her opening the door with the minimum of noise, stealing into the room with exaggerated care. She grimaced as one of the boards creaked in the course of her painful progress across the large, untidy room.

'Everything all right?' she hissed.

'Well, no: I'm afraid he had a fit. But he seems all right now.'

'Oh!' Dismayed, she sank on to the bed and looked across at her son. Her face, which had retained the stimulus of a lively evening, collapsed. She was wearing one of her strange evening dresses: this one was emerald green and decorated with little jewels of mirrored glass. With its matching green stockings, it was an optimistic, slightly frivolous outfit that suddenly looked incongruous. 'Oh, my dear! I am so sorry,' she said. 'I know how awful it is. I do hope it didn't upset you too much.'

'No, no. Don't worry about it.' I smiled reassuringly at her as I gathered my books together.

'Karen,' she said abruptly. We were still whispering, of course, but I could tell from the tentative tone of her voice that she was nervous about what she was going to say. 'Karen – do you think you – please feel free to refuse, that goes without saying, of course. You do more than enough as it is and Jacob is so fond of you. I always feel confident when he is with you. But do you think – I mean . . .'

'Whatever *is* it, Jenifer?' I asked, amused but slightly alarmed.

'Well, I wonder if you would consider taking Jacob to mass with you at Blackfriars.' In her embarrassment, the words tumbled out in a rush.

'What!' In my astonishment, I forgot to whisper, and we both froze and turned anxiously back to the bed. Fortunately, Jacob slept on. 'Sorry.' I spoke as softly as I could. 'But you must admit that this is a bit of a turn-around. I mean, I would have thought it was the *last* thing . . .'

'Yes, I know.' She smiled ruefully and made a helpless gesture. 'I know it must sound perfectly mad. Herbert and I, of all people! Can't you imagine what our friends are going to say? I know it seems illogical, inconsistent. But I've often thought that Jacob ought to have some kind of religion. All that ritual, for example – he'd simply love that. And religion is supposed to give some kind of comfort, isn't it?' She looked up at me tentatively.

'Well . . .' I tailed off, unwilling to go down that road, tonight of all nights. I couldn't resist a little sarcasm. 'You wouldn't feel like coming along yourself, I suppose? You haven't seen the light? And perhaps Herbert would like to join us?'

'Oh, heavens no!' We both laughed, as noiselessly as possible, at the absurdity of the suggestion. 'But seriously,' Jenifer continued, 'the Blackfriars mass sounds ideal, because presumably no one would mind if he made some kind of fuss. And he'd get to meet lots of new people at your coffee morning afterwards. I really think that it would do him good.'

She sounded as though religion were like an iron tonic: a regular dose each week would automatically induce peace of soul.

'He would probably enjoy it,' I conceded somewhat reluctantly. The very idea of Jacob or any Hart in a church was so astounding that it was difficult to imagine. 'But,' again I could hear the irony in my voice, 'I take it he'll just be going along for the show. You won't want me to give him instruction or anything like that?'

'Oh, Lord, no – he doesn't have to *understand* it!' Jenifer exclaimed, slightly scandalized. I stared at her hard: this really was a bit of a cheek. And yet, I reflected, how many Catholics truly understood the labyrinthine complexity of their doctrinal system? 'I don't want him getting any of those ghastly ideas you all have – God, Heaven and Hell or anything of that sort,' Jenifer went on, oblivious to any offence that her words might give. 'Of course, all those beliefs are nonsense anyway. Ludicrous, in fact! He doesn't need to know any of *that*!'

'He'll probably have to know something, though, to help him

into the experience,' I said, trying to see how the mass might look to a complete outsider. 'It would all be a sort of fantasy to him, of course, on a par with Guy Fawkes or Goldilocks. But he might grasp the point of some of the stories. Nothing heavy; just – I don't know – Jesus loves me and is my friend.'

'Well, I suppose that wouldn't do any harm,' Jenifer said doubtfully. She frowned, and I felt a sudden wave of affection for her. There was something heroic in what she was doing. She was sacrificing all her most cherished principles; her clever, sceptical friends would be merciless to her face and probably lethal behind her back. But what mattered most to Jenifer was what was best for Jacob. 'You see,' she continued, 'it's all very well for people like Herbert and me to reject religion. But Jacob – he needs something – he needs some kind of support.'

'What you mean is,' I said caustically, 'that religion is really just for idiots, weaklings and defectives.'

'Oh dear.' Jenifer grinned rather nervously at me. 'How awful. But yes . . . yes, if I'm honest, I suppose that is what I think . . .' she tailed off and looked at me sheepishly.

I couldn't in all conscience take issue with her. Had I not just dismissed God myself as an illusion? But Jacob deserved some consolation. 'All right,' I said at last, 'I'll take him.'

In finally relinquishing the last vestiges of religious belief, I had come closer to the mainstream than ever before in my life. During the 1960s religion had died in Britain, and church attendance plummeted. England was fast becoming one of the most secular countries in the world, topped only by the Netherlands. The Harts' principled rejection of religion had once seemed daring and iconoclastic, but it was now unremarkable, especially among intellectuals. But although the Harts regarded Catholicism as 'ludicrous', they were not crusading atheists. They were both admirers of the utilitarianism first enunciated by the nineteenth-century British philosopher, Jeremy Bentham. Jenifer's pragmatic approach to Jacob's churchgoing was essentially utilitarian. Actions are not intrinsically good or evil, but should be judged by their consequences. Right acts are those that produce the best results. There was nothing in itself wrong with attending mass, so, even though it was the product of a belief system that was palpably false, if it helped Jacob, then he should go to Blackfriars. Many of their friends, whose repudiation of faith was more militant, would find this faintly reprehensible.

The idea that somebody, like Jacob, might get something out of Catholic liturgy without accepting the creed that supported it was novel to me. As far as I was concerned, religion consisted essentially of belief, and now that I could no longer subscribe to a creed, I could not be a religious person. And yet all around me, at the same time as people were casting off the trammels of institutional Christianity, they were turning to alternative forms of faith. The Harts' two older sons, Adam and Charlie, for example, were both leading lights in Britain's counter-culture. Charlie lived in a commune near Cambridge, and had formed a pop group. Adam, who was my exact contemporary, was more radical, and regarded even the life of a performing musician as a cop-out. He lived in a commune in Northumberland in a house bought for the community by his father, and had no productive work. Their ideals, expressed in such typically 60s slogans as 'Do what you feel', 'Let it all hang out', 'Go with the flow' and 'Do your own thing', were, on the face of it, the antithesis of the ideals of my convent, and yet there was also a similarity.

Both boys had rejected the utilitarianism of their parents, yet, although they had no theological beliefs, they had embarked on what in other ways amounted to a religious quest. They had turned their backs on society, were seeking what gave life intrinsic value, and had rejected money and worldly success, just as I had when I had entered my convent. They had no time for institutional faith or the authoritarian structures of Christianity, but practised transcendental meditation in the hope of changing their thought-structures. Other post-war Britons also sought personal transfor-mation; they wanted to be 'somewhere else'. Some went off to Kathmandu; others merely took drug-induced trips. Even the Beatles, who had outraged Christians in the United States by declaring – correctly – that they were more popular in Britain than Jesus Christ, had spent months with a guru in India. People were beginning to experiment with new ways of being religious.

I could not see it at the time but, by asking me to take Jacob to Blackfriars, Jenifer was in tune with this trend. She understood that Jacob needed not a creed, but spirituality and rituals that could bring him a measure of peace. But for me, religion without belief was a contradiction in terms, and I had very little hope that the Church, which had brought me to the brink of despair, could help Jacob to make sense of his frightening world.

'Moon rises!' Jacob greeted me as usual, rushing along the narrow corridor to the kitchen. 'Moon rises twelve forty-nine a.m.! Karen! Where are we going this morning?'

'We're going to –' I waited for him to finish the sentence.

'Blackfriars!' Jacob roared with evident delight. He certainly seemed enthusiastic. 'Do I look smart?'

'You're looking very smart indeed.' He did, too: white jersey, brown cord trousers, and hair brushed and curly. 'Now, Jacob, you look at the papers, while I make our toast.'

'Karen.' He put his head round the door. 'You won't be angry, will you, if I spill coffee all the way down the front of my white jersey?'

'Not if it's an accident, no.'

'But if I do it on purpose?'

'Then I'll be very angry indeed.'

'Because, Karen, I'm going to do it!' He picked up his mug and regarded me hopefully.

'Don't you dare!' I thundered predictably.

'Oh, don't be severe!' Jacob beamed.

'I shall be very severe indeed, if you're not sitting in your place in two seconds flat!'

'Oh, don't be displeased!' As he returned to the dining room, I heard him mutter: 'Karen was extremely oppressive with Jacob. "Don't you dare do it!" she cried angrily . . . Jacob looked crestfallen and pleaded with Karen. "Oh, don't be displeased," he begged wistfully.'

When, an hour later, mass began, Jacob behaved beautifully. He stood with his eyes closed and his hands joined, fingers pointing heavenward. He must have learned this in school. 'You don't have to stand like that all the time,' I whispered. He nodded gravely. During the hymns and music, he listened intently, head averted, a strange half-smile of approval on his lips. Rapturously, he flung his head back and inhaled the incense. 'Karen,' he whispered luxuriantly between sniffs, 'I like coming to Blackfriars, I really do!'

Well, Jenifer had been right. Jacob really was getting something from this. But what was it doing for me? This morning, the ritual seemed remote, arbitrary and to have nothing to do with my own perplexities. This was the new vernacular mass, the creation of the Second Vatican Council. It was lively, fresh and cheerful – perhaps a little too cheery for my taste. It was all so sensible and matter-of-fact. It suggested that God was well disposed towards us, and could be approached in a casual, confident spirit, as though he were a congenial boss. But God was not my friend. I could see now that he never had been. And this service was so wordy. The old liturgy, punctuated by singing that gave the congregation time for reflection, had a silent, contemplative core. But we now seemed afraid to stop talking, and were reminding God insistently that he had created the world and redeemed us, as though he were too absentminded to recall these deeds. I cast my mind back to Mrs Moore in E. M. Forster's *A Passage to India*, confronted by the abysmal echo of the Marabar caves and finding no help in 'poor, talkative little Christianity'. Perhaps we were afraid that if we stopped chattering to God in this way, the empty silence would cause him to vanish. As perhaps he had.

When we stood for the Creed, Jacob looked around expectantly, hoping for more incense. I listened to the familiar words: 'I believe in One God, the Father Almighty, Maker of Heaven and Earth . . . and in Jesus Christ . . . Begotten not made, of one substance with the Father . . .' The congregation repeated these extraordinary propositions without surprise, as I had done so often in the past, but now I felt that I could no longer join them. I remembered a Jesuit telling us once during a retreat that faith was not really an intellectual assent, but an act of will. Christians could accept their essentially incredible tradition only by making a deliberate choice to believe. You could not prove or disprove these doctrines, but you could consciously decide to take them on trust. They might even turn out to be true. But somewhere along the line, I had given up. I could no longer summon up the emotional or spiritual energy to make that choice. I felt tired out, drained and slightly repelled by it all. I was finished with God; and God – if he existed at all – had long ago finished with me.

'Karen! Will you bring me to Blackfriars again next week?' Jacob asked as we crossed St Giles and hurried past the Lamb and Flag. He had had a wonderful morning. After mass, I had taken him into the coffee room, and again he had behaved beautifully, standing quietly beside me with his cup and listening as usual with averted face to the people who had come over to say hello. Geoffrey Preston had made a point of talking to Jacob and had asked him if he would like to serve on the altar one day. That had seemed a little too ambitious to me, but, as Geoffrey pointed out, Bernard, who had Down's Syndrome, regularly assisted at mass and carried the cross at the head of the procession. Jacob did not answer Geoffrey directly, of course, but he looked thoughtful and smiled to himself. He clearly felt at ease in Blackfriars and the community there had generously taken him in.

'Karen!' Jacob tugged at my arm and put his face close to mine, so that our noses almost touched. I smiled at him. 'Karen, we will be going to Blackfriars again next week, won't we?' It seemed that Jacob's religious life was beginning as mine was ending. And if I didn't take him to mass, nobody would.

'Of course we'll be going!' I replied, and, satisfied, Jacob broke away and trotted ahead in the lopsided gait that was so like his father's, looking back occasionally to see that I was still there.

Yes, I would continue to take him to Blackfriars. I did not believe in any of it any more; God had finally departed from my life, but it would do me no harm to sit for a while every week with those good people. And giving Jacob this new chance would be a positive thing to do. He had so few pleasures, and now that he had found something he so clearly relished, it would be cruel to take it away from him. It wasn't as though I had anything else to do on Sunday mornings. In fact, I really didn't have anything else to do in my life at all.

∻ 4 ∽

CONSEQUENTLY I REJOICE

I have no idea how it happened, but it was the result of a worrying new development. At least, it was of concern to me. Dr Piet had greeted the news with his usual nonchalance, but this latest symptom had been yet another sign to me that my mind was breaking down completely. I had started to lose control over my actions – only for a short period of time, and only infrequently, but I still found it very disturbing. The first time it occurred, I had been working in my room in Manor Place and decided that it was time for coffee.

'Another cup, Karen?' Nanny smiled as I came into the kitchen and lit the gas under the kettle. 'You must be thirsty this morning!'

'Sorry, Nanny? What do you mean?'

Nanny looked puzzled, as well she might. 'Well, you were here just half an hour ago.' I must have looked blank. 'I saw you going upstairs with your mug while I was tidying the drawing room. Surely you remember, Karen?' she added, disturbed about her own powers of memory. 'I saw you quite distinctly,' she added, to convince herself as much as anything.

'Oh, yes, of course. I do apologize, Nanny. I was miles away.' Poor Nanny, I thought, as I returned to my room. She was getting on in years, and old people were notoriously forgetful.

But when I opened the door, I saw the mug on the windowsill; when I examined it, I found it full of coffee that was not yet entirely cold. Try as I would, I could not recall making it. I must have gone downstairs, boiled the water, poured it on to the coffee granules, and returned to my desk. And I had no recollection at all of any of this.

Then, a few weeks later, I found myself unexpectedly sitting in the English Faculty Library. There I was, at a table in the upstairs reading room, with a copy of the journal *Notes and Queries* (known to us irreverently as *Quotes and Drearies*) open in front of me. And again, I had no recollection of leaving the house, taking the short walk down Manor Place, crossing the road, and entering the library. No recollection at all.

I was scared. It seemed obvious to me that I was breaking down. Yet again, I could see the locked ward, the padded cell, and a life in the twilight of consciousness. And there did not seem to be anything that I could do about it.

Dr Piet, however, did not seem perturbed. 'You're just becoming an absent-minded professor, Karen,' he said cheerily, grinning at me across his desk. 'This is what all you academics do, right? You're just reverting to the stereotype.'

'No,' I protested. 'It's *not* like that. I didn't just forget. I really didn't know what I was doing!'

'My dear Karen.' Dr Piet took a more bracing line. 'You really mustn't take yourself so seriously. You've probably just been working too hard. Or it could be a side effect of the medication. I'll take you off the Largactil for a while and we'll have a go at Librium. But I don't want to hear any more of this nonsense about padded cells and the rest of it. Believe me, if I committed everyone in Oxford who had periods of forgetfulness, the hospitals would be full to overflowing and city life would grind to a halt. This kind of mental abstraction is an occupational hazard for scholars. You've all got your minds on higher things, supposedly. You're just not focused on mundane reality. Try to get a sense of perspective about this.'

I stared mutinously at the carpet, unconvinced. I was not and never had been in the least absent-minded. I didn't forget things; I had an almost abnormally good memory. I could – and still can – recount entire conversations years after they have taken place, recall exactly what everybody was wearing and what we had eaten for lunch. I didn't float around in an academic haze. These were not bouts of forgetfulness but lapses into a form of unconsciousness, when I was quite *compos mentis* enough to boil a kettle or cross a road safely, but seemed unaware of what I was doing. This must, surely, be a symptom of something sinister. And yet a part of me longed to believe Dr Piet. It would be so wonderful if I really were simply behaving like a regular scholar. It would be such a relief to be 'typical' for a change, instead of a freak. And Dr Piet seemed to have no doubts at all; maybe he really *did* see a lot of this.

'And in any case,' he was saying, taking off his glasses and leaning seriously across the desk, 'all these symptoms that you're producing are just a smoke-screen. They're distractions from the real issue: the problems that drove you into the convent in the first place. You're taking refuge in the dramatic and the exotic because they make you feel important, whereas, in truth, there is nothing very special about your difficulties. They all spring from

145

identity issues, gender problems, and parental conflicts that are very common indeed. Shared by half the population, in fact. But you can't bear to be so banal. No, you have to turn it all into some kind of gothic trauma: convents, visions, voices, satanic terror – and now sleepwalking! Anything rather than be ordinary. Because as long as you keep producing these "interesting" psychic states, you are postponing the moment when you have to accept the unwelcome fact that, when push comes to shove, you're not that interesting! You're just another brainy girl who is having problems accepting her femininity. There is nothing very unusual about that, I'm afraid.' He glanced at the clock: 'You see – we've wasted nearly the whole of this hour discussing these moments of forgetfulness, which, as usual, you've beefed up into something extraordinary, and this has meant that we haven't been able to talk about what is *really* going on. It's a delaying tactic, Karen, an evasion.'

I stared back at him. What could I say? Perhaps he was right. There probably was a sense in which I didn't want to be ordinary. And it was certainly true that I was sick to death of grinding on and on about my early childhood. Perhaps I was warding off yet another discussion of my adolescence, which – Dr Piet was quite right here – was entirely without interest. He always seemed to be trying to force me to accept his version of events that he had not personally witnessed and his assessment of people whom he had never met. And yes, I could accept that I probably did have gender problems. I could see that my eating disorder had neutralized my body, making it neither male nor female. There probably was a whole lot of unfinished business, left over from the convent; I wouldn't have minded discussing this, but we were never supposed to talk about my years as a nun. That, apparently, was yet another exotic distraction that had nothing to do with the 'real' issues.

'So in future,' Dr Piet said pointedly, as he drew the session to a close, 'let's not waste any more time. Let us have no more agonizing about unimportant details. Let's get right in there to the basic difficulties, which are the cause of all these symptoms. And do me a favour – let's have no more histrionics about perfectly normal absent-mindedness. After all, Karen,' he smiled to soften his bleak conclusions, 'it's not as if you ever did anything very dreadful at these times. Making a cup of coffee? Going to a library? Come on! You, of all people, with your gothic imagination, can do better than that! Let's see what you're really like when you lose control. Surprise me!'

And so, a few weeks later, in the autumn of 1971, I did just that. I woke up in hospital throwing up an overdose of sleeping pills.

Again, I have no recollection of what happened. I do remember pouring myself a glass of the sherry that Jane had given to me for my twenty-seventh birthday. I had wanted to forget myself, to escape from the hallucinations, the fear and the perplexity, and to give myself a little treat. But I don't recall swallowing a large number of the purple sleeping tablets that Dr Piet had prescribed for my insomnia. I certainly cannot remember deciding to end it once and for all. There was nothing conscious or deliberate about the act. I could recall the sweet stickiness of the sherry, but of the pills, my discovery by Jane, the alarm, the ambulance, I had no memory, no recollection at all.

So the forced vomiting, the pain, the indignity and the curt orders of the doctors were devastating. I had no notion of what had happened or where I was. A nurse asked peremptorily for my name. Did I know how old I was? What was the date? Who was the Prime Minister? I remember Jane's anxious face, the succession of ceilings and doors, as I was wheeled down one corridor after another, and a numbing cold. As I was lifted on to a bed in the ward, I heard one of the other patients shouting officiously: 'She'll be cold! She'll need another blanket, nurse! She'll be cold!'

'Mind your own business, Brenda! Get back into bed,' somebody replied sharply. 'We can deal with this, thank you.'

But I reached gratefully for the word, which had eluded me, and was able to croak: 'I'm so cold!' I heard Jane giggle and say wryly, 'Spot on, Brenda.' Then a nurse leaned over my bed, her face lit grotesquely by the harsh beam of light.

'Where's your sponge bag, dear?'

I stared at her, bewildered.

'Your sponge bag! Surely you didn't forget to bring it with you?'

And dimly, as I sank into oblivion, I heard Jane's tart rejoinder, which would later tell me what had happened. 'She didn't think she'd need a sponge bag in the hereafter! When you're trying to kill yourself, sponge bags are not uppermost in your mind.'

I don't want to make too much of this. When I woke up the next day and gradually pieced it all together, I felt ashamed and could understand the scarcely veiled contempt of the nurses. When you are caring for people who are mortally ill and struggling desperately to live, it must be almost insupportable to have to deal with people who want to throw it all away. But I did not believe that I had really wanted to die, and, as I pondered the events of that night, I became more and more certain that it was not death that I had sought. The pills that I had swallowed were not lethal; I could have downed any number of them without doing myself irreparable damage. And I was almost certain that I was aware of that. This strange act had been another cry for help. What I was unconsciously trying to do that night was to make clear the depths of my desperation. I did not know how to live any longer. And nobody seemed to realize just how frightened I was. Nobody was willing to listen.

The trouble is that when people decide that what looks like a suicide attempt is 'only' a cry for help, they sometimes conclude that this appeal need not be answered. Indeed, they even decide that it is better not to respond, because the patient must not be encouraged to give way to such neurotic exhibitionism. He or she must learn to express pain simply and directly, without resorting to such outlandish symbolism. But I had tried to explain my fears and bewilderment, as clearly as I was able, and no aid was forthcoming.

Quite simply, I wanted help, and I didn't feel that I was getting it. That was probably what lay behind this unconsciously per-formed gesture. As I lay in bed that morning, amidst the confusion and the fear – what might I do next in this amnesiac state? – I was also aware of a definite sense of relief. I was sorry to have caused all this unnecessary bother, but on the other hand I was *so* weary and needy. I had spent years now fighting with demons, and the struggle had pushed me to an extreme. I felt exhausted, and it was good to have people looking after me instead of telling me briskly that I was perfectly well and getting along just fine. I knew that this could only be a temporary respite, but it was not altogether unpleasant to give up the struggle for a while. And something in me had been calmed. Instead of the familiar turmoil within, there was a new stillness. I had tried my best, and to no avail. I had expressed my fear and despair, and I could do no more. I had come to the end, had given up hope, and there was a certain peace in that.

Dr Piet, who came to visit that afternoon, seemed to take it all rather personally. He had challenged me to surprise him and I had taken him at his word. I was, he told me, clearly angry with him – and that, in his view, was a step forward. Even in my becalmed state, I felt faintly annoyed that he had placed himself so squarely in the centre of my personal drama. He seemed to believe that I had done all this just to grab his attention, whereas, in reality, he was by no means as crucial to me as he seemed to imagine. He had decided that the things that truly distressed me were peripheral, and had thus become a rather marginal figure in my emotional life. If a doctor had failed to respond in this way to Rebecca, I would have been furious. But you get angry only with people who are important to you in a way that Dr Piet was not. For months – indeed, for years now – I had felt increasingly insubstantial. As Tennyson put it, I saw myself as a ghost in a world of ghosts. I had existed for so long in this twilight state that nothing seemed quite real any longer, and therefore nothing seemed to matter very much.

I could also see that Dr Piet was no longer quite so dismissive of my amnesia, however.

'It would have been much easier, Karen, if you had made an extra appointment and told me that you were feeling this depressed,' he said, with a certain exasperation. 'I'm your doctor and I should know if you are feeling suicidal.'

'But I *wasn't*,' I snapped, stung momentarily out of my frozen calm. 'I didn't know that I was going to take the wretched pills. It was like the other times. I didn't know what I was doing.' He sighed. 'And I *have* been telling you how bad I've been feeling,' I went on, hopelessly. 'I've told you again and again.'

'But don't you see that this is another evasive tactic?' Dr Piet shook his head. 'We're going to have to work really hard now on the underlying causes of all this.' My heart sank. 'But you do need a bit of a rest, I think,' Dr Piet continued more kindly.

'You're going to need looking after. The hospital will let you out tomorrow. Where do you intend to go?'

'I can't go back to the Harts,' I said. This was one aspect of the whole *débâcle* that I could not contemplate with equanimity. They had been so kind, and how had I repaid them? 'No.' I waved away Dr Piet's next question. 'I can't ask them; it would put them in an intolerable position! How could they decently say no?'

We ran through my options. My parents were away on holiday, and I did not want them to know about any of this. I could not bear to think of their distress if they realized how bad things were. And whatever Dr Piet thought, this was not their fault. If they had had their way I would never have set foot in the convent. Nobody had forced me into the religious life; nobody had compelled me to stay there for so long. I had been responsible for the damage of my own mind.

'Well, you can't live by yourself,' Dr Piet said testily. 'We'll have to keep an eye on you now.'

The only alternative that I could come up with was Cherwell Edge. The nuns there had made a few wan overtures to me, implying that if I needed anything, I had only to ask. It was by no means an ideal solution, and I could see that Dr Piet was not entirely happy about it, but it was better than being admitted to a psychiatric hospital, which was the only other option. So we left it that I would ring the nuns and ask if I might stay in the convent for a while. It would at least be familiar, and a holiday from the endless struggle of trying to fit into secular life. And perhaps a little rest was all that I needed.

If a pall of gloom had hung over my meeting with Dr Piet, Jane treated the whole sorry affair as a tremendous adventure. She strode into the ward as if into a party, carrying a suitcase filled with my errant sponge bag, some clothes, a bunch of grapes, and a pile of novels. I glanced at the covers: John Updike, Saul Bellow, Margaret Drabble and Iris Murdoch. They looked a little daunting. Jane waved aside my embarrassed thanks and apologies.

'For God's sake! It was a marvellous piece of luck for me! I feel enormously noble and resourceful, though it was really just a question of dialing 999, and dealing with the Harts.'

I winced. 'How did they take it?'

'They looked pretty aghast, I must say. Jenifer hopped from one leg to another like an anguished stork, and Herbert was put right off his supper. Pity, really, he'd gone to quite a lot of trouble with it.'

She explained that she had made an impromptu visit, as she often did when at a loose end. Seeing that my light was on, she had let herself in through the kitchen door, as usual, to find Herbert concocting one of his elaborate late-night snacks in the dim light of the unshaded 40-watt bulb. He greeted Jane with enthusiasm, knowing that she was a good cook, and asked her advice. Should he add a touch more oregano? They had chatted amicably for a few minutes, and then Jane had run up to my room, tapped on the door, and getting no answer, had peered in to see me lying unconscious on my bed. Jacob fortunately had slept through the whole business.

'I'm afraid I didn't do anything heroic, like trying to make you sick,' Jane went on. 'I tell myself that I was afraid of doing more harm than good, but really I was just too squeamish. I must say,' she grinned, 'that it's never dull knowing you.'

I lay back on my pillows and contemplated Jane with amusement. She seemed determined to see the whole business as an entertaining tale on which she could dine out in the future. I listened as she relived the highlights: what the ambulance men had said, what I looked like, and the sturdy disapproval of the nurses. I knew that I could never be like that. I could not habitually view events in a positive or humorous light – nor did I particularly want to. But there was something comforting that afternoon in Jane's buoyant refusal to look on the dark side of the affair. As I watched her transform last night's mess into a highly crafted anecdote, it occurred to me that a little of her insouciance would do me no harm. Nothing else seemed to work. Even Dr Piet had seemed somewhat at a loss since his method had not yielded the result he had expected. If nothing could be done, maybe I should just stop fighting this peculiar malady of mine, and go with the flow, like the hippies. My mind seemed irreparably injured in some way, and perhaps I would never be wholly normal. But if I accepted this handicap as my lot, as other disabled people did, then perhaps I would discover a source of peace and endurance within myself. There was nothing I could do about the past that had brought me to this impasse. But I could deliberately cultivate the kind of robust gladness that seemed to come quite naturally to Jane. I recalled Wordsworth's decision, when he realized that the glory of the world that he had experienced as a boy had gone for ever:

> We will grieve not, rather find
> Strength in what remains behind.

Perhaps I could take that as a mantra.

Jane was horrified by the idea that I should go back to the convent to recuperate. 'You can't want to do that!' she insisted. 'It's that whole rotten system that put you in here, surely? That's the last place you should be.'

I shook my head. I wouldn't have that. The system hadn't worked for me, or for Rebecca, but it hadn't affected the vast majority of women who had undergone its disciplines in this way. I certainly could not lay it all at the door of the nuns. 'There was something in me – in my temperament, my genes, whatever – which was antipathetic to that kind of training. Antipathetic to religion, come to that,' I added gloomily.

'What do you mean?' Jane was immediately interested.

'I couldn't make religion work for me,' I explained. 'I really tried. I tried to pray, to meditate, but I never got anywhere. Oh yes, I know the ritual was wonderful – I remember how much it meant to you – but don't you see? That was just an aesthetic response. The real test is when you try to find God on your own, without props, without beautiful music, singing, and spectacle – when there is just you on your knees. And I could never do that.'

'Have you lost your faith, then?' Jane asked sharply.

'I don't know that I ever had any faith, not true faith. I wanted to believe it all; I wanted to have an encounter with God. But I never did. God was never a reality for me, never a genuine presence in my life as he was for the other sisters.'

'And what about now?' Jane went on. 'I mean, suicide's a mortal sin, right? Are you feeling guilty?'

'No,' I said slowly. 'No. Of course, I'm sorry to have caused so much trouble. But I'm not feeling guilty because I've offended God. No. I just don't believe that God is *there*.'

'Join the club.' Jane smiled dourly. 'If there *is* a God, he's doing a spectacularly bad job of running the world, that's all I can say. But anyway,' she seemed mentally to shake herself back into a more positive frame of mind. 'I really think you should reconsider this mad idea of going back to the convent. And I think you're wrong about the Harts. I'm certain they would have you back.

They're awfully fond of you, in their own way, you know – though they'd rather die than admit it. Jenifer rang up the hospital this morning to find out how you were.'

'That was kind.' I was touched, but determined. 'No. I just can't roll up tomorrow at Manor Place as though nothing has happened. I just can't.'

As it turned out, Jane need not have worried. When I rang up Cherwell Edge and spoke to the Superior, she had at first sounded genuinely pleased to hear from me. She had replaced Mother Praeterita, with whom I had clashed so stridently during my last year in the religious life, and was a kindly woman, whom I had known distantly in Sussex. But when I told her my story, she retreated at once. What I had done was truly terrible; she would have to take advice and pray about it, but she really didn't think that the community could accept this responsibility.

I was shaken when I put down the phone, and angry. How many times had I been told that nuns were never shocked, any more than Jesus had been? You can say anything to a nun; nothing about human nature surprises them. That was the theory, but it was not true of course. It is probably not the case with anyone, and now, almost thirty years later, I cannot say that I blame that Superior. I probably frightened her half to death. She would have remembered me as a timid little novice, unable to say boo to a goose, and here I was apparently deranged and dangerously sui-cidal. It was indeed a mad idea to imagine that I could go back to the convent to convalesce, and the fact that I had thought it feasible showed how confused I really was, despite my studied calm. But at the time the rejection seemed a slap in the face. And that too was salutary. It made me realize that I could not keep looking to the past; I had to move on. I repeated my new mantra: 'We will grieve not, rather find Strength in what remains behind.'

It was not so easy to be positive, however, when, a few hours later, I found myself sitting on a lumpy sofa waiting to be checked into a ward in the Littlemore Hospital, watching another patient making her slow crab-like progress down the corridor, limbs splayed in all directions, so that she looked disjointed. On her face was an expression of exaggerated terror as she took each painful step forward. While both her hands and feet made contact with the wall, she was all right, but each time she inched forwards, she broke her sole link with concrete reality.

'Come along, Mrs Saunders, you can do it!' a nurse said encouragingly every thirty seconds. But could she? And could I? My mantra seemed absurd in this context: it was, to put it mildly, difficult to find a source of strength in the psychiatric ward of my worst nightmares. True, there was no padded cell and this was not a locked ward. I had been breezily told that I would be able to come and go as I chose, just as long as I kept the nurses informed. But as I looked around the room at these other broken people, I feared that this was where I really belonged. I too had intimations of the kind of terror that was paralysing Mrs Saunders, making it impossible for her, try as she would, to take the next step. I stared glumly around the ward. There was a strong smell of sickness and disinfectant. Two brave souls were playing table tennis, but most were simply sitting on the ancient chairs and sofas, gazing at the walls or into space. I could be here for weeks or even months, until I found accommodation that would satisfy Dr Piet. But then I pulled myself up sharply. I had to get out as quickly as I feasibly could. I must not even begin to think that this was a natural habitation for me.

A short, middle-aged man with a beer belly plunked himself

down on the sofa beside me. 'Cheer up, darling. It's not so bad! In a day or two, it'll come to seem like home.'

That was precisely what I was afraid of. My new companion began to tell me a long, convoluted story about how he had ended up in what he called the 'loony bin': headaches, doctors, inconclusive medical tests, and then six months in the Littlemore for depression, though, as he explained, he'd never really *felt* depressed. But that, the doctors had informed him, was really the cause of his trouble. If he'd *allowed* himself to feel depressed, he wouldn't have had the headaches. And how were these headaches, after six months of group therapy, individual psychotherapy and Valium?

'Shocking.' He shook his head. 'I don't know. I really don't. Nothing's shifted them.' He was plainly bemused by the whole psychiatric approach. How *could* he be depressed without realizing it? I wondered how he would get on with Dr Piet, and looked at him thoughtfully. Perhaps there was something physically wrong with his brain? But now that he was stuck in here and branded a 'nutter' (his term), how would anybody ever find out?

A woman in a cerise knitted dress, her shoulder-blades sticking painfully through the thin material, her greying hair pulled neatly from her face, walked uncertainly towards us.

'Who am I?' she asked, bending down so that her lost, worried eyes looked directly into mine. 'I don't know who I am.'

'You're Mrs Sims, dear,' my companion explained patiently, with the air of one who had done this many times before. 'Got that? *Mrs Sims.*'

'Oh!' she cried in relief. 'I'm Mrs Sims!' she informed me happily, before wandering unsteadily to another part of the room.

'Karen.' A nurse stood at my elbow and picked up my bag. 'Would you come this way, please?'

'Off to register now, I expect?' my new friend said cheerily. 'See you later, sweetheart!' he called after me, as I hurried after the nurse, passing Mrs Saunders, who was still creeping down the corridor. I rounded the corner and there, standing as close to the door of the ward as possible and looking fastidiously alarmed, was Jenifer Hart.

'My dear!' She hurried forward and took my bag from the nurse. 'What are you thinking of? You can't possibly stay here – it's absolutely ludicrous!'

I had never been so glad to see anyone in my life. 'Do you mean –?' I asked, scarcely daring to hope for so swift a reprieve. Jenifer had already pushed open the door, nodded grimly to the nurse, and was striding resolutely out. 'Come on!' she called back to me impatiently, and I followed her down a flight of stairs, through the cavernous entrance hall, and out into the fresh air. I took a deep, luxuriant sniff, reminding myself of Jacob greedily snuffing up the incense at Blackfriars. 'What an extraordinary thing to have done!' Jenifer exclaimed. 'I telephoned the hospital to ask when they were going to let you out and they told me that you had come here!'

'Dr Piet –' I began, as we hurried across the car park towards the Harts' Morris Minor. The late autumn leaves looked more golden than I had ever seen them and the air smelled fragrant after the thick, heavy despair in the ward. I felt a thrill of pure exhilaration. Suddenly everything seemed possible. The battered, dusty car looked a chariot fit for the gods.

'Yes, I've spoken to him.' Jenifer flung my case on to the back seat. 'He told me that you didn't feel able to come back to us and that you had wanted to stay in the convent. My dear! I've never heard of such an insane scheme! You must be mad!'

'Yes.' I smiled to myself. 'I sometimes think I must be.'

'Here.' Jenifer scrabbled in the glove compartment and pulled out an already-opened packet of after-dinner chocolate mints, threw them into my lap, and turned the ignition key. 'These were left over from the guest night we had in college yesterday. There are quite a lot left. I thought they might cheer you up.'

As we drove back to Oxford, I felt a surge of returning life. There was excitement in the bustle of the streets, and the graceful curve of the High Street had never looked more beautiful. I smiled with real affection at the mints. It was so typical of Jenifer, whose frugality was almost miserly, to have pinched a box from college. A brand-new box would have been so uncharacteristic, a sign that something had irrevocably changed.

'Does Jacob know what happened?' I asked as we turned into Manor Place.

She shook her head. 'He knows that you haven't been well and that you went away for a rest. He's a bit suspicious – knows that there is something up, but that's all.'

It was almost dark by the time we drove the car into the garage and let ourselves in by the kitchen door. As I carried my bag through the hall, I passed Herbert, who was standing at the entrance to his study. He raised a hieratic hand in greeting.

'Moon rises!' he said.

That strange and frightening incident proved to be a watershed. Even though the external circumstances of my life had not changed, I was different. I was still plagued by panic and infrequent episodes of amnesia, I still felt cut off from the world in a capsule of unreality, but there seemed no point in fighting any of this. These things were permanent, and had proved to be untreatable, so now I resolved to ride with them. When the attacks came, I just tried to grit my teeth and let them carry me along, as though

I were trapped on a roller coaster, with no means of getting off. At least I knew now that, at some point, the ride always came to an end, and that even at their very worst, the attacks could not kill me. Come what may, I was determined that I would not end my days in a psychiatric ward.

But in real life, things are never as neat as they appear in a book. Inevitably in the coming months, there were setbacks, times when I seemed to have slipped right back to the beginning. When Dr Piet left Oxford, I saw other psychiatrists, who did no good, but by this time I had no great expectations and was not so disappointed when their treatment did not work. And that brief visit to the Littlemore was not my only sojourn in a psychiatric hospital. On two other occasions, I was admitted to the Warneford, its counterpart in Oxford, not because of a further suicide bid, but because I was simply worn out by the struggle – heartsick, discouraged, and needing the kind of rest that, I was told, could only be induced by chemicals. I cannot remember very much about these visits because I was so heavily drugged, nor – probably for the same reason – can I recall the particular events leading up to them. What they taught me was that, in my case at least, the kind of heavy medication designed to allay anxiety was worse than useless. I do remember sitting one day in the recreation room of my ward: it had once been a magnificent drawing room. Huge French windows looked out on to a terrace, walls and ceilings, decorated with elaborate cornices, were painted a gleaming white, and the doors were perfectly proportioned. But there the elegance ended. At floor level, the institutional armchairs, the floral hide-all carpets, and the dismal stench of sickness were all in nightmarish counterpoint to the original Victorian splendour. My eyes were fixed on the clock. Never had I been so acutely aware of the infinite elasticity of time. The minutes seemed to have become a new element. Each second seemed a millennium. Time had become something one had to wade through, like mud. And beneath the layers of heavy, turgid fug in my brain was a throbbing, high-pitched tension that no drug ever touched.

And then there were the problems of institutional life. It brought it all back: the way rules became absolute and could not be adapted to particular cases. I was sharing a room with a pretty, bulimic girl from Switzerland. Our beds were made up so that our heads were only inches away from a huge old-fashioned radiator, which gave off a thick, suffocating heat, smelling strongly of paint. Each night I turned the bedclothes around, so that my feet were beside the radiator and my head near the door. And each night a nurse would shake me awake and put me firmly back in the original position. Each morning I woke with a headache. Although I was supposed to be in hospital for a rest, I was yanked out of bed each morning at six, hustled down the corridor, and weighed with the other anorexic girls – and then told to go back to sleep. It was no use protesting; you were simply humoured by the ward staff and rarely saw your doctors who disappeared behind a phalanx of nurses and registrars. Both times, because I was so heavily drugged, it took me days to work out what to do. I would pretend to swallow the pills that the nurses gave me, spit them out, and then wait until my brain gradually cleared. When I had regained the necessary lucidity, I slipped out of the ward and ran down the corridors to my doctor's office. Both times, fortunately, she was there and was good enough to see me at once. 'I can't stay here,' I told her.

'No, Karen,' she agreed, adding, the second time around, 'Hospitals are not for intelligent people.'

After that I never went back again. Each time, the colour, vibrancy and sheer energy of the outside world greeted me like a gift. Food tasted better, the air smelled sweeter, and ordinary little privacies seemed the greatest of privileges. I would wake early each day, filled with anticipation. True, nothing had really changed. I would probably suffer from these anxiety attacks all my life, but at least I wasn't in a psychiatric ward. And as my doctor had reminded me, I had talents. I was intelligent – more intelligent, perhaps, than the nurses who had seemed omnipotent in the hospital. Maybe this was not the kind of intelligence that was of interest to the University of Oxford, but it was a potentially power-ful tool, a weapon that would help me to fight my way out of this apparent impasse.

I started to eat normally again, quite spontaneously, and with-out any real difficulty, which suggests to me that I was never truly anorexic. The pounds came back on and I barely noticed them. That phase was over. I had given up crying for help, because I had given up expecting any. Of course, I was grateful to the Harts and to Jane for their generosity to me during the crisis, but they could not touch the essential problem, nor could they ease my passage back to the world. Only I could do that, and towards the end of my third year of graduate study, I gave up psychiatry. Maybe this therapy could help others, but it had had no effect upon me at all. And besides, I told myself, I had submitted to other people's programmes and agendas for far too long. That, perhaps, was part of my trouble. It was now time to take my life into my own hands, instead of handing it over to other people, no matter how well intentioned. From now on, I was on my own.

Thus, during the third year of my doctoral studies and some four and a half years after leaving my order, I turned a corner. I may have imbibed some of the spirit of the time, because during the late 1960s and early 70s, laws that had hitherto seemed to be part of the very nature of things were being severely challenged.

It was starting to be impossible now to assume that men were superior to women, that homosexuality was a crime, that whites should rule blacks. Women were taking command of their own lives, were campaigning for equal rights – and beginning to get them. In November 1970, the Gay Liberation Front had held its first public demonstration in Britain. In the United States, South Africa and Europe, an unprecedented racial equality was beginning, slowly and painfully, to overturn centuries of enslavement and oppression. Nelson Mandela and Martin Luther King were heroes to students all over the world. People were beginning to think in new ways, to cast aside a discredited past, and were gradually transforming the world. In my own small way, when I left the religious life, I too had faced the unthinkable, broken a taboo, and crossed a frontier that had once seemed impassable. I too was beginning to think differently, and to realize that assumptions that had hitherto held me in thrall were by no means cast in stone. It was even possible that one day, I would able to sing 'We Shall Overcome' with the rest of my generation.

My new confidence showed in the fact that I was not particularly worried about the future. In the summer of 1973 I would come to the end of my government grant, but I had a new supervisor now, my thesis was going well, and we thought that it would be finished and ready for submission in about a year. This in itself was quite an achievement. Some people took at least seven years over their thesis, while others found it psychologically impossible to bring it to a conclusion. There was no point in even looking for a job without a doctorate but, thanks to my parsimonious regime, I had a considerable amount of money saved; living rent-free at the Harts', I could easily support myself during the intervening year.

It was probably because I had relaxed in this way that, in the

Hilary Term of 1973, I felt the first flicker of true recovery. I had gone to hear Dame Helen Gardner, the Merton Professor of English Literature, lecture on T. S. Eliot. She was known in the faculty as 'The Dame'. It suited her grand manner and her way of waving students into an auditorium as if she were welcoming them to a garden party. That day she was lecturing on the sequence of poems that Eliot had called *Ash-Wednesday*. The first of these, she explained, was Eliot's version of Wordsworth's 'Ode on the Intimations of Immortality'. I became immediately alert, because it was from this poem that I had taken my mantra, with its serene determination to let go of the past and cultivate new strength and joy. As I listened to the Dame reciting Eliot's lines, I felt for the first time in years profoundly and spontaneously moved by the poetry. I no longer had to wait for her to interpret it, and my appreciation was no longer wholly cerebral. It was an essentially emotional, intuitive response that somehow involved my entire personality, reaching something deeply embedded within. I had thought I had lost this capacity for ever, but now here it was again. There was a complete and satisfying 'fit' between my inner and outer worlds. The poem, with its quiet, haunting accuracy, perfectly expressed my own state, and endorsed it, showing that I had not weakly abdicated from the struggle for life and health, but had somehow stumbled upon a truth about the human condition and the way men and women work.

In some of the poems of *Ash-Wednesday*, the Dame pointed out that February morning, the experience of spiritual progress and illumination was represented by the symbol of a spiral staircase. This was, perhaps, reminiscent of Dante's *Purgatorio*, where the souls who are climbing to the beatific vision of God toil around the twisting cornices of Mount Purgatory, each of which constitutes a further stage in their purification. In the very first poem of the sequence, which is printed at the beginning of this book, the verse constantly turns upon itself in repetitions of word, image and sound. Repeatedly the poet tells us, 'I do not hope to turn again', and yet throughout the poem, he is doing just that, slowly ascending to one new insight after another. And even though he insists that he has abandoned hope, I felt paradoxically encouraged.

In my own minor way, I had also given up hope, and yet, Eliot seemed to be saying, that could be the way forwards. I too had understood that I could not hope to go back and undo the past. Ever since I had left the convent I had tried to be normal, to be just like everybody else. But I could not be the same as my fellow-students. It was now time to give up 'desiring this man's gift' or 'that man's scope' and to refuse any longer to submit to the 'usual reign'. At seventeen years old, when I had decided to become a nun, I had opted to be different, and now, whether I liked it or not, I *was* different. This was not because I was anything special, not because I was uniquely talented or sensitive, but simply because I had voluntarily and wholeheartedly submitted to a regime that had been carefully designed to put me fundamentally at variance with the rest of the world. The system had worked. It may in some ways have been destructive, but like any initiation, it could not be undone. I could not hope 'to turn again', and I must 'no longer strive to strive towards' what was normal for other people, whose experience had been dissimilar from my own.

But there were other things that I had given up – or perhaps it was truer to say that they had given up on me. It appeared now that I could not 'hope to know again' what Eliot called 'the infirm glory of the positive hour'. I no longer had a healthy mind that could contemplate the world in a wholly cheerful light. I had found that any such vision was indeed 'infirm' and weak, because

I had experienced the horror that lay just beneath our ordinary waking consciousness. Nothing could change that. Even if I never had another panic attack, I would never be able to forget what I had seen. And God had gone too. True, I had never known 'the blessed face' but (I had now concluded) that was because there was nothing to know. When I had embarked upon the religious life, I had been certain that, if only I tried hard enough, I would see the world transfigured by the presence of God and that I would, as the Bible promised, soar like an eagle. But now the world had shrunk, and I found that such wings as I had hoped to possess were 'merely vans to beat the air', which had become 'small and dry'. My hope of discovering eternity had died, and instead I knew that all we have is now; that 'time is always time' and place 'is always and only place'. What Wordsworth had called 'the glory and the dream' had faded, and the only strength to which I could aspire lay 'in what remains behind'.

But what thrilled me most about Eliot's poem were the words 'because' and 'consequently'. There was nothing depressing about this deliberate acceptance of reduced possibilities. It was precisely 'because' the poet had learned the limitations of the 'actual' that he could say, 'I rejoice that things are as they are'.

> Because I cannot hope to turn again
> Consequently I rejoice, having to construct something
> Upon which to rejoice

The sudden clumsiness of the syntax and language showed that this was no easy solution. It was not something that came naturally. The new joy demanded effort. It would have to be constructed as laboriously and carefully as I put together a chapter of my thesis or as engineers and aeronautical experts built an aeroplane.

It would be a lifelong task, requiring alert attention to the smallest detail, dedication and unremitting effort, but, as I listened to Dame Helen that day, I knew that it could be done.

My confidence sprang from the fact that the process had already started. I had resolved to stop fighting my malady, to accept what my life had become and – 'consequently' – for the first time in years I had responded spontaneously and with my whole being to a poem, just as I had before I had incurred this damage. It was a sign of life, a shoot that had suddenly broken through the frozen earth.

This must be the way that human life worked. He who loves his life shall lose it; he who loses his life shall save it. This was not an arbitrary command of God, but simply a law of the human condition. If you cast your bread upon the waters and were prepared to give it up for good, it would somehow come back to you – albeit in another form.

I experienced that poem as a gift. In the convent I might have said that it was a moment of grace. But I did not believe that it was the work of a God. I noticed that Eliot had not abandoned the deity, and that he still prayed. But that was his privilege; it was not for me. This moment of grace was precious for its own sake, because it was an earnest of recovery. Of course, I realized that there was still a long way to go, but I now knew that I could feel things, that I was not emotionally dead, as I had feared, and that my mind was beginning to come to life again.

I was also aware that my full recovery depended upon my obeying certain rules. I was especially struck by Eliot's line 'I rejoice that things are as they are'. For years I had told myself that black was white and white black; that the so-called 'proofs' for God's existence had truly convinced me; that I might not be feeling happy, but that I really *was* happy because I was doing

God's will; that sewing for hours at a machine without a needle was the most profitable way of spending my time. I had deliberately told myself lies and stamped hard on my mind whenever it had reached out towards the truth. As a result I had warped and incapacitated my mental powers. From now on I must be scrupulous about telling the truth, especially to myself. I realized that this would not be a popular stratagem. I had noticed how frequently people rushed to put an optimistic gloss on a disaster or a difficulty, even when their interpretation seemed at obvious variance with the facts. As Eliot had said in another poem: 'Human kind / Cannot bear very much reality.' It was probably natural for us to deny pain or at least to try to push it out of sight. I could see that this could be a useful survival technique. While you were marvelling at your silver lining, you could be making all kinds of unconscious adjustments so that when the storm finally broke you were in fact prepared. But I could not afford to do this. I was like a recovering alcoholic, who could not allow herself even a sip of this positive elixir, because it could awaken old destructive habits. That was why I could no longer go along with Dr Piet and his theories. For me, they did not reflect the way things really were. By making a habit of gazing unflinchingly at reality, however unpleasant, I too might learn to rejoice in it. So now I had a new project: to construct my own recovery by correcting the bias of my mind towards delusion, thus helping it to regain its former integrity.

But I was only on the very first steps of Eliot's winding stair; I had no idea how far I still had to go.

For one thing, I was not nearly as resigned to my fate as I pretended. As the year progressed, I sometimes felt that life was leaving me behind. Everybody else seemed to be moving on. Even

Charlotte had decided to break out of her tranced existence in the moated grange of the Iffley Road, waiting for the lover to show up.

'I'm getting out,' she told me one evening. 'I'm going to go to London, breaking with Mike. I'll get a job there.'

I had looked at her with respect. Charlotte's decision was, in its way, heroic. She was dismantling the prison she had made for herself and was going out into a completely unknown, empty, Mikeless future. She was renouncing everything that had given her life meaning. She did not hope to turn again. But why did I feel so uncomfortable when she asked: 'Why don't you come too?'

I had shaken my head. 'I have to finish my thesis,' I said, 'and my grant is running out. I'll need to stay on at the Harts', at least until I finish the degree.'

Charlotte had looked sceptical. 'You see, I don't think you should be doing this academic stuff. It's all too confined for you, love. I don't know how you can bear it. You're just putting yourself in another kind of convent, cut off from the world . . .'

'. . . With limited horizons, and a lofty conviction of belonging to an elite,' I capped. Was that why I yearned so towards it? Was I really seeking to escape yet again from the confusions and ambiguities of my time and enter another safe and separate world? Trying to be above it all? Perhaps I was, after all, hoping to turn again. 'Well, what do *you* think I should do?' I demanded, somewhat fretfully.

'Oh, you should write,' Charlotte replied, as though it were so obvious that it was scarcely worth mentioning. 'Not this thesis – that's just an exercise in writing what other people want, but something of your own. You're a writer: that's what you should do.'

'*Write!*' I repeated incredulously. I, who could not string a paragraph together unless I had found somebody else's ideas to act as a framework? To face the empty page every day and – still worse – the inner vacuum that would ensure that it would remain blank? 'No, Charlie,' I said firmly. 'You're the writer. And anyway, surely you're not suggesting that I should abandon the thesis? After three years of hard work?'

'No, you probably should finish it,' Charlotte conceded, as she got up to refill our glasses. 'But after that . . . You really should do something that will free you up a bit . . . take you out of the straitjackets that you keep tying yourself up in. Not yet awhile, perhaps. But soon.'

I was reminded uneasily of that conversation when I visited Rebecca in the London convent, a few weeks later.

'I'm leaving,' she said. The words had fallen heavily into the room. Rebecca was staring ahead, looking, as I knew only too well, into an unimaginable future. She had had a long, slow climb back to health, but though she was now back on her feet and able to do light tasks around the house, she was still painfully thin and could not sit down without a cushion, which she carried around with her as a child might carry a security blanket. Her skin looked transparent; her eyes still appeared enormous. Her whole body had suffered an enormous shock. 'I'm leaving the order,' she said again, more to herself than to me, as though trying to convince herself that she really was going to do this.

I could hardly say I was surprised. 'How do you feel?' I asked.

She sighed and huddled into the bulky cardigan she was wearing, cold despite the fact that it was a warm spring day and an electric fire was burning in the grate. 'It's the right thing,' she said slowly. 'But I cannot imagine what it will be like. Not to be here. But of course, you know all about that.'

I nodded. It would be an insult to offer hearty reassurances, telling her that she would soon find her feet. I had found it almost impossibly difficult after a mere seven years in religious life; Rebecca had been in for twelve, and was leaving in much worse shape than I had.

'There's just no place for me here.' Rebecca poured out more tea. I looked around her room. It used to be one of the students' rooms, when the convent had been a teachers' training college. There was a pretty fireplace, an electric kettle, a delicate collection of cups and saucers, and a chenille bedspread. The order had also travelled a long way since I had left. 'And I should go soon,' Rebecca went on. 'They can't forgive me, you see.'

'For the anorexia?' I asked.

She nodded. There was no need to explain. Despite their attempts to seem welcoming when I had arrived that day, I had sensed wariness in the nuns here. They knew what had happened to me, of course, and did not know how to deal with it. Rebecca and I had demonstrated the flaws of the system. The nuns, I knew, were good women, and it must be almost unbearably painful for them to realize that they had damaged us. It is always difficult to forgive people we have harmed.

'But it should be different,' I said, gesturing around the room. 'From the outside, at least, things have changed so much!'

'Yes, it *is* different. And they know they've got to change,' Rebecca said. 'But they can't do it as quickly as they need to. Oh, they can wear different clothes, put us all into bed-sitting-rooms . . . but inside, they are the same. How can they be anything else? That training was meant to last a lifetime.'

'And it does,' I concluded. If I had found it impossible to beat the conditioning, why should the nuns find it any easier to adapt? Rebecca and I looked at each another bleakly. There was no need to spell out the implications for us. That, I thought, was the best thing about talking to Rebecca. She knew what it was like, and nobody else really had a clue.

'What are you going to do?' I asked.

'Oh, my father has got me a job with *The Tablet* . . . Nothing much; nothing too onerous. But it will be interesting, I think.'

'Is that a good idea?' I asked, startled. I didn't want to be discouraging, but *The Tablet* seemed far too depressingly familiar. It is the chief intellectual Catholic journal in Britain. It was, no doubt, a very worthy and, in its own way, even an excellent paper, but frankly I had no desire ever to set eyes on it again, let alone help to produce it. 'Isn't it a little . . . er . . . Catholic?'

Rebecca smiled. 'Very Catholic indeed. Yes, I know what you mean. But I'm not sure that I could cope with anything more challenging. Not yet, at any rate. No, it will be nice. There's a tiny office – just three or four of us. It will be quite a little community, in a way. Quite comforting, in fact.'

I could see it all: a small enclosed world that viewed everything entirely from the Church's perspective, and whose radius of interest rarely extended beyond Catholic preoccupations. At an instinctive level, I could understand exactly why Rebecca wanted to work for *The Tablet*, even though I felt it to be a mistake. But it was then that I recalled my conversation with Charlotte. Was I really any better?

'So we're leaving,' Jane told me grimly, as we left the English Faculty Library and headed for her flat. 'It's definite. Keswick – here we come!'

Jane and Mark had married the previous summer, and Mark, who was currently a lecturer in a teachers' training college in

London, had just accepted a promotion in a similar college in the Lake District. And, as a good wife, Jane, of course, was going with him.

'How do you feel about it?' I asked cautiously. This could mean the end of Jane's career, or, at least, of a certain kind of career. Unlike me, Jane had been pegged for stardom. The powers that be wanted to keep her in Oxford.

'Not great.' Jane grimaced, until her ebulliently positive nature asserted itself. 'But hey – it's beautiful up there. We've rented a lovely old eighteenth-century manor house – it's even in Pevsner. It's mess at the moment. We'll have to paint it from top to bottom. But when that's over and Markie has started in college, it will be just the sheep and me. *No* distractions. It will force me to finish the damn thesis.'

'And then what?' I pursued. I had recently been discovering feminism, which as yet was only of academic interest to me. So far men had scarcely impinged upon my life, though I could see that in the future, when I had to compete with men for jobs, my gender would count against me. We entered Holywell Manor and climbed the stairs leading to Jane's apartment. It did seem unjust that Jane, who was by far the abler of the two, should sacrifice her career for Mark's.

'Then what? God knows!' Jane shrugged. We entered the lovely modern flat that had come with her prestigious Junior Fellowship. 'The outlook is fairly bleak. I told Dorothy Bednarowska the news yesterday, and she just said: "Oh, Jane, I am so sorry!" Not exactly a ringing endorsement for the plan! But there is a university at Lancaster – and if I got a job there I could commute, I suppose.' She put on the kettle for coffee. 'If not, it'll be me and the kitchen sink – not forgetting the sheep, of course.'

She looked thwarted. And indeed, what became of highly

educated women who married men less clever than themselves? I didn't know what I should do, if ever I were in Jane's position. I knew that I would resent any man who would take that kind of sacrifice for granted, and I did not envy Mark. Jane was a powerful person and I did not fancy his chances if she were cooped up in an isolated manor house for too long. Now my sister Lindsey was quite different. She had called in to see me a few days earlier to tell me that she was emigrating to Canada. I began to tell Jane the story as we sat down with our coffee.

'Your sister – the famous actress?' Jane asked with raised eyebrows. 'I thought she was starring in *Crossroads*. What's she doing in Canada?'

Lindsey had trained as an actress, rather to my parents' dismay. For a time they had the dubious pleasure of saying that they had two daughters: one was an actress and the other a nun. We did not meet very often, since we had such different lives and interests. Lindsey led a highly precarious life in London, doing odd typing and waitressing jobs while 'resting' between plays. She had grown up tall, sexy and glamorous and always made me feel an ugly duckling that had no hope of turning into a swan. During the last year, I had seen quite a lot of her on television because she had landed a part in a popular soap opera. Nanny and I had become quite addicted to it, and even Jane had watched the odd episode with us.

'She's been written out of *Crossroads*,' I explained, 'and now she's going to Canada to join a man she met on holiday in Cyprus last summer.'

'A holiday romance? Is that wise?' Jane asked. 'How long has she known him?'

'Only a weekend,' I said. 'I know – it's crazy in a way. But as she says, she's not the world's greatest actress, and a new man in a new country seems better than going back to that hand-to-mouth existence in London again. And you know men are much more important to her than any career.'

'A nice old-fashioned girl?' Jane smiled sardonically. It was a description that in one way seemed wildly inappropriate, since Lindsey was a 60s girl *par excellence* and had cast off the restraints of Catholicism with never a backward look. But on the other hand . . .

'I think she really is, underneath all the modern trappings. You know: "Follow your man . . ." '

'Even to Keswick,' Jane capped gloomily. 'Well, I'm doing it. But not willingly, I have to tell you. Would you do this? You've just left one confining situation; would you give up your new freedom?'

I had shrugged. My situation was so different from Jane's. There was no prospect of my being enslaved to any man; men generally looked through me as though I did not exist. The problem simply did not arise.

And yet, I asked myself as I got up to go back to the little room at the Harts', where I spent the greater part of my life, how free was I? Were not Jane and Lindsey really more adventurous than I was? Would I ever love anything or anybody enough to leave it all behind? I had done that once, when I had entered the convent, and I wasn't sure I had the courage to do it again.

That Easter, as usual, I accompanied the Harts to Cornwall. They had an extraordinary house on the south coast, which had been built by Jenifer's father for her mother as a wedding present. Because of the strong winds, the Cornish usually built behind the cliffs, but Lamledra, as this house was called, stood bravely on the seaward side. It was a massive pile, with a servants' wing and an amazing baronial-style hall, which had probably been spectacular when Lady Williams had first set up house, but it had now succumbed to Hart-like chaos. From the terrace there was a spectacular view of Dodman Point and, beyond the red slash of the fuchsia bushes, the startling blue of the Atlantic. In the sloping paddock in front of the house, which curved steeply towards the small beach below, horses from the local riding school grazed peacefully, silhouetted nobly against the sea.

I usually travelled down with Jenifer in the Morris Minor, with Nanny and Jacob squeezed together into the back seat. It was a long, difficult journey, and my task was to talk to Jenifer, who had to do all the driving, while Nanny tried to keep Jacob amused. As soon as we arrived, we had to rush through the house, removing all the signs of the occupancy of Jenifer's sister Mariella, who had the house during the winter months. Her elegant ornaments were thrust disdainfully into a cupboard ('Can you imagine choosing this?' Jenifer would ask, brandishing a quite unexceptionable lampshade. 'Ludicrous!') and replaced by Jenifer's more unconventional objects. There had almost been outright war between the sisters when Jenifer had defiantly painted the kitchen wall a brilliant orange, Mariella apparently preferring magnolia. Herbert generally followed us in comfort on the train, and by the time he arrived, the house was ready for habitation.

Staying at Lamledra had always been an education. It had given me, as it were, a crash course in the permissive society. Adam and Charlie often turned up, each with a large entourage of wives, girlfriends and other members of their respective communes. I often wondered whether Adam was more successful at meditation than I had been, but never dared to ask. I always found Adam and Charlie somewhat daunting, even though they were always perfectly, if rather distantly, friendly, and I was quite intimidated by Adam's wife, Mary, who treated me with the scorn she reserved for somebody who had clearly sold out to 'the system'. I much enjoyed Herbert's account of an afternoon he had spent at Throstle's Hole, the house he had bought for Adam's commune. To preserve the spirit of equality, Adam and Mary used her surname as well as his, and so were listed in the telephone directory as 'Hamilton Hart'. On the afternoon in question, two members of the local Conservative Party who were out canvassing and, not unnaturally, thought that the Hamilton Harts of Throstle's Hole would be a pretty safe bet, visited them. Herbert gleefully described the horror of these stalwart Tories when they confronted the communal scene, with various stoned communards crashed out on the floor, another couple meditating in yogic positions, refusing to acknowledge their presence, while Mojo, Adam's daughter, ran naked amidst the general squalour. For once, Jenifer's favourite adjective, 'ludicrous', seemed entirely appropriate.

Whenever Adam or Charlie visited Lamledra, Jenifer would turn the servants' wing over to them. 'Just make up all the beds,' she told me the first time. 'I have no idea who is sleeping with whom.' Not only did Charlie have a number of different partners, but Adam and Mary were often otherwise engaged. This was the sexual revolution with a vengeance and I was amazed by Jenifer's lack of concern. Alan Ryan, Joanna's former husband, was also a regular visitor, with his girlfriend Katie. In addition, Jenifer and Herbert would invite their own friends. So it was a rather strange house party on that Cornish cliff, with distinguished Oxford academics living cheek by jowl with hippies and other members of the alternative society. But everybody coexisted amicably. On one evening, Herbert and Isaiah Berlin gave a spirited reading of Max Beerbohm's 'Savanarola Brown' in the drawing room, and had us weeping with laughter. In the hall, next door, the air was thick with marijuana, while the communards sat dreamily listening to Charlie's guitar.

I drifted between these two worlds. I had no desire to be with my contemporaries in the hall, though they would politely invite me in for a joint from time to time. I also, just as politely, declined. I did not need to cultivate exotic states of consciousness; I was able to engineer quite enough bad trips of my own, and my experience of drugs in the Warneford had given me a lifelong aversion to this type of recreation. But neither was I at home with the Oxbridge celebrities, though they too were reasonably welcoming on the few occasions when I plucked up the courage to join them. In any case, nobody took much notice of me. I was just the 'skivvy' and, when not on duty, could wander around the house, left peacefully to my own devices. This suited me very well. I spent a lot of time on the terrace that Easter, not reading much but gazing out to sea. At night there was sometimes the extraordinary spectacle of the full moon casting a path of shining light on the ocean all the way to the horizon.

Those contemplative moments occurred within the benign hubbub of the household. I walked into the kitchen one afternoon to find Herbert and two philosophers sitting solemnly in front of Mariella's dishwasher, which one of them had tried to repair, contemplating it with the same kind of rapt attention as I had bestowed upon the moon the night before. 'It has just completed its second cycle,' Herbert informed me with wonder in his voice. That was also the year when Charlie arrived one afternoon with a grand piano, which he had picked up cheap. The entire household had turned out to propel the piano up the steep winding path on a rolling sequence of broom handles, until we managed to manhandle it into the hall. For the rest of his visit, Charlie and Jenifer played pieces for two pianos together – he flamboyant on the grand, she lean, intense and dry on the old upright – calling encouragement to one another above the Mozart and Beethoven.

Exotic as my life with the Harts often was and different from anything I had ever known before, there was much that was reassuringly familiar. Jenifer's frugality made her as stringent about economy as any of my former superiors. We were not allowed to vacuum the carpets or wash our sheets too frequently, lest we wear them out. She was adamantly opposed to the newly repaired dishwasher – 'a ludicrous waste of water!' – and there were constant arguments about the electric fire in the drawing room, a miserable little contraption which should probably have been banned for safety reasons rather than for the pathetic amount of power that it splutteringly consumed on its three ancient bars. 'You had the fire on this morning, Herbert, just because it was a little chilly! There is absolutely no need for such waste! If you want a fire, there's plenty of wood and –'

'The same discussion', Herbert had beamed around the table, quite unabashed, 'is probably going on at this moment in boarding houses in Worthing.'

And so, in a way, I felt quite at home. Asceticism was certainly central to the whole Lamledra experience. Every morning after breakfast, the guests were frog-marched by Jenifer with spades and mattocks to do battle with the ubiquitous nettles and thistles in the grounds. Nobody was excused from this forced labour, unless they had a physical disability or an article to write. 'There goes the Chain Gang!' Herbert would murmur gleefully, as he left the breakfast table for his room, resolutely refusing to take part. I too was exempt from the *corvée*, since I had housework to do. This included helping Nanny to cook lunch for the conscripts, who returned home hot, scratched, stung and dirty – with no hope, of course, of a hot bath, since that too was regarded as a ludicrous extravagance. In the afternoon, everybody was expected to bathe from the beach at the foot of the cliff, but nobody was permitted to utter the word 'cold' in case we put Jacob off. Tight-lipped, with muscles clenched, we strode into the icy water, calling strangled cries of encouragement to Jacob, who showed good sense in his reluctance to join us. Sometimes he would agree to sit on a lilo, which Herbert dutifully towed up and down, wading at thigh-level through the freezing blue sea, his hair blowing patriarchally in the breeze. 'How are you getting on?' I asked once, as I swam briskly past. 'I am unaware that I have legs,' he replied calmly, adjusting his spectacles.

After we had dressed, each of us was required to fill one of the backpacks that we had brought down from the house with pebbles from the beach (few of us were ecologically-minded in the early 1970s) in order to replenish the gravel on the terrace, which was constantly being blown away by the high winds. We used to struggle up the cliffs bowed under the weight of our burdens, looking for all the world like the Vainglorious, who, to expiate their sin of pride, had to toil around Dante's Mount Purgatory, bent double under massive stones.

But this remote literary echo was the only reference to religion for me that Easter. For the first time in my life, I took no part in the rituals of Holy Week: the mass of the Lord's Supper on Maundy Thursday, the Veneration of the Cross on Good Friday, and the solemn mass of the Resurrection on Easter Sunday morning. The strange thing was that I did not feel at all odd. I experienced no nostalgia and no guilt during my first wholly secular Easter. In fact, I felt a good deal better. The beauty of my surroundings and the general good-will of the Harts and their guests were healing me in a way that religion had never done. In my first years with the Harts, I used to make the effort to hear mass every Sunday at the Catholic Church in Mevagissey, which meant getting up extremely early and walking five miles over the cliffs. It had been a pleasant walk, even though I had to brave a field full of bullocks and sometimes tore my clothes on barbed-wire fences. The service itself, however, was less rewarding, the words of the mass soullessly intoned by a priest who seemed bored and irritated with his congregation of holiday-makers, who were patently longing to get back to the beach as quickly as possible.

But this Easter, I did not attempt the trek to Mevagissey. If anybody at Lamledra noticed this, they all tactfully forbore to mention it. I was surprised, even slightly shocked that such a final break with religion had affected me so little. From the Harts' atheist stronghold, the events of that first Holy Week – the suffering and death of Jesus and his rising from the tomb – seemed an obvious fiction; a mere myth, an arbitrary sequence of improbable events that bore no relevance to life in the twentieth century. But in the convent, when we had lived that myth step-by-step, moment-by-moment, from Ash Wednesday, through the long journey of Lent all the way to Golgotha, the myth had meant something entirely different. Holy Week, the culmination of Lent, had always been a special time. We had sung the whole of the divine office every day, instead of chanting an abridged version. Each novice had to sing a chapter from the Lamentations of Jeremiah. The plaintive cadences of the Gregorian chant had penetrated our hearts; then there had been the drama of the Easter Vigil. I had never seriously questioned the myth itself because the liturgy, the fasting and the strict silence of the convent during these days had re-created it, so that, in some sense, whatever had happened in Jerusalem two thousand years ago was not as important as the fact that the events had somehow been brought to life here and now. But without these rituals, the myth was dead. If you wanted to preserve your faith, the trick clearly was to keep practising. If you stopped and looked at those rites and stories from the outside, they seemed absurd. Ludicrous, in fact.

'Isn't it Easter tomorrow?' one of the guests asked at supper.

'Don't talk about Easter and all that boring stuff!' Jacob commanded. Everybody laughed but broke off raggedly, looking rather warily at me. 'Karen, do you insist on doing the washing up, so that Nanny can come upstairs with me?'

'Yes, of course,' I said, grateful for the diversion.

'As long as you don't use the dishwasher,' Herbert muttered darkly.

'I absolutely forbid anybody to use that dishwasher. It's an absurd waste of –'

'Karen, do you absolutely insist?'

'Karen.' Jean Floud, the Mistress of Newnham College, leant across the table. 'I've got to go back to Cambridge tomorrow. I'll be leaving pretty early. If you'd like to come with me, I could drop you off at Mevagissey for mass.'

My heart sank. I really didn't feel like making a public announcement of my loss of faith. 'Well, Jean, it's very kind –' I began.

'Oh, for God's sake, don't take her to mass,' Jenifer exclaimed, helping people to more lasagna. 'She always comes home in such a bad temper!' She dropped a second helping on my plate.

'Do I really, Jenifer?' I was astonished.

'Yes, you do! I must say I don't approve of a religion that makes people so gloomy.'

Neither did I. What had religion ever done for me but make me ill, make me unhappy and dissatisfied with myself, and, now,

182

apparently, make me cross into the bargain? I would be better without it.

Some weeks later, after we had returned to Oxford, I looked apprehensively at the envelope that Jenifer had pushed under my door, but forced myself to open the letter and read it. Then I read it again. I had got a job. I had been appointed Tutorial Research Fellow at Bedford College in the University of London.

It was Jane who had seen the advertisement. She had marched into the kitchen, where I was heating up some soup for lunch, and waved the newspaper under my nose. 'You should apply for this!' she said. It was a three-year appointment. It would enable me to finish my thesis, and – even more importantly – would give me some teaching experience. I wanted that job. I wanted it very much. I looked at Jane and knew that she wanted it too. We didn't have to say anything, because we both knew that if she had been able to apply, she would certainly have been the one to get it.

But Jane was going to Keswick, and I had applied and been summoned to an interview. Dorothy Bednarowska had written me a reference. This was the kind of junior post that she thought I could handle, and it was 'only London', a university, which, from her Oxbridge perspective, was almost beneath serious con- sideration. 'I've written her up terrifically,' she had told Jane. And she must have done, because at my interview the two young lecturers seemed to assume that I would be coming. They wanted me to teach nineteenth- and twentieth-century poetry, and, because they themselves wished to concentrate on the drama of the period, I would be teaching the twentieth-century novel. 'Malcolm Lowry, John Fowles, Graham Greene, Iris Murdoch, Doris Lessing? Is that all right?' one of them had asked me.

'Yes, of course,' I lied, realizing that if I got the job I would have a great deal of reading to get through during the summer. But they seemed to think that it was not *if* but *when*.

I had returned home to Oxford, scarcely daring to believe it. But it was true. I had been offered the job. All I had to do was sign the contract. It was a step up the ladder, a foot in the door ... all those things. It seemed that, after all, it really might be possible to become an academic. It was a new start.

Three years now stretched invitingly ahead of me. In three whole years in London, anything could happen.

~: 5 :~

DESIRING THIS MAN'S GIFT AND
THAT MAN'S SCOPE

The English department at Bedford College, located in a Regency house beside the Regent's Park lake, was a haven of quiet in the hubbub of London. From the lecture rooms you could see herons swooping over the water and landing on the wooded islands, yet only a few hundred yards away the traffic roared incessantly in Baker Street. This would be the centre of my world for the next three years, and very pleasant it was too. My teaching duties were so light that I had plenty of time to get on with my thesis, which was now nearing completion. The faculty was welcoming, especially Richard and Jackie who had interviewed me and now treated me with extraordinary kindness. Since we were responsible for teaching the literature of the nineteenth and twentieth centuries, we soon formed a triumvirate within the department, meeting regularly for coffee in Richard's room, which was the largest. I was slightly disconcerted by the way the course was organized. The students seemed to run from one class to another. They could well have been still in high school. When did they have time to read and explore for themselves? To me they seemed over-taught, but I kept this criticism to myself. It was probably just an Oxford prejudice. All in all, Bedford was an amicable place and I seemed to have fallen on my feet.

In fact, it was all so easy-going that I began to look for a catch. There must be more to university teaching than this. For the past three years, my mentors had told me that I should not even think of an academic career, implying that it would be too much of a strain, perhaps beyond my intellectual capacity, and bad for my fragile 'nerves'. But I appeared to be managing all right. I had no problems with the students, and Richard and Jackie gave me very positive feedback. Indeed, everything seemed to be going very well. Why had people been so negative about my prospects? The faculty did not seem to consist of intellectual giants. My 'nerves' were no worse than usual. I certainly didn't feel that I was being unduly challenged – or stretched in any way at all. It was, indeed, pleasant. But wasn't it already a little . . . predictable? Was it not a trifle . . . dull?

I remember when I finally allowed this question to surface. It was towards the end of my first term and I was hurrying home to my flat in north London. The underground station at King's Cross was packed with commuters and I tried to find a quiet place in my mind away from the crowds, the noise and the bustle. Two free research days lay ahead. I could stay at home, finish the chapter that I was working on, and go to the British Library. Wonderful! Two whole days away from college! But then I stopped short: why was I so delighted? For the last couple of months I had been telling myself how lucky I was to have landed this job, but now, as I stood on the crowded platform, I asked myself: 'Is this *it* then?' Was this what I really wanted to do with the rest of my life? Of course, it was all very . . . pleasant. That was the word that continually came to mind when I tried to describe my new life. But it seemed wrong somehow. 'Pleasant' sounded so insipid, so bland. They had been wrong at St Anne's, I thought. I *can* do this job, very easily indeed. Perhaps it was too easy? Had that entire struggle, all that striving led to something that was merely . . . pleasant? Of course, I enjoyed it all. It was fun gossiping with Richard and Jackie. Moreover, I was hugely privileged to have a job that *was* pleasant, for heaven's sake. And it wasn't as though there was anything else that I wanted to do. There was no other profession for which I was remotely qualified. But somehow I had always thought that life should be more than merely . . . pleasant.

I tried to push the thought away. I am doing a useful job of work, I told myself firmly as I boarded the train and stood crammed against other bodies, swaying in unison with them through the dark subterranean tunnels. But was I? Only that afternoon, I had been giving a tutorial on the Romantic period to three students. They had been quiet, docile and attentive, carefully noting down my every word – even the jokes – but had not seemed at all excited by Coleridge's poetry. None of them had asked me anything, except how to spell a word or to repeat a date. But then, who was I to talk? I knew what it was like to feel tongue-tied in class, to have nothing to say. But these students *had* worried me. However empty and numb I may have felt, I had always been caught up intellectually in what I was studying. I always wanted to find out more, to see things clearly. And once an idea had been suggested to me, I got real pleasure from it – even if I could rarely come up with ideas of my own. But these three might as well have been studying quantum mechanics.

'What do you want to do next week?' I had asked at the end of the hour.

They gazed at me blankly. 'Dunno,' one of the boys eventually volunteered.

'You must have *some* idea,' I had said, a little testily. Silence. 'What about Keats?'

'Oh, no,' the girl groaned. 'Oh, no – anything but Keats.'

'What have you got against Keats?' I demanded. What *could* anyone have against Keats? Didn't they admire those extraordinary odes, the sonnets – the letters, for heaven's sake? The students continued to look at me expectantly, and for a wild moment I longed for one of them to get up and yell that he absolutely hated Keats, that he thought Keats was insufferably indulgent, pretentious and overrated. I would have welcomed any sign of involvement or commitment. 'Do you really not like Keats?' I asked again, hoping to coax them into a reaction.

They shrugged and smiled, sweetly. There was no hostility; they were perfectly . . . pleasant. I gave up. 'Well, what about John Clare?'

'OK,' the girl replied equably, 'I'll do Clare.'

I had given them a reading list and an essay title, which they had written down diligently, and we had parted cordially. But now, as I hurtled northwards on the rattling train, I wondered what on earth was the point. Of course, not all the students were so passive. Only last week I had had a splendid session with two highly intelligent girls. But what had those three students actually learned this afternoon, and what would they learn about Clare? Certainly they would acquire a little information about him, but was their course teaching them to think? Was it enhancing their lives? Would the world be a better place because they had shared Clare's insights? Or were they simply passing the time pleasantly? I shook myself irritably out of this reverie. I was glad to have this job. I couldn't expect the moon. And yet, I had thought, at some absurd level of my being, that if only I could get an academic post, everything would fall neatly into place. I had believed that I would find a new vocation.

When I arrived home that evening, my flat did little to cheer me. I had been rather spoiled by life at the Harts, where there was always something interesting going on. I had also been horrified by the exorbitant rents charged for the most meagre of rooms in London and had been lucky to find this quite reasonable apartment near Highgate. It consisted of a bedroom and sitting room, with a minute kitchenette portioned off behind the bed. There was no garden or balcony, but my bedroom overlooked Highgate Wood. I had done my best to cheer the place up, but the furniture and curtains were not really to my taste, and the flat had an unloved air. Nothing quite came together. But it was spacious and quiet, so I was able to work there quite successfully. The chief problem was the landlady, who tended to lurk in the hall ready to pounce on me when I came home. On several occasions I had been waylaid for nearly two hours, while she told me endless tales about her deceased husband and unsatisfactory daughter. The old lady was so obviously lonely that I didn't have the heart to cut her off. When she wasn't regaling me with lugubrious stories, she would descend upon me in a fury because she had inspected my flat earlier in the day and found a cobweb or an undusted shelf. This impertinent surveillance enraged me. I'd had enough of that kind of supervision in the convent and it was not good for me to experience it here, when I was making a bid for independence.

But I managed to make a life for myself in London. Richard and Jackie frequently invited me to join them and their partners in a visit to the theatre, a dinner or a walk in the country. I started to entertain the handful of my former classmates who were now living in London. I would meet Rebecca for lunch or spend an evening with Charlotte in her room in Kilburn. There were visits to Jane in the Lake District and trips home for weekends in Birmingham. These last became more frequent as the work on my thesis drew to a close, because a woman in my mother's office was typing it for me. It made sense for me to review the typescript in my parents' home, so that my mother could take any corrections in to work with her on Monday morning. I was starting to feel more relaxed with my family. As I no longer looked skeletal and ill, they were not so worried about me, and the shared project of my thesis brought us all together.

I had made a niche for myself in the world, something that had once seemed to be beyond my powers. True, I still experienced occasional moments of terror when my brain cracked open and the world became suffused with dread, but in other ways I could feel that my mind really was coming back to life. There were times when I still encountered the familiar emptiness, but sometimes I could feel a text calling to me and I was able to reply. I noticed that this tended to happen when there was some pressure. If I had a lecture to prepare for the following day, for example, I found that the thoughts and arguments would come while I was actually writing the piece, which took on a new life. Sometimes I needed another critic to start me off, but then I discovered that I could continue by myself and that, almost without realizing it, I was supplementing his insights with some of my own. It was like learning to ride a bicycle. I remembered pedalling confidently, convinced that my father was still holding the bike steadily, and then found that I was balancing perfectly by myself. Interestingly, this tended to happen when I was writing about authors with whom I had initially felt no particular empathy: with the poet Philip Larkin or with the novelist Ivy Compton-Burnett.

I was especially moved by the novels of Iris Murdoch, who had once been the philosophy tutor at St Anne's. I noticed that her characters often had what seemed to be a religious experience while they stood in front of a picture or contemplated a powerful landscape. These passages were so characteristic and so vivid that I felt certain that Murdoch herself must have been transfigured in this way, though, as Jenifer Hart had told me, she had no conventional religious beliefs. Certainly Murdoch did not interpret the ecstasy of her characters in a traditionally theistic way, and yet it was clear that these were numinous encounters. It seemed that Murdoch had developed a form of secular mysticism, so that natural objects, works of art or the experience of falling in love revealed a transcendent dimension that seemed natural to human beings. These experiences were clearly a revelation, similar to what religious people described as God or the sacred. Something similar had happened to me when I had listened to Dame Helen Gardner reading *Ash-Wednesday*. If traditional religious disciplines had failed to enlighten me, perhaps I would find in literature what had eluded me in the convent chapel. And this raised all kinds of questions about the nature of religion. If an unbeliever could experience the same kind of ecstasy as a Christian mystic, it seemed that transcendence was just something that human beings experienced and that there was nothing supernatural about it.

Now that I no longer had to take Jacob to mass on Sundays, I did not go myself. I had woken up on my first Sunday in London, registered what day it was, and decided to stay in bed for a while with a novel and a cup of coffee. My landlady had given me the address of the local Catholic Church, but I knew that I was never going to set foot in it. Indeed, I now felt distaste for the whole churchy enterprise. It seemed not only a colossal waste of time and energy, but positively harmful too. If I saw somebody reading a theological or devotional book on the underground, I felt an involuntary twinge of disgust, and would even turn away as though I had seen something abhorrent. The words 'God' or 'Jesus' or 'church' filled me with a lassitude akin to nausea. Conventional religion had worn me out and I wanted nothing more to do with it. If possible, I would have liked to forget that it existed.

It was quite easy to ignore religion in London. In Oxford, there had been constant reminders: cloisters, church spires, bells that sonorously called worshippers to service, formal grace before dinner. All had recalled the age of faith when the university had been established. It was true that the religious customs often seemed quaint anachronisms, and that many of those who actually attended a service simply wanted to hear one of Oxford's fine choirs. 'Oh, I don't think that any of them are *believers!*' a choir master had said of his choristers during a radio interview; he had given the impression that the very notion of faith was outlandish. 'No, no, none of them actually *believes.*' He had sounded anxious to reassure the host that the virus of religion had not contaminated his choir. Nevertheless, wherever I had looked in Oxford, there had been mementoes of faith.

But life in London was very different. There I often passed churches that had been converted into warehouses, theatres or art galleries. I even went to a dinner party in a flat that was cunningly constructed in the shell of a massive Victorian church: we sat under its rose window. None of the guest felt in the least uncomfortable about this sacred ambience; the ecclesiastical touches had simply been an amusing talking point. They had found it hilarious to ring the front door bell and enter what had once been the church porch. Religion, it appeared, was quite risible. I noticed that I myself was reducing my convent past to a series of entertaining anecdotes. Hostesses often introduced me as an 'ex-nun', as though pulling a rabbit out of a hat: Look what I've got! Top that! My fellow-guests might look faintly scandalized – 'Do people truly *do* that any more!' – or would ply me with endless questions about nuns' underwear or convent hygiene. It did not usually occur to them that the religious life could be anything other than a joke. 'You really should write all this up, Karen,' they would say. 'It's such a hoot!'

I was uncomfortable about this, but did not know what to do. Rebecca told me that she tried to hide the fact that she had been a nun, and would ask her hostesses not to mention it. But that didn't seem right either. I didn't want to make those years a dark secret. After all, I hadn't robbed a bank or been in prison. But neither did I want to get unduly heavy and ruin the party. Despite all my negative feelings about religion, I still felt protective about the nuns, and still felt sorrow and regret for a lost ideal. I still mourned the girl I had been, with her sense of high adventure, the hope and the crazy optimism that had led me into the religious life. None of this was suitable conversational fodder for a dinner party. So it was really easier to fob my fellow-guests off with a couple of funny stories and leave it at that.

I realized that these days I scarcely knew anybody who was religious. There were one or two churchgoers at college, but they were not soul mates and I didn't see much of them. It was odd to think how completely my life had changed. Just five years earlier I had been enveloped in a monastic atmosphere, and now I had swung a full 180 degrees and was living in a wholly secular environment.

Some people in my life were still involved in religion. Jacob continued to attend mass, because a member of the Blackfriars congregation had volunteered to take him. And then there was my sister, Lindsey. She had not stayed long in Canada. The man she had pursued had been a disappointment, and she hated the long winters. So she had married an Englishman whom she had met in Winnipeg and had driven all the way to California with him and their two Siamese cats. She had also become a Buddhist of the Nichiren school. I had no idea what that involved, but apparently it did not require her to wear a yellow robe or become a vegetarian. She chanted a mantra for about an hour each day, my mother told me. I found it hard to imagine this. Lindsey and I seemed to have changed places. 'I don't know what it is with this family and religion,' my long-suffering mother said in mock bewilderment. 'Where did I go wrong?' Well, at least she didn't have to worry about my religious obsessions any more. My involvement with God was well and truly over.

Pleased with myself, and with a mounting sense of excitement, I patted the bulky parcel containing three copies of my thesis, duly typed and bound in important-looking black covers with gilt lettering. It was a very satisfying sight. It had not been easy, but I had managed to complete this task. Against the odds, I had persevered, had shaped an idea and argued it through – like any other doctoral student. During these last few months, all the different themes had come together and fallen elegantly into place, almost of their own volition. My supervisor was pleased, and two professors whom I had consulted were impressed. Another, it was true, had been extremely rude about it, but my supervisor assured me that he did not approve of the close linguistic study of literature that I had attempted. Because he was known to have this bias, he would not be my examiner. So it all seemed hopeful. Here at least there had been no disaster. My mind still boiled with visions and paralysing panic attacks, but this piece of sustained work was a guarantee of its ultimate integrity. The thesis was my passport to a job and a career, an earnest of my survival in a world that had once seemed so impossibly alien.

I watched the girl behind the post-office grille slap on the stamps and the registration forms. Then she put the parcel in a pile at the end of the room, whence it would be conveyed to Oxford.

In some bewilderment, I stared around the art gallery. A student was copying William Dyce's *Pegwell Bay*, and one or two other people were strolling round the Tate's Pre-Raphaelite exhibits. I was stiff, as though I had been sitting for some time in an uncomfortable position. I got up and stretched. In front of me, John William Waterhouse's *Lady of Shalott* reared up in her fragile little boat. Her tapestry, the fruit of so much dedicated toil, floated away downstream, waterlogged, stained and ruined. The Lady's face had already assumed the pallor of death and her skin looked as grey as the sky behind her – Tennyson's Lady of Shalott, who for so long had been my *alter ego*. She had tried to break out of her prison, as I had mine, but the effort had destroyed her. Waterhouse had caught the Lady at the moment when she realized the folly of her rebellion.

I shook my head hard and looked around the room again. On the other side of the gallery was John Millais' *Ophelia*, who lay supine in the water. Having succumbed to madness, she too was about to die. Her hands were lifted slightly, as though she welcomed her fate; her expression was one of surrender. They were disturbing pictures, but that was not what was bothering me. My head was aching and my mind was foggy. I groped through the mists and suddenly – there it was. What on earth was I doing in the Tate? I was supposed to be in Greenwich with Richard and Jackie. We were taking a group of students to a matinée performance of Jean Genet's *The Maids*. I looked at my watch. Too late: the play had started almost an hour ago.

Weak with fright and trembling slightly, I sank back on to the leather banquette, staring at the Lady of Shalott without really seeing her. What had happened? The last thing that I could remember clearly was getting on to the tube train at Highgate. I had been due to meet the party at Charing Cross station at 2.15 but I had no recollection of the intervening period. My mind racing now, I realized that I must have left the tube at Charing Cross, and instead of taking the escalator up to the mainline station, I must have walked all the way down the Embankment to the Tate. As I struggled to remember, I thought I could dimly recall the steely grey Thames, the wet cloudy sky, umbrellas and mackintoshed figures. But nothing else, nothing at all.

How was I going to explain this to Richard and Jackie? Dazed, I got up and walked groggily through the other galleries. My colleagues' reaction, I told myself grimly, was the least of my problems. Nothing ever got better. My mind was as infirm and as unreliable as ever. I seemed quite unable to function as a normal human being. Again, I glimpsed the locked ward, the padded cell. I felt sick, and had a strong desire to lie down on one of the long benches and sleep for hours. Outside the mid-winter rain cut into my face and the wind penetrated to my bones. As I walked towards Pimlico station, the white peeling houses, decayed relics of a splendid past, looked blank and shuttered.

As soon as I opened the envelope, I knew that it was hopeless. The terse official letter from Oxford told me that my academic career was over. The professor who had been so hostile to the very idea of my thesis had been appointed as my examiner.

Friends, family and colleagues told me that I was despairing too soon. I wondered how they could be so certain about this, but after a while I realized that their remarks were not really considered statements, but were more in the nature of denial. It *had* to be all right, because the alternative was unthinkable. 'Let's face it, Karen,' Jane exclaimed cheerfully on the phone, 'if you fail, there's no hope for any of us.' So for the next three months, while I waited for the viva that was to be held (a cruel irony, this) on Valentine's Day, most people refused to discuss the matter. 'It will be fine!' they said airily. 'Don't even think about it!' Even my supervisor seemed unconcerned. 'It's such a lovely piece of work,' she assured me. 'It simply cannot fail.' Mind you, she admitted, there were irregularities. She had protested against the appointment of the hostile professor – let us call him Alistair Courtney – who had long been on the Oxford faculty but now occupied a Chair in a provincial university. She had pointed out to the Academic Board that I now had two 'external' examiners. The other examiner, who was favourably disposed to my work but not nearly such a big-shot as Courtney, was at the University of Birmingham.

'It's against the regulations for Miss Armstrong to have two external examiners,' she had complained. 'Oxford should also be represented.'

She herself had taken her first degree at Birmingham, and, in the patrician climate of Oxford, felt at a permanent disadvantage. 'My dear,' Dame Helen Gardner had replied suavely, 'Alistair is much more internal than somebody like you!'

So for the next three months I waited. However hard I tried, I was not reassured by these confident predictions. I remember spending whole afternoons sitting on the floor of my flat, staring ahead, sick with apprehension. I found it impossible to read; I could not even listen to music, but was in a state of continuous, slow-burning panic. I should have liked to have somebody to talk to. I had lost some of the reserve that had inhibited me when I first left the convent, and could see that it would be helpful to discuss my options. What could I realistically do if the worst happened? What were the chances of an appeal? How would I endure the shame and the disgrace? But since everybody I might have talked to about these things refused – seemingly on principle – even to discuss these possibilities, I was on my own. I used to read the thesis over and over, feeling alternately elated at some of its felicities, and in despair when I came across a passage that I knew, with chilly certainty, would antagonize Professor Courtney.

As I had expected, the viva was a rout. Courtney was brilliantly sarcastic; the co-examiner, who had been so encouraging to me earlier, was clearly daunted by Courtney's reputation and looked at me helplessly across the table. I argued back, of course, but I could see that it was no good. As I walked from the Examination Schools to the station, the glowing shops festooned with the hearts and cupids of Valentine's Day seemed an unkind joke. During the journey home, I opened the corridor window and threw my copy of the complete works of Tennyson out into the dark, rainy night. I felt calmly pleased by this gesture, which seemed to release some of the tension that had accumulated over the last months. I felt stalled, almost in a state of suspended animation. Sometimes that evening I seemed to look down at myself as from a great height, as though all this was happening to somebody else.

So when the letter came informing me that I had indeed failed, I found that I did not feel nearly as bad as I might have. I read the letter, nodded grimly to myself, tore it up, and continued my preparations for a morning's teaching, feeling the same curious detachment. I told myself that I had, after all, known this was going to happen. There was nothing surprising about it. During those lonely weeks before the viva, I had lived with my failure and grown accustomed to it. Not so my colleagues. Richard and Jackie looked at me dumbfounded when I told them the news that morning. For once even Richard, a naturally voluble and ebullient soul, was lost for words. And when I phoned Jane with the news that night, I was astonished and touched when she burst into tears.

I know perfectly well that if this had happened to somebody else – to Jane herself, for example – I should have been angry on her behalf. Yet because it had happened to me, all I could feel was cold, fatalistic acceptance. I was not simply in shock. For years, people had told me that I was rubbish, and this proved it. I had tried to convince myself that I had talents, but I think that I had been waiting subconsciously, but with a dread that I dared not acknowledge, to be finally, fatally unmasked. Now it had happened. There was, if not relief, a grim sense that this was *right*; it had to happen. I should have known better than to imagine that I could succeed. For all the spurious success that I had enjoyed, I was just no good – and I should have known this all along. This latest *débâcle* was, in the original sense of the word, a revelation: it had 'unveiled' a reality that had been there all the time but which I had not seen with sufficient clarity.

But that was not the whole of it. I still felt at some profound level that it was wrong to feel distress. For years I had been castigated for being too sensitive. I had spent the three years of my novitiate weeping like a broken waterspout. Reduced to tears by a pitiless rebuke for a failure, or a mishap, I would then be chastised for weeping. And the tears would flow again. It became a vicious circle. I became obsessed with my sensitivity, and would include these lachrymose episodes in the list of sins for my weekly confession. Eventually I learned to keep my feelings at arm's length, and refused to allow myself to feel anything at all. It was part of the residual damage that I had incurred as a result of my training, and had still not completely overcome. This, coupled with the fact that my 'weird seizures' made me see everything in a remote, distanced way, meant that I was unable to connect with my feelings at all. Friends later told me that I imparted the bad news about my thesis with an uncanny, unearthly smile. 'I've failed,' I would say calmly. 'Yes, failed.'

This icy calm persisted for days. Then I had a call from my supervisor.

'No, listen!' she said urgently, after we had exchanged greetings and commiserations. 'There is a crisis. People are furious. This is a scandal, my dear. There is going to be a row.'

And so there was. If a thesis is failed – not simply referred back to the student for correction, but failed outright, as mine had been – the examiner is expected to write a very detailed report, going through the text page by page, point by point, and drawing attention to errors and flaws. Professor Courtney, however (at least, this is what I was told), had written half a paragraph to the effect that I was a clever young woman, but that in his view the topic of my thesis was unsuitable for a doctorate. This reflected badly on the university, which had approved the subject, and the Faculty was furious. Now, apparently, when it was too late, the Academic Board was also incensed that I had not had an internal examiner, and insulted by what they regarded as Courtney's arrogant brevity. They wrote back, I was told, telling him that he had failed as an examiner on eleven points and that it would be a long time before he was invited to examine for Oxford again.

But what were they going to do with me? For five months, the Faculty discussed my fate. In any other university, I expect that the thesis could have been re-examined, but Oxford was a law unto itself. There had not been a case like this before (though a few dons darkly recalled something similar happening fifteen years earlier in the History Faculty) and many felt that re-examination would create a dangerous precedent. Any student could demand the right to get a better result. To my surprise, I found that I had powerful champions. Some of the most distinguished members of the board pleaded my cause and argued for me with passion, and this I found consoling; not everybody, apparently, thought I was a fool and a failure. Some remembered my very nice under-graduate degree and were outraged by what had happened. For months there was deadlock. I had very little hope of a favourable outcome, and knew that, whatever happened, there would always be something questionable about me in academic circles. In any event, in July 1975, Dame Helen, the chairman of the board, settled the matter. An injustice had been done, she told the Dean of Graduate Studies who was staunchly on my side. She was very sorry for Miss Armstrong, but the sanctity of the Oxford doctorate could only be impaired by re-examination.

So that was that. To this day, some of my friends – even those who did not know me at the time – insist that I could still have reversed this decision. I cannot imagine what they think I could have done. Chained myself to the railings outside the Examination Schools? Picketed the Dame's house? Prostrated myself in front of the Sheldonian Theatre and stopped the traffic? Gone on hunger strike? It was quite clear to me and my supporters that the game was up. I found it very comforting that there had been such a row, that people had fought on my behalf, and that I had not gone quietly. I was glad that I wasn't simply an ordinary failure, though there was something disturbing about all the notoriety. There seemed to be something irremediably odd and freakish about me.

I tried to behave with dignity, but I still experienced the final decision as a body blow. It would be a long time before I could hear the words 'Tennyson', 'doctorate' or 'thesis' without pain. I was not angry with Alistair Courtney. I suspected that, for all the fuss, he had been right. I was no good, and he had unmasked me. I had failed as a nun; I had failed as an academic. I was cracking up mentally. I could not see what I could usefully do with the rest of my life.

As I travelled between the college and my flat, the city seemed to mirror my depression. 'SAME THING DAY AFTER DAY,' read a famous graffito, snaking between Ladbroke Grove and Westbourne Park tube stations, 'TUBE – WORK – DINER [sic] – WORK – TUBE – ARMCHAIR – TUBE – WORK – HOW MUCH MORE CAN YOU TAKE – ONE IN FIVE CRACKS UP.' 1975 was a grim year in London. Britain was in recession, the IRA had brought their terror campaign to the mainland, and the tabloid newspapers were apocalyptic, calling for a return to law and order. The unemployment figures were among the worst since the Second World War, and I took perverse consolation from the fact that even if I had got my doctorate, I probably wouldn't have got a university post. The colourful interlude of the 1960s was over. The hippie commune had been replaced by the 'squat', an ideological protest against the futility and absurdity of work, and the young seemed afflicted by what was termed 'a poverty of desire'. The dream of a brave new world, which had seemed almost palpable during my Oxford years, was over.

Yet despite my depression and my fear for the future, I could not quite succumb to the prevailing despair. The worst had happened, but that meant that I no longer had anything much to lose, and increasingly I found that quite liberating. I had recently moved from my Highgate flat into the house of a college acquaintance in West Finchley. Her husband Barrie had died, almost overnight, of viral pneumonia, at the age of twenty-six. Susan had been six weeks pregnant at the time of his death, and decided that she did not want to live alone. Her tragedy put my own woes into perspective, and Susan was also a marvellous support to me. Together we looked forward to the baby, and when her daughter was born later that summer, I helped to look after her, changing nappies and even getting up to do the night feed. Susan's Jewish family generously welcomed me into their midst. Neither Susan nor her parents were believers, but they did have family dinners on Fridays, and I was introduced to chopped liver and challah.

On the baby's naming day, I attended my first synagogue service. Sitting in the women's gallery, watching the men below transformed by their white prayer shawls and listening to the strange chant, I was aware that this was quite different from any religion that I had experienced. People talked throughout the service, taking apparently little heed of the long Hebrew readings and prayers. But there was a warmth in the room that was moving and intriguing: the men embraced one another and came over specially to talk to us women, admiring the baby, and congratulating Susan's and Barrie's parents with tears in their eyes. I did not think about it much at the time, but that service planted a seed: there were other ways of being religious than those I had been accustomed to. Not everybody felt that it was unworthy to feel emotional and to show your feelings.

Yet again, in the spirit of *Ash-Wednesday*, I found that relinquishing hope had released something within me. My love for reading came back in full. Even though I had started to respond to literature again, there had still been something rather dutiful and anxious in my approach. I would read a new novel, desperately casting around for a clever thing to say about it that would impress my colleagues. But now that I had been ejected from academia so publicly, I no longer needed to impress anybody. It didn't matter whether I came up with any brilliant insights or not. When I read a novel or a poem now, I no longer had an ulterior motive; I was no longer trying to use literature to promote myself, but was simply immersing myself in the text for its own sake – as, of course, I should have been doing all along. As a result, I found myself inundated with ideas and with the words to express them. The mind that I had bludgeoned into a stupor had been given back to me. Again, I did not reflect upon this much at the time. I simply noted it as an irony.

And yet my renewed delight in the written word was a gift and a grace. This too planted a seed of perception. Insight does not always come on order, and there will certainly be no renaissance if you are merely trying to 'get' something for yourself. As soon as I stopped trying to exploit my literary skills to advance my career or enhance my reputation, I found that I was opening myself to the text, could lose myself in the beauty of the words and in the wisdom of the writer. It was a kind of *ekstasis*, an ecstasy that was not an exotic, tranced state of consciousness, but in the literal sense of the word, a going beyond the self.

Then, in February 1976, just over a year since the viva that, I thought, had wrecked my life, I received the greatest gift of all, though at first it seemed like another setback.

It had been a perfectly ordinary day in college. Richard was producing some short plays by W. B. Yeats and I was his assistant, dogsbody and stage manager. That evening I stayed late for a rehearsal. My role was chiefly to administer moral support. I could not contribute directorially, because the plays were so cryptic that I couldn't really understand them. But there was a nice sequence that I always enjoyed, in which Nicky, one of the most gifted of our students, performed a magical dance to the accompaniment of strange, haunting music. A curious feature of these somewhat arcane plays was a chorus of four women, who had to fold and unfold a large cloth, which they displayed to the audience. I hadn't a clue what this signified, and never quite dared to reveal my ignorance to Richard, but I guessed that the women were the Irish equivalent of the Fates or something of that sort. That evening, the girls made us all laugh when we reached the end of the play, since when the cloth was unfolded for the last time, we saw that it was inscribed with the words, 'That's All, Folks!' Richard was not amused – he took this venture very seriously – but I was still smiling to myself when I reached Baker Street station to begin the long journey home to Finchley.

The rush hour was over, and the large, dank ticket office looked desolate and grim. A few commuters hurried past, the collars of their coats turned up against the cold. Outside it was raining and the drunks had taken up their usual places near the turnstiles. Everything seemed as usual.

But just after I had gone through the ticket barrier, it hit me: the smell, the acrid taste, the flickering quality of the light and the terror. But the experience was more intense this time. I was dimly aware of lurching around, trying to get away from something – but from what? I grasped the railing, as my thought processes splintered and the fluorescent station lights began to flash violently with a ferocity that was almost blinding. And then there was a change. Suddenly, at last, all the conflicting pieces of the pattern seemed to fuse into a meaningful whole. I had entered a new dimension of pure joy, fulfilment and peace: the world seemed transfigured, and its ultimate significance – so obvious and yet quite inexpressible – was revealed. This was God. But no sooner had I realized this, than I began to fall down that familiar dark tunnel into oblivion.

A couple of hours later, the attending doctor in the A and E department of the Middlesex Hospital told me that I had suffered an epileptic seizure, and arranged an appointment for me in the neurology department. I truly did not know whether to laugh or cry. I was an ex-nun, a failed academic, mentally unstable, and now I could add 'epileptic' to this dismal list. Every time I thought I had turned a corner, I seemed to get knocked back. Even God, for whom I had searched so long, was simply the product of a faulty brain, a neurological aberration. I went to bed that night in despair.

'So it is epilepsy, then?' I asked Dr Wolfe, the consultant, some weeks later.

'Yes, I'm afraid it certainly looks that way.' He nodded briskly, a lean, elegant man with a sharply intelligent face. His eyes held mine kindly. 'The electro-encephalograph shows a small but definite abnormality.' A few days earlier, I had had a preliminary EEG, during which numerous small electrodes had been inserted into my scalp to measure the brain rhythms. 'But we didn't find anything very terrible,' Dr Wolfe continued. 'That's good news. Epilepsy isn't the end of the world, you know. It is even curable, if we get it in time. We can do a lot nowadays with drugs and you can learn how to avoid unnecessary risks.'

'How did I get this?' I asked wearily, expecting to be told that my unstable 'nerves' had brought me to this sorry pass.

Dr Wolfe shrugged. 'We can't be sure, but I would suspect some kind of brain injury. It could have been a bad knock on the head, or a birth trauma, which had left some scarring on the brain. Are you aware of anything like that?'

I shook my head, but later my mother recalled that my birth had been difficult. When the contractions had become severe, she had been given a shot of morphine and had passed out. It seems likely that I was deprived of oxygen for a few critical moments and suffered mild brain damage. I am lucky that I was not as badly injured as Jacob.

'There are one or two questions I would like to ask you,' Dr Wolfe went on, 'just to give me a clearer idea of what part of the brain has been damaged and what kind of epilepsy you have. Epilepsy is a generic term, you know; it covers a multitude of very different conditions.'

I nodded vaguely, though I had little idea of what he meant. For me, epilepsy meant the *grand mal* seizures that I had seen in Jacob. I did not know that there could be any other kind.

'Tell me, I know this was your first *grand mal* attack, but are you ever prone to fainting? Loss of consciousness – anything of that sort?'

There was a moment when, as they say, the world stood still. I felt literally blank, and could not even begin to think what this might mean. There was a pause, and then I told him about the blackouts. 'And you were about eighteen when this started?' Dr Wolfe made a note, and nodded, as if to himself. 'This condition quite often appears in late adolescence – with the hormonal changes, you see. And the good nuns didn't advise you to check these medically?'

'No. We thought it was all due to emotional disturbance.'

Dr Wolfe sighed impatiently. 'I do wish people wouldn't play psychiatrist and make these facile assumptions!' he said, his lips taut with suppressed irritation. 'It's the current fashion to see every illness as psychosomatic, but epilepsy is a physical disease and needs physical treatment, though there are often quite traumatic emotional *effects*. You see, I am interested in the fear that you say you experience, the distress and the smell. This is what we call an aura, and it is associated with a particular kind of focal epilepsy, centred in the temporal lobe, the part of the brain responsible for the retention of memories, and for the senses of taste and smell.'

So all that anguish about my feeble will power had been entirely misdirected. I could have been as emotionally stolid as a sloth and it would have made no difference. I felt a dawning sense of vindication, but Dr Wolfe's next question took me completely by surprise.

'Now – please don't be afraid to speak honestly about this; nobody will think that you are mad or deranged in any way if the answer is "yes", but have you ever had any hallucinatory experience, seen or heard things that aren't there?'

Again, the silence in the little consulting room vibrated and I sat, afraid almost to move or speak, in case the hope that I was beginning to feel should prove to be yet another delusion. But slowly, in response to his careful probing, I began to answer his questions. 'And have you found things looking rather strange? Or have you done things without realizing it? Started to go to one place, perhaps, and ended up somewhere completely different?'

Almost winded by the implications of what I was hearing, I answered, hesitantly at first, but then the words almost tumbled over one another in my eagerness to explain. And – more wonderful than almost anything else – was the fact that Dr Wolfe was nodding as though this was only to be expected.

'Yes,' he said at last. 'These are all classic symptoms of temporal lobe epilepsy.' He took some more notes, and then looked up, frowning slightly. 'But forgive me, I'm puzzled: this must have been very alarming for you. Why on earth did you not take these symptoms to a doctor?'

I explained about Dr Piet, the hospitalization, the therapy and the drugs. Dr Wolfe covered his eyes with his hand, shook his head, and looked up again. 'Do you mean to tell me,' he asked, with devastating calm, 'that you were treated by psychiatrists for over three years – men and women who were all fully qualified doctors – that you presented these symptoms, and that none of them, not one, in all that time suggested that you have an EEG?'

'No, they didn't.' I was beginning to be invaded by an enormous astonishment, a confusion of feelings that included anger but also a relief so great that I was close to tears.

Dr Wolfe uttered that explosive sound that novelists used to transcribe as 'Pshaw!' 'It's not even as though temporal lobe epilepsy were an obscure condition,' he snapped. 'It's the most common of all the focal epilepsies, and very well documented. And, as I say, you are almost a textbook case!' He tailed off. Then his face cleared, and he wrote out a prescription for the drug that, he hoped, would eliminate the demons that had haunted me for so long.

As I got up to go, he looked at me sternly. 'I don't think you need waste any more of your time with these *psychiatrists*.' He made the word sound like an obscenity. 'No amount of talking about your problems will make the smallest impression on your condition, and I'm very sorry indeed that you have had to wait for so long before getting adequate medical help. By the way,' he added, as I reached the door, 'it's interesting that you were once a nun. People with temporal lobe epilepsy are often religious!'

*   *   *

I walked down Mortimer Street in a daze. For many people, I am sure, a diagnosis of epilepsy must be unwelcome news, but for me it was an occasion of pure happiness. As I looked at the grimy buildings, the diseased London pigeons flapping untidily round the gables, the littered streets and the overflowing dustbins, this urban detritus seemed a vision of beauty. For the first time in years, I felt that I could trust my perceptions. I knew now that my mind was neither broken nor irretrievably flawed. I was not mad, and need not expect to end my days in a locked ward. The world had been given back to me and, perhaps for the first time ever, I felt that I could take charge of my life.

The disease itself did not trouble me unduly. The experience of looking after Jacob had taught me that it was a manageable condition. It was also very common. Dr Wolfe had told me that each year twenty-five thousand people contract epilepsy in Britain alone. It was even a rather distinguished illness: Dostoyevsky, Van Gogh, Gustave Flaubert, Edward Lear, Julius Caesar and Alexander the Great had probably all been epileptics. Later I would learn that Tennyson had also suffered from epilepsy. No wonder I had been drawn to his poetry, with its haunting descriptions of tranced states of mind and of life seen through a veil of unreality. But Tennyson had lived in terror of the disease, which had darkened his whole life. His brother Edward, also a sufferer, had been confined for years in an asylum for the insane. A hundred years ago, epilepsy was a disgrace; it was thought to be the result of a disordered sexual appetite. Epileptics were thus castrated, circumcised or incarcerated. But that was no longer true. I had a prescription in my pocket for a drug that would control these symptoms. I might never again have to experience that periodic descent into hell. And even if I still suffered further temporal lobe attacks, at least I would know what was happening to me. By far the most frightening aspect of the whole experience had been the fear of losing my mind.

I was, therefore, rather surprised that my friends not only found it difficult to share my relief, but that some positively resisted the diagnosis. This has been the only aspect of the disease that I have found truly troubling. Something of the old shibboleths remains. Epilepsy is still, in some sense, an unacceptable disease; as I have found, people need to turn it into something else. Friends will look puzzled and mulish when I explain that it is a purely physical disease, the result of a birth accident. They seem to *want* it to be the expression of psychological strain or neurosis. They can become quite dogmatic on the subject, even though their know-ledge of neurology could be written down on a small postcard. Others simply change the subject, if I mention my condition, as though I had made a remark in bad taste. I am quite sure that I would not experience the same kind of reaction if I suffered from diabetes or hypertension.

This has meant that, even though nobody would dream of incarcerating me in a mental hospital because of my condition, my epilepsy has been an isolating factor. I tended to retreat from close contact with people during the years before the diagnosis, because I was afraid of having one of my 'weird seizures' in front of them. This made my return to secular life far more difficult than it need have been, and I should not have been abandoned for so long in that Bosch-like hell, which has left me with an indelible memory of the darker regions of my mind.

But when I left Dr Wolfe's consulting room on that bright spring morning in 1976, I did not know that I would have these difficulties. I felt simply a joyous relief that has never entirely left me. I still feel a sense of reprieve. All I wanted to do, when I first received the diagnosis, was to revel in this wonderful reversal. As

I walked down Mortimer Street that day, I knew that I had a viable future.

Later that year, I travelled up to Oxford and walked through the city streets to Blackfriars to meet Jenifer Hart. She wanted Jacob to be baptized. 'But *why*?' I had asked. 'You don't believe in any of it! Why do this?'

Jenifer had sighed. 'I want him to have the whole thing,' was all she could say. 'I want him to do it properly.' Jacob wouldn't understand the theology of baptism, of course, but maybe the rite could speak to him at some other level. The Dominicans, who were no fools, had agreed to the christening, and the ceremony was to be held that afternoon. As a final twist in this strange story, I was to be Jacob's godmother. I had been the person who had brought him into this world of religion, even though I did it at a time when I was losing my own faith. Jacob seemed doubly my *alter ego*. I had now discovered that we were also bound together by an illness that could make our environment appear demonic and was grateful that the experience of looking after him had prepared me for my own diagnosis. Now he was taking my place in the Church.

Geoffrey Preston had decided to perform the ceremony in a small chapel upstairs. Jenifer was already waiting there, tense, hands clenched tightly in her lap, and clearly ill-at-ease. But Jacob was sitting quietly, his head to one side in a listening posture, his face thoughtful. 'This is a special occasion, isn't it, Karen?' he hissed, as I went and sat beside him. Nobody else was present. We made a strange quartet of belief, unbelief and – for Jacob – something else that had nothing to do with theological conviction.

'Jacob,' Geoffrey said, 'would you like some incense for your baptism?'

His eyes lit up. 'Oh, Geoffrey,' he breathed. 'Can I make it?' I smiled at Geoffrey. We both knew that this was a long-cherished dream.

'Come over here.' With his hands on his knees, Jacob bent low over the thurible, his blond head close to Geoffrey's tow-coloured one. 'Snap, crackle and pop!' he whispered gleefully, as the charcoal spluttered. 'Karen, watch this! Just watch me now!' He carefully spooned incense on to the glowing pellet and a cloud of fragrance rose up and filled the small room. I glanced warily at Jenifer, fearful that this popish flummery might be one step too far. But she was watching Jacob as he swung the thurible to and fro, with a rather sad smile, acknowledging that he had gone to a place where she could not follow. His face was transfigured; his head flung back, as he snuffed histrionically.

'Right.' Geoffrey nodded, and Jacob instantly replaced the thurible on the stand. 'Did you see me, Karen? Mummy, did you see me?'

Geoffrey cut the ceremony to the minimum. There was no complicated creed for me to recite on Jacob's behalf, an affirmation of faith that, as Geoffrey knew, I could not honestly make and which had no relevance in Jacob's case. The exorcisms were omitted: Jacob was not to be frightened by the idea of a demon trapped inside him. Instead, we had just the bare essentials. I stood behind Jacob and made the responses; Jacob knelt on a prie-dieu, bolt upright, his hands joined and his eyes fixed sternly ahead.

'What do you ask of the Church of God?' Geoffrey asked.

'Faith!' I replied in Jacob's stead, catching Geoffrey's eye for a moment. He smiled at me, kindly, accepting the irony. What did faith really mean? If you could leave out the creed, as we had just done, could faith be liberated from belief? Could it mean that we sought the kind of trust and confidence we feel when we say that we have faith *in* a person or an ideal? Maybe the Church could give Jacob this kind of faith – I looked at his rapt face – but it had signally failed with me.

'What does faith bring to you?' Geoffrey continued.

'Life everlasting,' I replied. No, I couldn't believe in the prospect of immortality. But could faith not simply bring an enhanced life, here and now? A more abundant life, as Jesus had promised, even though my so-called faith seemed to have diminished my own mind and heart.

'If, then, you desire to enter into life,' Geoffrey went on, 'keep the commandments: You shall love the Lord your God with your whole heart, and with your whole soul, and with your whole mind, and your neighbour as yourself.'

Put like that, it sounded so simple. Why had we tied ourselves up in such knots? Sewing at needle-less machines, performing archaic penances, and treating one another so coldly? And how could we have loved our neighbours and sisters in religion, when we had been taught to despise ourselves? At each phrase, Jacob nodded to himself. There was poignancy in the phrase 'with your whole mind', but Jacob did know how to love, and Blackfriars had welcomed him lovingly. He approached Geoffrey slowly and stood quite still, while Geoffrey made the sign of the cross on his forehead and breast. I quailed slightly when he put a few grains of salt on Jacob's tongue: at any other time, he would have spat it out with scant ceremony, but now he swallowed it gravely, while Geoffrey said the prescribed words: 'Grant, we pray you, Lord, that your servant who tastes the savour of salt may no longer hunger but be filled with heavenly nourishment.'

Jenifer had been right. Jacob did hunger for something that he could never have put into words. And I too had once had a similar hunger. I had wanted to be filled with God, transformed by a holiness that would bring me a fuller and more satisfying existence. But instead I had starved my mind and my heart, and that hunger had atrophied, died, and been replaced by a malaise with all things religious. And yet when I looked at Jacob, I felt nostalgia for what I had once been. Jacob did find something at Blackfriars, though none of us could explain what that was. His face was clear and peaceful; he was enjoying a little respite from the demons that plagued us both.

'Now, bend forward, Jacob,' Geoffrey said gently. Sprinkling a few drops of water on Jacob's head, he raised his voice, which filled the little chapel triumphantly: 'Jacob, I baptize you in the Name of the Father, and of the Son, and of the Holy Spirit.'

Jacob gave a long, audible sigh of satisfaction, while Jenifer and I, excluded from the source of this peace for very different reasons, exchanged glances and smiled slightly.

The long, hot summer of 1976 was my last at Bedford College. In the autumn, I would begin a new career as a schoolteacher, a prospect that filled me with gloom. Thanks to the failure of my thesis, I had no luck in my applications for academic posts, but when I started applying to schools, I got the very first job I put in for. It was a good position in a prestigious school in south London, and there was a strong possibility of my being promoted to head of department in a year or so. But I just did not want to do it. I felt shades of the prison house begin to close around me, and I was determined, during these few sultry months, to have fun. I was befriended by a group of mature students at Bedford who were about my own age, and they invited me to their parties, introduced me to their friends, and life took on the hectic, crazy quality of a delayed adolescence.

And, of course, there were men. I would not dignify these encounters with the term 'love affairs', but there was at least some good humour and affection. I have not spoken at all in these pages about my so-called 'love life', because it has been a dead-end. My more serious relationships have (to paraphrase Hobbes) been nasty, brutish and not as short as they should have been. Last summer, I was having dinner with two gay friends in upstate New York. They quizzed me about my single state, perhaps expecting me to 'come out' to them. But to their delight and to the utter astonishment of the young waiter, who was uncorking our bottle of wine, I explained that I was a 'failed heterosexual'. I added that, though I liked men very much, and had often been in love, men did not seem to see me as female. They either look through me with an indifference that is almost comical, or see me as a dear old pal – 'one of the boys'. Throughout our relationship, one of my former lovers, who was not English, persistently used the masculine form of the local endearment – as it were, *caro* instead of *cara*. Now that I am older, I no longer expect male attention, and, as I explained that evening to my gay friends, the problem has been compounded by the fact that I have enjoyed some success and have money, which men of my generation sometimes find difficult. 'Sounds good to me!' said our waiter.

When I wrote *Beginning the World*, I did try to chronicle some of my early sorties into the world of love. Writing about these relationships was a lowering experience for me, and the result must have been even more demoralizing for my readers. I see no reason to dwell on these episodes here, because none of them developed into anything significant. Like my failed thesis, they were doors slammed in my face, precluding me from a certain way of life and forcing me into another direction. Just as I was prevented from becoming an academic, so too I have never been able to achieve a normal domestic existence, and this, like my epilepsy, has also ensured that I have remained an outsider in a society in which coupledom is the norm.

Nevertheless, I do speculate on the reasons for my lamentable failure with men. It is odd to be so inept at something that most people appear to manage naturally. I have always been reluctant to blame the convent for this since I am the exception rather than the rule: most former nuns seem to find partners quite quickly after leaving the religious life. Even Rebecca, who became so ill in the convent, is now happily married. But we all respond to things in different ways, and it may be that a touch of frost entered my soul during those years. The constant and abrasive rebuffs, which we all experienced as a matter of course during the novitiate, may have made me chronically unconfident of my ability to inspire love. The distrust of my wretched 'sensitivity', which was so carefully cultivated by some of my superiors, and my consequent habit of repressing strong feelings may have left me emotionally impaired. One of the purposes of the initiation rites of traditional societies is to confirm adolescents in their sexuality. It may be that my initiation into the religious life, which virtually ignored gender issues, transformed me into an androgynous anchorite rather than a virginal woman. Or there may be a simpler reaction against those years. Men of my age tend to be big on control, and I have found that when I have let a man into my bed, I have suddenly found my life invaded by a mini-dictator, who has to have his own way in the smallest matters. My last partner, for example, who had seldom composed anything longer than a letter, used to give me minute but peremptory directions about how I should go about researching and writing my own books; and after the convent, I cannot tolerate this type of supervision and restraint.

But I also think that the years after my departure from the convent took their toll. At a time when most people are supposed to find a mate, I was engaged in a solitary battle with an undiagnosed illness, and locked into a private hell. If you cannot trust the integrity of your own mind, you cannot fall in love, and neither can anybody fall in love with you. The strange sensation of talking to people at a distance, through a glass screen, or seeing them through the wrong end of a telescope, which dissipated once I was properly medicated, made real contact very difficult indeed. Because I received no adequate help during this time, I turned in upon myself, and this tendency may have become habitual.

But was I pushed into solitude, or did I jump? It was my idea to go into a convent, and nobody forced me to stay in the religious life so long. Recently I have started to wonder whether my solitary state may in fact be due to some deeper imperative within myself, which I am only just beginning to understand.

During that last summer at Bedford College, I played hard. I taught at the Summer School organized by the University of London for graduate students from overseas, and for six weeks I lived in Bloomsbury, in the centre of town. I had participated in this school before but, on this last occasion, I was a great hit. My lectures and classes were popular and crowded, and I found that I had acquired a little circle of literary disciples. It seemed ironic that I was being forced to leave the academic world just as I was beginning to feel at home there. By day we worked hard, but every night, students and staff partied. 'You're so different,' one of the administrators said to me at lunch one day. 'I wouldn't have dared to speak to you last year: you were quite unapproachable. What happened?'

What had happened was that I was at last receiving proper

treatment for my condition, and I had relaxed. Because I felt that I had nothing to lose, some residual barriers had come down, and I found that I was able to relate easily to other people for the first time since leaving the convent. I liked being with my students and colleagues, and they seemed to like being with me. I remember one night lying on my back in the gardens of Russell Square, staring up at the stars with a group of fellow-revellers, quite untroubled by the fact that in a few hours' time I would be delivering a lecture on Philip Larkin to three hundred people. I was happy. It was an unfamiliar sensation, but in spite of everything, I felt a sense of well-being and gratitude. There was nothing above those stars, I reflected hazily. There was no God, and the heavens were empty. As T. S. Eliot had noted: 'time is always time, And place is always and only place'. This was all we had. But that night for once I was wholly present in the moment, not looking before or after, nor pining for what was not. And the present moment was not a bad place to be.

~: 6 :~

THE USUAL REIGN

A few weeks later, however, in September 1976, I started my new job and did not feel so sanguine. The school looked like a Victorian jam factory; it was a clumsy building in red brick with large, ungainly windows. Over the years, they had added a haphazard series of new wings, so that the whole pile sprawled awkwardly over a huge area of the leafy, prosperous suburb of Dulwich in south-east London. As I went through the front door, I did not feel that I had started an exciting new phase of my life, but as though I were beginning a prison sentence.

I knew that I was lucky to get this job. This was one of the best private girls' schools in London. It was academic, and still taught Latin and Greek as well as the sciences to a high level. I had been appointed an 'assistant mistress' (I was amused by the archaic ambiguity of my title) but the following year I would become the new Head of English, and run my own department. At my interview, Pearl, who was currently in charge of English studies, told me that she hoped to retire soon and that I would be nicely placed to take over.

'I'm beginning to find it all rather a grind,' she told me in her rather arch drawl. 'I've been doing this job for over twenty years, you see.'

'*Twenty years!*' I was aghast; I had been wondering how I was going to endure the next twenty minutes.

'Well, you've got to spend twenty years *some*where,' was her unruffled reply.

True. But not here, I pleaded with the absent, non-existent God during school prayers on that first morning. Because of my experience in higher education, I had been made a sixth-form tutor, so I was standing with my new charges in the gallery, looking down on the serried ranks of girls in the hall below, all clad in an unbecoming navy uniform. The headmistress walked on to the stage: 'Lift up your hearts!' she murmured, in a listless, lifeless tone, and I felt my own heart plummet to my boots. I just did not want to be there.

Yet there really seemed no alternative. I had come a long way in the seven years since I had left the religious life, and in recent months I knew that I had made great strides. I no longer feared for my sanity; I had a new circle of friends; I was having fun. And for the first time in my life I had a home of my own. Because I now had a secure job and a stable income, I had become eligible for a mortgage and was now the possessor of a tiny one-bedroomed flat in Highbury, near the stadium of the Arsenal Football Club; henceforth my Saturday afternoons were punctuated with great roars from the fans who crowded into the neighbourhood for the weekly match. The flat was a symbolic step. I now had a place in the world – something which had once seemed psychologically impossible. But despite all this undoubted progress, the failure of my thesis and my consequent explusion from academia had severely wounded my confidence. I had managed to recover my equilibrium, but I had very little belief in my talents. The idea of striking out into an entirely different field was beyond me, and I was too exhausted by the struggle and drama of the recent past even to contemplate such a venture. I needed a rest. I was in a convalescent state, and was simply not fit enough for anything more ambitious. I had been fortunate to get this job, I repeated to myself over and over again, and I must just settle for what I had. Not hope to turn again. Find strength in what remains behind.

Yet the location of my new flat showed that I had not really settled for this at all. Highbury in north London, on the other side of the city, was miles from my new school. There were, I thought, sensible reasons for my choice. Because of my epilepsy, my doctors told me firmly, driving was out of the question. Southeast London is badly served by public transport: Dulwich is not connected to the underground railway, and without a car, life is very difficult there. Most of the new friends I had made during the last few months lived in north London, and, I argued, they were going to be very important to me now. If I could not have a satisfying career, at least I could have a good social life. But the real reason for choosing Highbury was that I did not want to live anywhere near the school. In the evening, as I headed north, my heart became lighter with every mile, and when the bus finally lurched into Rosebery Avenue, passed the Sadlers Wells Theatre, and began the approach to Islington, I felt a new woman. Conversely, as the bus crept through the morning traffic, passed the Houses of Parliament, and crossed the Thames at Westminster Bridge, I felt gloomier by the minute.

In one sense, it was crazy to live so far away from my work.

The journey was horrendous. Because the mortgage gobbled up much of my meagre salary, I could not afford to travel either by tube or the overground train, which would have cut the trip in half. Instead, I had to rely on a most unreliable bus that took me to south-east London by an extraordinarily circuitous route. In the morning, I had to leave the house shortly after 6.30 looking most peculiar in a moth-eaten fur coat, which had once belonged to my grandmother (I could not afford a new winter coat), and my face glistening with baby oil to protect my skin from the elements (I could not afford to waste make-up on the other passengers of bus 172). If all went well (and all too often the journey did *not* go well – the bus would fail to arrive, and once even broke down), I would arrive in Herne Hill at about 8.15, and then had to walk a mile to the school. In the evening, I sometimes had to wait for over an hour for the wretched bus. But I felt that all this was worthwhile. I wanted to put myself at some distance from my new job, because I knew that it was doing me no good at all.

This, I must emphasize, was not because there was anything wrong with the school. Indeed, I was very impressed with it. Most of the girls seemed to like being there, the staff was excellent and standards were high. It was also a humane place. I had passed my own school days alternately bored and frightened, but that was clearly not the case here. I even quite enjoyed the teaching, though not extravagantly so. People expected me to like my classes with the older girls best but, to my surprise, I much preferred the little ones. It was fun to watch them encountering Dickens and Shakespeare for the first time, and to catch them before they realized that a cool teenager was supposed to find these authors boring. Occasionally I would find myself completely wrapped up in a lesson. You cannot be a good teacher to every student, any more than you can be a good friend or a satisfactory lover to just anybody. But I could see that in the main I was doing a useful job, and I was grateful to have financial security for the first time since leaving the convent.

The trouble lay not in the school but in myself. It was bad for me to be in another highly authoritarian institution, and I was keenly aware that I was slipping back into old craven habits of obedience and conformity. Instead of moving on and away from the constraints of the religious life, I felt that I was standing still. Indeed, sometimes I feared that I was actually losing ground, because in many ways school life seemed a parody of my convent years. The Headmistress was a charismatic, unusual and gifted woman, but listening to the tales of other teachers over the years, I have noted that this job has its dangers. A headmaster or head-mistress has almost complete power in an enclosed world, and this often seems to go to their heads. Thus the Head at Dulwich tended to treat her staff like a temperamental parent would treat her children. One day you were flavour of the month, the next, for no apparent reason, you were in the doghouse, your every request and suggestion refused, often discourteously, and your projects stymied. Then, a few weeks later, you were back in favour again. We were supposed to jump to attention if the Head so much as sneezed. 'The Head is hopping mad!' the deputy would report, as though this were a catastrophe comparable to the out-break of World War Three.

One of the Head's foibles was a near pathological sensitivity to noise – an unfortunate affliction if you happen to be working in a building crowded with adolescents. At every hour of the working day, one of us had to do 'corridor duty', sitting outside the Head's office to prevent any child from walking past and disturbing her; students often had to make absurdly long detours to get to their classes. We all resented this ridiculous waste of our time. This was not why we had been put on the planet. The Head's office was situated directly beneath the staffroom, where we were supposed to have coffee and relax, so she continually complained about the noise we made. I was one of the worst offenders. All too often the school secretary put her head apologetically around the door. 'Miss Armstrong, this is awful, I am *so* sorry, but would you please laugh more quietly.'

Then there was the drama of the stapler. During the examination season, we had to staple together the pages of hundreds of question papers, and the only place we could do this was the staffroom. Two or three of us would be engaged in this essential task at any one time, using perfectly ordinary office staplers, which made the discreetest of thuds and clicks. As we had very small desks, we liked to spread our papers on the floor and staple them together down there, but that caused such a volley of lamentations from below that we had to find an alternative method. 'The floorboards amplify the sound!' the Head moaned. 'You simply would not *believe* how intolerably loud it is.' We didn't, but we tried everything. First we stapled on our laps, but again there were furious complaints. Next we tried to muffle the sound by stacking cushions on our knees, but to no avail. It reminded me of the fairy tale of the princess whose royal blood becomes apparent when she is kept awake all night by a pea buried under scores of mattresses. On one occasion, I returned from class to find four of my colleagues crouched in the corridor outside the staffroom, stapling with their bottoms in the air: they had been banished from the staffroom by an irate Head, who insisted that she could not possibly work to the accompaniment of this appalling din. We became hyper-cautious about noise. Once, a stolid, sensible member of the French department tripped over a coffee table and fell headlong; she struggled to her feet, ashen-faced, clutching her right wrist (which subsequently proved to be broken), muttering in terror: 'Oh, my God! I made a noise!' Before any of us came to her aid, we sat, frozen in our seats, eyes fixed on the ground, waiting for an explosion of wrath from below.

There were other frustrating rituals. We were never allowed to use the photocopier, because it 'wasted' too much paper. The Head gave us long, firm lectures on the need for this economy. If we wanted material printed specially for our lessons, we were expected to use an archaic machine called the Banda, whose impossible intricacies I cannot explain, as I never attempted to use it. This restriction meant that we tended, boringly, to rely on 'chalk and talk'. Then there was the Biscuit Book. We each had to bring our own jar of coffee to school, in order to make ourselves a drink during recreation. The school munificently laid on milk and hot water free of charge, and also provided tins of biscuits, but we had to pay for these. Every time we took a biscuit, we had to note down our purchase in a little notebook, together with the exact time we made the transaction. Each type of biscuit had a different price. As there were about seventy members of staff, the entries became labyrinthine.

10.45 a.m. Miss Hicks: 3 Royal Scots = 4½ pence + 1 Custard Cream = 2 pence

10.46 a.m. Miss Layton: 2 Ginger Nuts = 3 pence

10.48 a.m. Mrs Soames: 1 Custard Cream = 2 pence + 1 Royal Scot = 1½ pence

And so on. By the end of each day, there could be scores of entries, and at the end of each term, some hapless junior member of the Maths Department had the appalling job of calculating how much each of us owed. It took hours. I several times suggested that we simply divide the expenditure equally, but this daring innovation was unacceptable. After a while I decided to leave well enough alone, fearful that, to punish my temerity, they might devise a byzantine method of making us pay for our milk and hot water.

This brought back too many memories. It recalled the sewing machine, and the reprimands designed to destroy our self-will and self-esteem. Indeed, during one of my run-ins with the Head, Pearl, who seemed to find it difficult to keep away from the school once she had left, told me that the Head had said to her: 'I really must *break* Miss Armstrong!' Her behaviour was, of course, preposterous, but I could not laugh it off as easily as my colleagues. I could not see it in proportion, and found to my disgust that I actually *minded* being out of favour. This was not surprising; I had been programmed to relate to authority in this way, and the Head's leadership sometimes seemed as perverse and irrational as that of some of my former superiors. When, for example, I was called up for jury service and had to spend two weeks at Knightsbridge Crown Court, she was almost beside herself with fury. 'The Head is *hopping* mad!' her deputy informed me on the phone each night. But what could I do? She had got it into her head that I need only serve for a couple of days, but that was simply not the case. I asked if she would be prepared to pay the fine I might incur for contempt of court, or stand bail if I were hauled off to prison. When the judge finally released me and I went back to work, she was so unpleasant that there were moments when I felt that gaol would have been preferable. She was not always as bad as this. She could be very kind indeed, was excellent with the students, and when she was not trying to *break* me, went out of her way to be appreciative of my efforts. But the experience of being cursorily ordered around and 'owned' in this manner was bad for me, and I knew it.

There was also the problem of my health. I was now much better. The *jamais vu* of a temporal lobe attack was almost entirely a thing of the past, but I occasionally still suffered from *petit mal*. Anti-convulsant drugs do not work automatically. Nobody fully understands how they prevent seizures, and as the various epilepsies are all so different, it is sometimes hard to find exactly the right pill and the correct dosage for each patient. It can be a matter of trial and error, and, at first, in my case it was often error. It was some years before my doctor brought me into hospital and, by carefully monitoring the dosage, found some truly effective medication. I had been advised to conceal my condition from the authorities. My doctors warned me that even though we lived in an enlightened age, the condition still carried a stigma, and that epileptics often found it difficult to gain employment. As I had been appointed to the post before my epilepsy had been diagnosed, I did not have to lie directly, so I just kept quiet about my disease. I was beginning to learn that virtually the only people who reacted to my problem in a balanced way were those with a medical training and those who had had some first-hand experience of epilepsy.

One of these was Sally, whose older sister had been a life-long sufferer. Sally had come into the English Department in my second year at the school. We became friends after I had a seizure during the staff Christmas lunch. This had been so mild that it was easy to pass it off as a faint, due to end-of-term exhaustion, but Sally knew at once what had happened. It was useful to have an ally. Teachers tend to pick up all kinds of germs and fevers from the children, and a high body temperature can bring on an epileptic attack. This meant that whenever I caught one of these viruses, it took me a lot longer to recover than my colleagues. I had to take a great deal of sick leave, and this did not go unnoticed. Nor did the fact that I so often looked haggard and ill. Schoolteaching is an extremely exhausting job: it is like doing a one-woman show, in which you are on stage for about seven hours every day. By the end of term, we all looked at death's door. At coffee-time, we no longer laughed and chattered, and the Head had no need to complain about the noise. We all sat around silently, staring into space like zombies. Sometimes – horror of horrors – we actually forgot to record our purchases in the Biscuit Book. My particular difficulty was that my drugs were debilitating, and this increased my natural weariness. Fatigue is one of the things that trigger my seizures, as does sleep-deprivation. So it all became a vicious cycle. The more tired I was, the less resistance I had and the more flu-bugs I caught from the children; the more seizures I had, the more exhausted I became.

During my absence from school, Sally did a splendid PR job, elaborating on the symptoms she could mention in great detail in order to allay suspicion. And for a while our system worked well. But this could not be a long-term solution. All in all, I was beginning to miss at least six weeks a year, and even though I looked far from healthy, the Head began to suspect me of malingering. Finally, I came clean and she responded perfectly, with one of those leaps of sympathy that reminded us of how humane she could be when she was not trying to control every detail of our lives.

'I am so relieved,' she explained. 'I can quite understand why you didn't tell me. Of course, I can. But this is something physical, something that we can work with. Far more worrying is a vague neurosis that produces psychosomatic symptoms that nobody can ever get to the bottom of!' I was an asset to the school, she said, and if I had to take time off for unavoidable illness, so be it. It was worth it – for the time being.

And so I settled down at Dulwich. It was not what I had wanted to do with my life, but I had a secure job and friends. Sally and I had our own little coterie of the livelier and less conventional members of staff; we had a couple of holidays together in Yugoslavia and the Soviet Union. And I also had my north London life. I was uneasy about my inability to rise above the institutional idiocy of the school, and I was disturbed that I seemed to be wishing my life away. I spent the whole week longing for Friday, the weekend dreading Monday morning, and the whole term pining for the holidays. I knew that this was all wrong, and yet for the first time in my life I felt safe and ordinary. Nothing much happened to me during these years. I was no longer being carted off to hospital; I had no scandalously public failures; I was beginning to be like everybody else at last. And I have no doubt that, even though it was dull, this was a valuable period. It gave me some 'time out'. I could rest and, as I thought, heal.

As for prayer, God, holiness – all that seemed to have happened to somebody else. I sat through school prayers every morning in a daze of bored abstraction, incredulous that these ideas had once been so important to me. 'How on earth did you stick it out in the convent?' my colleagues would ask me in astonishment. 'You don't seem religious at all!' A few members of staff were churchgoers, but they were in a minority. Many of the children I taught had never heard of basic Christian concepts. One day, my class of eighteen-year-olds seemed to be making very heavy weather of John Donne's poem 'Good Friday. 1613. Riding Westward'. Eventually, to my astonishment, one of them cried in bewilderment: 'Miss Armstrong, what exactly *did* happen on Good Friday?' I used to look with pity at the young teacher who was the sole member of the Religious Department, and taught only a tiny number of students at the advanced level. What a dead-end subject!

In fact, however, in other parts of the world, this sceptical indifference was becoming eccentric and even old-fashioned. The countries of northern Europe were indeed responding to the peculiar strain of the late twentieth century by renouncing religion. For many, God had died in Auschwitz. The churches had been implicated in the Holocaust, and the traumatic experience of two world wars, fought on European soil, had left a legacy of unanswered questions. But other regions reacted differently. The United States, whose experience of the twentieth century had been more positive, was becoming more religious all the time: by the year 2000 it would be the second most religious country in the world after India. In the Middle East, as the Arab–Israeli conflict entered its third decade without hope of resolution, the secular ideologies of socialism and nationalism seemed increasingly bankrupt; after the wars of 1967 and 1973, there was a religious revival among both Israelis and Arabs, and on both sides the new religiosity became sucked into the conflict. In 1978–79, a bemused world witnessed the Iranian revolution, when an obscure mullah overthrew what had seemed to be one of the most stable and successfully secular countries in the Middle East. People were shocked. 'Whoever cared about religion?' cried a frustrated official in the United States State Department. But 1979 also saw the eruption of Jerry Falwell's Moral Majority into American politics. Even though its success was short-lived, it proved to be a watershed. Henceforth presidential candidates often found it advisable to sport their born-again credentials. In the middle of the twentieth century, it had been assumed that secularism was the coming ideology and that religion would never again play a major role in world events. But there was now a swing away from this position. Increasingly, people who were disenchanted with modernity felt impelled to push God from the sidelines to which he had been relegated in secular culture, and back to centre stage.

The extremists grabbed the headlines, and at this point I regarded them simply as a lunatic fringe, a dangerous bunch of fanatics. Because I was – on principle – not interested in religion, I was unaware that 'fundamentalism', as this militant piety was called, was only the most visible element of a much more pervasive trend. By the late 1970s, a significant number of people all over the world, who were never in the news and who would not dream of taking part in acts of terror and violence, were demonstrating in all kinds of ways that they wanted to be more religious and to see faith reflected more prominently in public life. There was a new interest in spirituality and mysticism. Religion was making a comeback.

It was easy to remain in ignorance of this in Britain, which was going in the opposite direction, even though people there certainly shared the widespread disappointment with modernity. The depression that had festered in London during the mid-70s had now exploded into the absolute nihilism of punk. Young men and women made themselves as ugly and cadaverous as possible. They sported wild Mohican hairstyles, caked their faces with white make-up, mutilated their bodies with razors and safety-pins, and destroyed their minds with drugs. The Sex Pistols, the chief punk rock group, vomited on stage, denounced the Queen, God and Jesus Christ, loudly proclaiming the death of all values, all principles. This was a public flouting of belief *per se*, but like the religious fundamentalists, other Britons were looking for certainty. The old ways had been dismantled, but as yet nothing new had appeared to take their place. Traditional boundaries and markers had come down, and many lacked a clear sense of identity. In America such people followed Jerry Falwell or Pat Robertson; in Iran, they turned to Ayatollah Khomeini. In Britain they voted for Margaret Thatcher, who became Prime Minister on 4 May 1979.

Margaret Thatcher went into Downing Street with the prayer of St Francis on her lips: 'Lord, make me an instrument of thy peace!' In fact, she was highly combative, and played on tabloid fears of internal decay. In her very first party conference, she issued a ringing attack on those 'who gnaw away at our self-respect, rewriting British history as centuries of gloom, oppression, and failure'. She was going to put the 'Great' back into 'Britain'. To many she seemed the answer to the long decline of the 1970s but to me she was a symbol of the dangers of certainty. With her hectoring rhetoric, upholstered, buttoned-up clothes, rigidly upswept hair and unfaltering propriety, she seemed to epitomize an attitude of unquestioned and unquestioning superiority. I remembered my flickering distaste when confronted with certainty in the person of poor, ineffective Miss Franklin. Watching Mrs Thatcher, I knew that I wanted no such certainty in my own life. Under the influence of Thatcherism, British people became preoccupied with money as never before; some prospered, but others were impoverished. For the first time, large numbers of homeless men and women started sleeping rough on the streets of London. An underpass near Waterloo station, where people erected shelters made of boxes, became known as Cardboard City; there was a soup kitchen for the destitute on the South Bank. In the Middle East, religious certainty led to such atrocities as the assassination of President Anwar Sadat in October 1981; in Britain, Thatcher's economic and political certainty had pushed people on to the streets.

As far as I could see, certainty made people heartless, cruel and inhuman. It closed their minds to new possibilities; it made them complacent and pleased with themselves. It also did not work. The new regime in Iran seemed just as oppressive as that of the Shah, the murder of Sadat did not lead to a new era in Egypt, and Thatcherism too would prove to be an expensive mistake. This type of certainty was unrealistic, and out of step with the way things really worked. Religious people seemed particularly prone to this dogmatism, and even though there was nothing remotely religious or Christian about Mrs Thatcher's regime, the experience of living in 'Maggie's Britain' made me even more leery of faith, dogmatism and orthodoxy, which so often – even in a good cause – made people ride roughshod over other people's sensitivities. That kind of certainty had damaged me in the past, and I wanted no more of it.

Sally was one of the first people I had met in my own generation who had been totally untouched by religion. Unlike the Harts or Susan, my former housemate, she did not recoil from religion in principled disgust, but regarded it as a strange, incomprehensible eccentricity, like swimming in the Serpentine on Christmas Day. Why would anybody want to do anything so bizarre! The basic doctrines of Christianity had passed her by. When she was having difficulty in her classes on Milton's *Paradise Lost*, I tried to explain the concept of Original Sin. Sally was appalled. 'You're not serious!' she exclaimed. 'All that fuss over eating a piece of fruit. What a system!' I could see her point. What kind of God would damn the whole human race because of one momentary lapse? Only one that I wanted nothing to do with. In fact, the more I thought about God these days, the more I realized how much I had probably always, subconsciously, disliked him. These days it seemed that he had lurked in my life like Big Brother in George

Orwell's novel *Nineteen Eighty-Four*, spying on everything I did, thought and felt, endlessly dissatisfied, and doling out favours and punishments indiscriminately. Sally was quite right. What a system!

When I met Sally's parents, I could understand her detachment from any form of faith. They had rejected the religion of their childhood so thoroughly that it now had little reality for them. Lady Phyl, the title she preferred to the more correct Lady Cockburn, was one of those people who didn't seem to need Christianity. Her painting was a form of contemplation that had nothing to do with any kind of deity, and she seemed naturally kind, gentle and creative, able to make the best of any situation, including being married to Sir Robert, which could not have been easy. He was a brilliant, pugnacious physicist, one of the small team of scientists who had discovered radar during the Second World War. But his achievements meant very little to him. He certainly had no self-righteous certainty. A depressive, he was profoundly disturbed by life in the late twentieth century, but it would never have occurred to him to seek comfort in religion, which he found obscurely troubling. He worried at theological concepts, rather as a terrier belabours a bone. The existence of God might have been a recalcitrant equation that refused to come out right.

'Now, Karen,' he would boom in his strong Hampshire accent as soon as I had put my foot over the threshold of their house. 'Let's get to the bottom of this question of God.'

'For goodness' sake, Bob!' Lady Phyl would exclaim. 'Let the poor girl get her coat off first!'

Yet ironically Sir Bob seemed to inspire the confidences of religious people. To the derision of his wife, in order to save a few pence, he would repair to the local unisex hairdressing salon, somewhat ambiguously called Blow Heads, on Thursday afternoons, when there was a cheap rate for senior citizens. He looked an incongruous figure, having his short back and sides amidst the youthful stylists with their Mohicans. One afternoon, when he had as usual been lugubriously lamenting the lack of honour in public life, the greed and triviality of the times, and looming ecological disaster, one of the stylists, with purple hair, tattoos down his bare arms, and clothes duly festooned with safety-pins and razor-blades, wordlessly thrust a card into his hand. Sir Bob stared at it with blank astonishment: it was an invitation to a special mission at the Church of the Lamb the following week. Then there was the time when he had paid a friendly visit to an elderly couple who were moving into the house next door. 'Moving is hell, isn't it?' he had commiserated affably to his new neighbour.

'Terrible.' The old man nodded in agreement. 'But fortunately I have a friend who makes the whole thing bearable.'

'Oh, really?' Sir Bob rumbled amiably, assuming that he was speaking of a helpful chum, but to his amazement, the 'friend' turned out to be Jesus. Sir Bob returned home shaking his head in utter perplexity.

'I can understand the idea of God – at a pinch,' he told me afterwards, still shocked by this revelation of the aberrations of the human mind, 'but I simply cannot – *cannot* – understand how anybody can imagine that he has a personal relationship with *Jesus*.'

I could only agree, especially since the historical Jesus would have been more likely to tell the couple to give all their possessions to the poor rather than helping them to convey their worldly goods around the country in heavily insured vans.

Yet it was in part due to this godless family that, even while I was recoiling from the very idea of faith, I had already taken the first step in a process that would, without my fully realizing what was happening, bring me back to religion. The Cockburns were great writers. Each one of them kept a diary, in which every evening they recorded the events of their day; it was, I could see, another form of meditation, or even an examination of conscience; it was a way of making sense of their lives. Sally had kept her diary since she was eight years old, and I used to marvel at the thick volumes, one for each year, lined up on her shelves.

'I don't know how anybody manages without a diary,' she used to say. 'You should have kept one in the convent. I bet you would have got out sooner; you see things so much more clearly when you write them down.'

Both Sally and her parents constantly urged me to write about my years in the convent. 'After all, it's over ten years since you left,' Sally argued. 'You'll forget it all, and that would be such a pity.'

In fact, I had been thinking along these lines myself. I was growing uneasy about the way these years were being trivialized, reduced to a series of funny stories to tell at dinner parties. It had been a crucial period and I needed to find out what it had really meant to me. I used to look thoughtfully at Sally's diaries, which had clearly been a means of creative self-appraisal and discovery. Maybe I should try something similar. My mother agreed. She had recently given me a typewriter which had been thrown out of her office. 'But you can only have it on one condition,' she said. 'Use it to write your story!'

As it happened, I even had a literary agent lined up. Charlotte had invited me to a dinner party in her flat to meet June, who had edited an anthology of short stories to which Charlotte had contributed. June had become professionally alert as soon as she heard that I had been a nun. 'You should write about that,' she said immediately. 'That could be a terrific book!'

'You could call it *I Was a Teenage Nun!*' her husband Greg quipped caustically.

June looked at him reflectively: 'Actually, that's not bad . . .' She was just about to leave publishing and set up her own literary agency. 'Remember,' she said at the end of the evening, 'if ever you decide to write that book, let me know.'

Things were moving a little too fast for me. The only major piece of writing I had attempted was my ill-fated thesis, and the kind of book that June had in mind was something very different. It would mean that I would have to reveal myself at my most vulnerable. It would be like stripping naked before hundreds of strangers. And writing books was something that other people did – people like Charlotte. The whole process seemed daunting. How would I know what incidents to select? How could I shape the material so that it made a point without imposing an artificial pattern that would distort it? How would I know what kind of style to use? I could see from Charlotte's typescripts that she would sometimes put a line right through a paragraph: how did she know that it hadn't worked? And besides, I didn't really enjoy writing. I had always rather dreaded the moment when I had to write a chapter of my thesis or an essay. It had never been easy. Writing was a grim, exacting, frustrating process, because you never said *exactly* what you wanted to. How on earth could I embark on a whole book? Especially since, with my track-record, it was bound to be yet another failure.

I might have dithered indefinitely, but Sally intervened. It was a summer evening in 1979, and I was staying overnight in her flat in Dulwich. I quite often did this, since it saved me having to do the gruelling journey to Highbury every night.

'Now look here.' Sally led me into her sitting room, where we usually had a glass of sherry to celebrate the end of another school day. But on this particular evening, Sally had other plans. She had cleared her little white desk in the corner of the room. Her father had made it himself; indeed, he had sat at that desk struggling with the calculations that had led to the discovery of radar. 'This is a historic desk,' Sally said. 'It will bring you luck.' She had already laid out an exercise book and a new felt-tipped pen. 'I'm going to go out now for an hour,' she continued. 'I'm going to go for a walk, do some shopping – maybe I'll call on Brigid. But I'm going to be away for a whole hour. So get started. Just sit down now and write the first two pages of your book. Just two pages, that's all! And then, when I get back, we'll have a drink to celebrate.'

She pulled back the chair, turned on the desk-lamp, looked at me firmly, and left the flat.

And so there was nothing for it. I sat down and started to write.

'Miss Armstrong, I'm afraid we've reached the end of the road.' The Headmistress spoke pleasantly, and looked relaxed, but her words were ominous. It was a dark, windy summer day in 1981, and we were approaching the end of the school year. The Head looked down at her hands for a moment, then turned back to me and smiled: 'We're going to have to let you go.'

I stared back, feeling a cold clutch of fear. I had seen this coming. My doctor was trying new combinations of pills, and I had been off sick a great deal recently, as my brain and body struggled to adapt to the changes in medication. When my dosage had been increased by a half-tablet, it had poisoned my system and become toxic, making me stagger round like a drunk, unable to walk across the room in a straight line. I had also had to ask for time off to see my consultant, and that had not gone down well at all.

'Leave the school, you mean?' I asked stupidly, playing for time. Perhaps if I could get my wits together, I could talk my way out of this – until next time. But one look at the Headmistress's face dashed these hopes before I had even begun to articulate them to myself. She was positively beaming with benevolence, her face a mask of kindly implacability. She nodded.

'For a long time, it has been marvellous to have you here – worth it for all of us,' she said, leaning back in her chair and gazing reflectively into the middle distance. 'You've given a lot to the school. You don't need me to tell you how much we've appreciated your contribution and how we've all been enriched by your talents. And I hope we've given something to you too.' She waited, while I hastily forced a gesture of assent, unable as yet to smile. 'And yes, we've accepted your illness as the price we've had to pay. But now the demand is becoming too heavy, you see, and it isn't worth it to us any more.' She leaned forwards, her face suddenly grave. 'We can carry a sick member of staff, but we *cannot* carry a sick head of department.'

I was silenced. I could see the justice of her words. I probably wouldn't have lasted nearly so long in any other school. But what in heaven's name was I supposed to do now? I tried again: 'Perhaps I could go back to being an ordinary member of staff?' I flinched at the thought of the drop in salary. With my heavy mortgage, I could scarcely manage on my far from munificent earnings as departmental head, but even a severely reduced income would be better than no income at all.

The Head made a decisive gesture of refusal. 'You know that isn't the answer,' she said. 'You know that wouldn't work. Miss Cockburn, to whom I'm going to offer the department, would be

miserable with you working under her. And you should know –
you of all people – that nobody should ever, ever go backwards.'

I gazed out of the window, trying to stifle my rising panic. A
group of girls passed outside, laughing loudly. The Head winced
at the noise but, controlling her irritation, turned back to me.
'And anyway, the job itself is too much for you. Look at yourself,
my dear. You look ill; you *are* ill. I'm told you've been spending
your weekends in bed.' I could not deny it. Gone were the days
when I had partied in north London after a school day. Now I
would crawl home on Friday evening and fall into bed, exhausted
by the demands of the week. The Head let the point sink in and
continued: 'This is no good for you. You're still a young woman.
You are – how old are you? – Thirty-six? That's nothing at all,
believe me. You shouldn't be struggling like this, with no life at
all outside school. You know that this isn't right.'

'But what am I going to *do*?' My voice had thickened with tears,
which I firmly tamped down. I wasn't going to beg. And my
financial prospects were no concern of the Headmistress, who
now dismissed any thought of perpetual penury with an airy laugh.

'Oh, any *number* of things! You have remarkable talents, Miss
Armstrong. You're wasted here, my dear. A lot of people could
teach English literature to the level required here, but you have
an exceptional mind and you're not using it to anything like its
full capacity. There is nothing here to stretch or challenge you
intellectually. You *know* that. You must be bored stiff a great deal
of the time.'

Again, I had nothing to say. She was quite right, of course.
When I went into a classroom preparing to teach a class of four-
teen-year-olds how to use the semi-colon, I sometimes wondered
how I could face the next forty minutes. But at least it was a job.
This talk about my intellectual superiority was all very fine, but

it had no market value outside the classroom that I could see. Feeling the familiar sensation of utter defeat, I looked down at my lap, unable for a moment to speak.

'And, anyway, we're not asking you to leave us immediately,' the Head continued in bracing tones. I looked up, hopeful of a stay of execution. 'Of course not, my dear, what do you take us for? At the very least, we're obliged to give you a term's notice, and the school year finishes in just a few days' time.' She gave a silvery laugh. 'You surely don't imagine that we'd throw you out just like that, do you? No, listen, this is the plan I've worked out with the governors. Next year you will work part-time only, but on a full-time salary. You will earn exactly the same amount as you are earning now. Miss Cockburn will take over as Head of Department, and we'll get somebody else in too. You can have a year with very light duties and take the time to recover your health and look around you for something fresh. Now, how does that sound?'

It was a humane, even a generous settlement. I gave a watery smile to acknowledge this, but I was convinced that the words the Head had spoken at the beginning of the interview were closer to the truth than this false cheer. This was indeed the 'end of the road', for me. I would never get another teaching job. My dismissal on grounds of ill health would always stand in the way of employment. And what else – realistically – could I hope to do?

'In any case, Miss Armstrong,' the Head said in a more steely tone that startled me out of my reverie, 'I don't think that money can be much of a problem for you. You must have made a lot of money from your book.'

Ah, the book. I had wondered when we would get to that.

*   *   *

Through the Narrow Gate had been published six weeks earlier. Writing it had been one of the hardest things that I had ever done. It had taken three full drafts to get it right. The first had been very angry; I had poured out all the bitterness and rage that had accumulated over the past ten years, fulminating about the absurdities and cruelties of our training. June, my agent, had looked at the draft, suggested different narrative techniques to vary the tempo, but had then asked a crucial question: 'If it was really as bad as that, why did you stay so long?' That had hit home, and I returned to my script and started again. This time, I made myself remember some of the more positive things about the convent years. I recalled the excitement of those first days in the Postulantship, when I had been convinced that I had embarked on the road to holiness; the beauty of the liturgy, the kindness of some of my superiors; and the grief that I had felt when it had become clear that I must leave. I realized that the order had itself been undergoing a painful period of transition. For the first time in years, I allowed myself to feel the attraction of the ideal that had propelled me into the convent and kept me there.

June had been far more satisfied with this second attempt. A final draft, with some fine-tuning and additions, took only a few weeks, and the manuscript was ready for the publishers. It had been sold at auction just a year after Sally had sat me down at her father's desk and forced me to make a start.

I had told the Headmistress about the book, of course, and promised that I would confine my writing to the school holidays and weekends, so that it did not detract from my schoolwork. She had smiled and wished me luck. I see now that she probably expected the book to creep humbly into the back of the bookstores, gain a couple of kind notices in some obscure religious journals, and die an early death. That did not happen. June had sold the serial rights to a tabloid newspaper, which had also run a big interview with me, complete with photographs, in the Sunday edition. There were more profiles and photographs in some of the women's magazines, and I had appeared on several radio and television programmes. The children were agog, arriving in school each day brandishing copies of the *Express* and looking at me with new eyes. I was no longer just a boring teacher, who nagged them about their punctuation, but had suddenly acquired celebrity status and had a kinky past. Of course, it was only a nine-days' wonder and by the time I received my quietus from the school, the excitement had long subsided. The Head had never remonstrated with me about the fuss, but she did not need to. A grim air of disapproval and reserve had made her position quite clear. This kind of notoriety was not what she expected from her staff.

I myself had doubts about the wisdom of this publicity. Writing *Through the Narrow Gate* had been an act of restoration and self-discovery. It had redeemed the time I had spent in the religious life and set it in proper perspective. As I had unearthed more and more layers of the experience, I felt that I was reclaiming my past. But now my inner journey had become a sensational story in the popular press. Any subtlety that the book might have had had been lost in the *Express*'s abridgement, especially when the newspaper text was punctuated with such subheadings as 'Whip', 'Tears', 'Anguish' and 'Blood'. When I had written the last pages of *Through the Narrow Gate*, I had realized that those years had probably been the most significant of my life; they had changed me for ever. I might have lost my faith, I could no longer believe in God or the doctrines of the Church, but I still longed for the sense of heightened intensity and transcendence that the convent had promised to give me. Was I a still a nun, living in the world and yearning for a deity that did not exist?

I was uncomfortably aware that I should reflect further on this strange ambiguity, but there was no chance of that during the publicity campaign. I had some sensitive interviews at the BBC, but the cheaper newspapers and journals had turned me into something called 'A Survivor'. These interviewers took it for granted that the convent had been a ghastly aberration and that I was now completely at home in secular life. Look, the *Express* pictures said, here she is in her own flat, taking a casserole out of the oven! There she is chatting like any other girl on the telephone, wearing dungarees, having a glass of wine in the pub! *Woman's Realm* even photographed me leaping over a puddle in Highbury Fields, presumably jumping for joy at my release. I did not know how to counter this, because there was an element of truth in the survival myth. It was true that I was no longer a Roman Catholic; it was true that the convent experience had been damaging in many ways; and true that I had no intention of going back. It was true that I wasn't even a Christian any longer, and that the mere thought of going to church made me feel physically sick. Interviewers constantly congratulated me on my triumph over adversity, and for getting rid of an imbecilic religious worldview. And each time I admitted that I had indeed severed all links with convents and churches, my dissociation from the spiritual became more of a reality, in the way that elusive matters do when you put them into words. Yet I was uneasily aware that this was not the whole truth. I was not that joyous girl, leaping in the air, happy and at ease with the world, wholly integrated with secular life. And I could no longer maintain, as I had on the day of Jacob's baptism, that I no longer had any hunger for what I used to call God. By writing *Through the Narrow Gate*, I had recalled and thus reawakened some of that longing for the sacred that had carried me into the religious life. But what could

I realistically do with this nostalgia for transformation and trans-cendence? In a world that was now empty of God, I could see no place for it and did not understand what, if anything, it meant.

The shock of the sudden demise of my teaching career pushed these vague worries to the back of my mind. I was, quite simply, terrified. All my old fears about money came to the surface again, with good reason. My situation was indeed alarming. My neurologist was disturbed to hear that I had lost my job. 'You won't get another,' he told me. 'I know how these things work. Now that you've been invalided out of one post because of your condition, no one else will want to know.' It was ironic that, thanks to this wonderful doctor, my epilepsy improved dramatically during the summer of 1981. Just after the Head had asked me to leave the school, he had brought me into hospital for two weeks and put me on a regime of medication that at last gave me effective control over my condition. But it was too late to convince the school authorities of this.

So I began my final year at Dulwich in good health, and because I was no longer working full-time, I was rested and felt immeasur-ably better. Emotionally, however, I was a wreck. I would spend whole evenings in tears and days in a state of sheer panic. I simply did not know what to do and could see no solution. As the doctor had pointed out, there seemed little point in applying for another teaching job, and I could not imagine how I could finance any training for an alternative career. Friends assumed that I had made a lot of money from *Through the Narrow Gate*, but that was not the case. Because of the recession, the advance against royalties had been very modest. The money might tide me over for a year, or, if I was very frugal, even two, but what then? 'Well, you must write, of course!' was the continual response. But write what? The publishers had commissioned a sequel and I used this fallow year to write *Beginning the World*, but I obviously could not continue to write volumes of autobiography. As it was, I was struggling hard with this second memoir and realized that I had not begun to assimilate these last difficult years.

In the summer of 1982, as the school year came to an end, *Through the Narrow Gate* came out in paperback, so that meant more talk shows and more publicity. I was expected to be positive with my interviewers, and confident about the future, but I felt as though I were heading into an abyss. One evening, after a day in school, I got on to the bus and found tears rolling down my cheeks. I could not stop them, but sat throughout the long journey home to north London weeping quietly. There seemed no hope at all. The next morning I woke up feeling empty and hollow. Looking into the mirror, I winced. Not a pretty sight. And today, as ill luck would have it, I had an appointment with a television crew. Perhaps I could get out of it! I could always ring up and say that I wasn't feeling well. It wasn't as though this project would do anything for the book; in fact, it seemed I would simply be doing the film company a favour.

'Don't feel you have to do this, Karen,' Jacqui, my publicist, said when she had included it on the schedule. 'It's only a pilot for Channel 4, the new television channel starting this autumn. The film company is doing a few programmes to persuade the channel's editor to give them a commission for a series. So nothing may come of it. If you don't want to do this, please feel free to say no.'

But I had agreed to go along and had spoken with the producer. He asked me to think of a topic on any subject that I felt I could talk about. As long as it was punchy and controversial, it didn't matter what it was. I had not given the programme a thought and spending the morning in a hot studio was the last thing I felt like. All I wanted to do was crawl under the bedclothes and shut out the world. I even dialled the office of the production company, but of course there was no reply. They would all be waiting for me at the studio, 'setting up', as they called it. A car was coming to collect me in forty-five minutes. I often wonder how my life would have turned out if I had managed to get through to the producer, offered my excuses and pulled out.

Strangely enough, once I was in the cab, I found that I was feeling better. It was a beautiful day, and London was looking its very best in the June sunlight. Outside I passed women wearing brightly coloured clothes, looking like exotic birds, and preening themselves on the grey pavements. Men walked with their shirt-sleeves rolled up, their jackets slung over their shoulders. There was that air of excitement, that pulse of life, which becomes almost comically evident in England whenever the sun makes a brief appearance. I found myself picking up the mood. I remembered the strange lightness that had come upon me in the hospital the morning after I had swallowed those sleeping tablets, the feeling that I had nothing to lose. I felt a similar freedom that morning and I realized that I too looked a part of this cheerful summer scene. I had washed my hair, slathered on some make-up to hide the ravages left by my tears, and put on a bright pink dress. I could almost feel my mood shifting in my mind.

This tentative optimism got a further boost when I arrived at the grimy studio. The team seemed friendly and genuinely pleased to see me, and explained again what they wanted me to do. They were hoping to make a series for Channel 4 called *Opinions*. Every week, somebody with a strong or interesting viewpoint would discuss an idea in front of the cameras for thirty minutes. There would be no visuals, no interviewer, and no TelePrompTer. The idea was that the speaker would simply explore his opinion with the viewers, and carry through an argument by him or herself from start of finish.

'I mean, how often do you see this on TV?' Nick, the producer, demanded rhetorically. 'All we are given these days are bite-sized ideas, everything cut down to size. Channel 4 wants to make different kinds of programmes and this will be new! This will be the ultimate talking head! A lot of people think it can't work, but we're convinced that it can.' Sometimes, he explained, the person would be a celebrity; sometimes somebody like myself, who was not famous but might have something interesting to say. The thing to do was to go in front of the cameras and enjoy myself. This morning, as this was just a pilot, they weren't expecting a thirty-minute talk. They would just film me for fifteen to twenty minutes.

So into the tiny studio I went, and was told to talk directly into one of the cameras. During the journey, I had hastily concocted a little argument. I remembered that some years ago, while I was still living in Oxford, I had dropped into Blackfriars one evening. The Dominicans had been celebrating the mass together and had just reached the consecration, pointing toward the Eucharistic bread and saying in unison, 'This is my body'. The words had suddenly struck me as horribly ironic. At the time, I weighed about ninety pounds; I was in my anorexic phase, and was doing my best to make my body disappear. I thought of Rebecca; I thought of the way our bodies had rebelled against the religious regime we had endured. Of all the great world religions, Christianity should value the body most. After all, it taught that God had in some sense taken a human body and used it to redeem the world; everything about the physical should have been sacred and sacramental. But that had not happened. Instead, the churches had found it almost impossible to integrate the sexual with the divine and had developed a Platonic aversion to the body – particularly the bodies of women.

So that morning, in the hot little studio, I told that story. I also spoke of my anorexia and my epilepsy. I recalled my blackouts and the way I had been instructed by my superiors to subjugate my body to my will. I recalled the physical penances we had used to keep our bodies in line. And then I branched out and spoke of the failure of the churches to make creative use of their cult of the Body of Christ. I remembered how Francis of Assisi had called his body 'Brother Ass', as though it were simply a stupid, sexually rampant beast of burden. I mentioned the women saints, such as Margaret Mary Alocoque, who had suffered from anorexia; Catherine of Siena had starved herself to death with the Church's approbation. I spoke of the barely concealed disgust felt by the Fathers of the Church when they were forced to contemplate the female body, recalled that in the convent at Matins each Saturday, we had listened to readings from St Bernard or St Augustine, who had speculated about the virginity of the Mother of God in a way that even then seemed prurient to me: how exactly had Mary remained a virgin *after* giving birth to Jesus? Did her hymen remain intact after the birth? I finally concluded my little talk by suggesting that a religion that found it impossible to accommodate the physical make-up of half the human race had a grave problem. I looked at the clock. My twenty minutes was up.

It was a clever piece, and I use that word advisedly. There *was* truth and insight there, but it was not profound. It was also very angry. As I spoke, I realized that I still had a lot of scores to settle with the Church. When I had finished, the cameraman raised himself slowly into an upright position and gazed at me. 'Phew!' he breathed, wiping his brow. When I went out into the control room, I found the rest of the crew staring at me dumbstruck. Even the cool Nick. 'Wow!' he said. And then he grinned. 'You,' he told me, 'are embarrassingly good!'

Apparently nobody else had been able to do this. Without a TelePrompter, most of the contributors had dried up after a few minutes. 'And what you said was *terrific*,' Nick continued. 'We'll call it *The Body of Christ*. John is going to *love* it!'

John apparently was the Commissioning Editor for Religion at Channel 4. 'But surely if he's religious, he won't like this?' I asked.

'No, no! You don't understand,' Nick beamed at me. 'John *loathes* religion! He'll really go for this. Look, I know it's a lot to ask, but would you mind doing it again? Just so we can show him the best of two pilots?'

As I drove back to north London, I felt not merely light-hearted but elated. After the second filming, which had gone even better than the first, Nick had swept me off with the crew for a celebration lunch. All kinds of nice things had been said, but the flattery, though very welcome, was of secondary importance. It was only when I was on my way home that I realized what I had done. I had walked into a studio and talked for twenty minutes about an idea of my own. Nobody had suggested the theme to me; it was an eccentric – perhaps even original – idea that I had thought up for myself. I remembered all those years at Oxford when I had sat tongue-tied in class, my mind able to function only when somebody else had kick-started it. In one small but vital respect, I had recovered. And the wonderful thing was that it had seemed so effortless. It had never occurred to me that I would not be able to talk coherently and persuasively. The healing had happened without my realizing it.

It was partly due to all those years in the classroom. Day after day, hour after hour, I had been compelled to talk to a captive and often reluctant audience of adolescent girls. To hold their attention and convey the ideas and information that they needed, I had learned to think on my feet and make my material lively and interesting. And as a result, what had once seemed an impossible feat had become second nature. Not only that, I realized. I had positively enjoyed talking seemingly to myself in that dark studio, cut off from the rest of the world by the blinding lights, but conveying my message all the same. I had thought that the school had arrested my progress. I had feared that I was slipping backwards into old habits of timidity, but all the time I had been developing a new skill. And if I could do that, I might be capable of other things. Maybe my future was not as hopeless as I had feared.

And so, a few weeks later, on the last day of term, I found that I was neither distressed nor frightened to be leaving the school, even though I had no definite plans and no prospect of another job. I had imagined that I would be distraught. But instead I felt a great calm and an occasional flicker of excitement. It was time to go, I acknowledged, as I stood with the other members of staff at the back of the hall for the final assembly. I recalled my first morning at the school, when I had stood up in the gallery with the Sixth Form, looking down at the hundreds of girls in the hall below, and felt suffocated by the all-too-familiar rhythms of institutional life. Against the odds, I had gained something from these years, but now it was time to move on. I listened to the very generous words of the Headmistress as she thanked me for my contribution to the school in her detached way, almost as if she were speaking of somebody else. It felt as though I had already gone. Later that morning I was able to joke in my farewell speech to the staff and admire my present: a set of elegant cocktail glasses with dark red stems. I smiled to myself. Not an obvious present for an ex-nun.

As I left the school grounds to wait for the bus that had been the bane of my life during the last six years, I felt as though I were beginning a new journey. Other people seemed to progress much more smoothly through life, I reflected wryly, as the bus finally crested the hill and roared towards me. They went through college, chose a career and a partner without all this drama. But that didn't seem to happen to me. I kept getting derailed, ejected from one job, one lifestyle after another. Doors kept slamming in my face. But had I really wanted to be ordinary; had I really wanted what T. S. Eliot had called 'the usual reign'? I forced myself to remember all the times I had been bored and frustrated by the school, despite the regular salary. I couldn't have it both ways. And now, here I was again, heading into the unknown, and yet I felt in some strange way as though I were back on track. The bus was taking me away from my nice safe job, but it seemed to be going in the right direction.

∴ 7 ∵

INFIRM GLORY

This could not be happening. I stared incredulously at the gentle-man sitting opposite me and asked him to repeat his question. The room was noisy, after all, and I might have misheard. We were in the BBC studios in Glasgow, having dinner before going on to make a live television programme. But this was a dinner party with a difference. There must have been about a hundred guests, most of whom would make up the studio audience, and apparently they were all prostitutes, pimps, strippers, drag artists, porn dealers and other members of Glasgow's vice ring. There were also a number of bathing beauties and beauty queens. As one of the principal discussants, I was placed at the top table. A few seats to my right was Linda Lovelace, the notorious star of *Deep Throat*, now in her feminist phase, slightly overweight and clad in a tent dress and sneakers, earnestly explaining to one of the transvestites that her little boy was starting school that autumn. To my left was Oliver Reed, who was downing malt whisky as though it were lemonade, and already looked the worse for wear.

A few weeks earlier, I had been invited by the BBC to take part in a new talk show, which would deal in depth with the seven deadly sins. It was billed to me as a serious enterprise, and my publishers were excited by the idea. It would go out live in a prime slot on Saturday evening, and would give me a chance to show that I could talk about other things than being a nun. I would contribute to the very first programme, which would focus on lust – presumably because my years of chastity gave me an interesting angle. But already *Sin on Saturday* was turning out to be very different from anything that we had expected. The cheery Scottish gentleman opposite me was the agent of many of the strippers in the room. He had asked me what my job was and why I was taking part in the programme, and I had replied that I had been a nun and was currently unemployed. His eyes brightened; he had leaned across the table in his enthusiasm, and asked me the question that I now wanted him to repeat.

'Would ye be interested in doing an act called "The Stripping Nun"? . . . No!' he continued vehemently, as I gazed at him, flabbergasted. 'I'm quite serious – I think it would go down wonderfully! You'd be great!'

I replied that it was not quite the career that I had in mind.

The programme was a catastrophe. I was on first with Linda Lovelace, who explained that she had done what she did in *Deep Throat* only because her then lover had put a revolver to her head and threatened to pull the trigger. I can remember none of the questions I was asked, but recall vividly the lurid set and my stunned horror at the unfolding nightmare. During the interval a scantily clad band played a song called 'I Wanna Spend the Night With You!' Then Oliver Reed joined us, but he was so drunk by this time that he had to be almost carried on to the stage by the fourth guest, a hefty woman whose Mills and Boon bestsellers had made her a multi-millionaire. Once settled in his chair, Reed was uncontrollable, and embarked on a fifteen-minute rant, which lasted until the show mercifully came to an end. The critics panned it, of course, and the BBC was forced to cancel the series after the second sin, which, I think, was covetousness. I particularly remember the brilliantly funny piece written by Nancy Banks Smith in the *Guardian*, because her only kind words were for me: 'a relatively sane ex-nun.' She noted her bewilderment that all the members of the studio audience had Scottish accents. Did the BBC think that lust was a peculiarly Scottish vice? If so, that would put an entirely new slant on the song 'The Campbells Are Coming'. She concluded that she had always maintained that the sins of any show should be forgiven if it was live, but that was before she had seen *Sin on Saturday*.

The experience convinced me that I could not make a career out of being a former nun – even a relatively sane one. I would have to find something else to write about. But what? After its demise, *Sin on Saturday* achieved a posthumous fame. Periodically, during a holiday season, it appears regularly in programmes that show clips of the worst television programmes ever made. And there I am, in a green silk dress, twenty years younger, walking on to the set behind Linda, with no means of knowing what was about to happen.

A fortnight later, I was sitting in my flat desultorily reading *Little Dorrit*. My former colleagues had all returned to school, and though I did not really wish to join them, it was hard to find anything truly constructive to do. My current project was to re-read the works of Charles Dickens, but it was difficult to work up any enthusiasm for the task. I still had no inkling of how I was going to spend the rest of my life, and knew that sooner or later I would have to find some kind of job. And then, as if on cue, the telephone rang, and yet again my life took a new turn.

It was John Ranelagh, the Commissioning Editor for Religion at Channel 4. He had seen my pilot film 'The Body of Christ' and loved it. He was going to commission *Opinions*, and looked forward to working with me in the future. Would I, for example, like to write and present a six-part documentary series on St Paul? It would take about a year; there wouldn't be much money in it; and it would mean working with an Israeli film company in Jerusalem.

Of course I said yes. I had, after all, nothing else to do.

So that was how I came to be sitting on a British Airways flight to Tel Aviv at the end of January 1983. The months that had elapsed since John's phone call had been strange. To my surprise, June, my agent, was dismayed by the project. This was not what she wanted for me at all. She had seen me as a popular novelist, writing blockbusters with a vaguely religious theme, along the lines of *The Thornbirds*. Religion was a dead-end, she argued. I would never make a living by writing about theology, and she didn't trust the people at Channel 4. She also scolded me severely for responding to John's invitation with such obvious delight. 'Now they *know* you want to do it!' she snapped. 'We can't possibly get you a good deal.'

June was not alone. Nick, the producer of *Opinions*, told me that if I had any doubts about this project, I should walk away from it. Right now. 'It sounds a rum set-up to me,' he said. Nobody knew anything about these Israelis, and Channel 4 was giving them a quite unrealistically tiny budget. The proposed schedule looked impossibly tight. I would be filming in the Middle East, Italy and Greece for about three weeks; there was no way anybody could complete a six-part series in that time! 'I know how frustrating it is to work on a programme that never gets screened,' Nick said. 'So if you're not happy – don't do it! John will find you something else.'

Then there were the Israelis themselves, who had arrived in London shortly before Christmas and gazed at me in frank dismay. Joel, the director, a large bear of a man, slumped morosely in a corner of John's office, chain-smoking and glaring in my direction. He wanted a Big Name to be his presenter – Conor Cruise O'Brien had been his first choice – but John made it clear that either they settled for me or the deal was off. In any case, in view of the miserable fee, nobody with a 'name' would have touched this project with a bargepole.

'I've nothing against you personally,' Joel explained, while John was out of the room, 'but you have no experience. Nobody knows you – you are not even . . .' he broke off, gesturing hopelessly at me but saying nothing. 'Pretty' was clearly the word that, with a restraint that I would later realize was quite uncharacteristic, he had managed to bite back. The only thing that gave him any hope at all was that I had once been a nun. 'Perhaps we can make some scandal out of that,' he sighed, blowing the blue cigarette smoke out from his nostrils like a disconsolate dragon.

In fact, the only person who had any faith in the project was John. 'It's going to be wonderful, darling!' he told me repeatedly. 'You're going to be a big hit. I'm going to make you a star!' I took all that with a pinch of salt. But for some reason, I wanted to make this film. I sensed instinctively that this was what I had been waiting for.

It was odd that I should feel this. For years I had wanted nothing to do with religion; the thought of reading anything remotely theological had filled me with visceral disgust. But this was different. The reading I was doing now in preparation for the series was not devotional. It would have no bearing on my life, after all, but would be a purely academic exercise. The slight quickening of spiritual interest that I had experienced while writing *Through the Narrow Gate* had been submerged. In the robustly secularist atmosphere of Channel 4, any form of faith seemed absurd, and my early life an aberration. Where Nick found religion faintly upsetting, John hated it with the passion of a zealot. This, I was told, was one of the reasons why Jeremy Isaacs, the Controller of Channel 4, had put him in charge of religion. This new channel had a remit to be different from the other three. There was to be no 'God slot', no *Songs of Praise*, no edifying discussions for the devout. 'I want to open up religion and discuss it as critically as any other subject,' John was fond of saying. And he did, conducting his mandate as an anti-religious crusade. 'They're all bonkers, darling!' he would exclaim incredulously when yet another pious broadcaster came to talk to him about the possibility of a commission. He had also decided to put on a highly provocative series called *Jesus: The Evidence*, designed to explode the Christian myth once and for all. Indeed, as he gleefully explained, the director actually intended to blow up a statue of Jesus at the very beginning of the first programme. 'Blast it to smithereens!' John predicted exultantly. 'That'll show the bastards!'

It transpired that I was to be the chief weapon in John's anti-religious arsenal. 'You're so bright, darling,' he repeatedly exclaimed. 'God – you're clever!' he would breathe ecstatically, after I had uttered what seemed to me a perfectly commonplace remark. Constantly he and Nick would congratulate me on having escaped from the clutches of the Church. Like the tabloid newspapers, they treated me as a heroine, who had, with great resourcefulness, escaped from deadly peril. 'How *did* you come to be the person you are?' Nick once wrote to me on a postcard. I was amused and flattered. After all the years of failure, of being told that I was simply not up to the rigorous demands of a university career and being treated like a tiresome child at Dulwich, this adulation was delightful. Of course, I could see that it was over the top, but I wouldn't have been human if I hadn't enjoyed it. And it was all such fun. This was the 1980s, and John was constantly sweeping me off for delicious, bibulous lunches and dinners, where we all discoursed wittily on, among other things, the absurdity of the religious enterprise. And the more I gave voice to the distaste that I still felt for the Church and its claims, the more repelled I became.

There was also something cathartic in this iconoclasm. For years I had kept quiet about my frustration with religion, and even though writing *Through the Narrow Gate* had redeemed certain aspects of the convent years, there was still a residue of anger. I hated the high-handed way that the Christian authorities had behaved over the centuries, haranguing the faithful on their sexual lives, telling them what to believe, and what kind of contraception they could use. I was appalled by their attitude to women. I was incensed by the way they claimed a monopoly of truth and had persecuted others for not submitting to the theological niceties that they endorsed. A cursory glance at Christian history with its crusades, inquisitions, persecutions and bloody wars of religion was surely proof enough that on the whole faith had done more harm than good. This was what certainty did for you! For years I had kept these thoughts to myself. But now I could name my anger, give it a definite form and shape. This was liberating and healing, like lancing a boil. I was chiefly angry about the churches' obsession with intellectual conformity. Of course, I had not been tortured for my false beliefs by inquisitors nor massacred like the victims of the crusaders. But in my own small way, I had suffered from this intolerance. I remembered the scene with Mother Greta: No, the arguments for the historicity of the resurrection are not true, Sister, but please don't tell the others.

'How can anyone *believe* all this stuff?' John or Nick would ask incredulously, and we would look at one another, wide-eyed in genuine astonishment. It did indeed seem incredible that in the late twentieth century people could still accept the idea that a personalized deity had brought the world into being and supervised human history, or that a young Jewish teacher, who had died in an obscure province of the Roman Empire, had been divine. And if you could give no credence to these doctrines – and I could not – you had lost your faith. That was the end of the matter, and truth demanded that you should say so honestly.

I was convinced that I had not been alone in my doubts: there must be hundreds – thousands – of Christians who suppressed similar misgivings, stamped on their rebellious thoughts, and felt all the while a sinking loss of intellectual and personal integrity. These people must be crippling their minds as I had done by confining them within an untenable doctrinal system. Channel 4 had commissioned me to liberate them. I would show the absurdity of these dogmatic constraints. People could walk free and rediscover the joy of an unfettered mind, as I was doing right now. This was arrogant, of course, but I still felt slightly intoxicated by my newly recovered mental agility and I wanted others to feel this way too. I could not get over my luck in getting this commission; it was a privilege, and I wanted to spread the 'gospel' that had, I thought, saved me. So I was not simply carried away by the flattery, the attention and the expense-account lunches. I was a woman with a mission.

St Paul seemed a great place to start. I was convinced that many if not all of the failings of Christianity could be traced back to this pugnacious apostle. The churches' obsession with complex doctrine, their denigration of women and the body, their intolerance and authoritarian corruption could all be laid at his door. He had perverted the simple, loving message of Jesus, and the religion that came after him had never fully recovered. But as I started to read a little more deeply, I found that the role of Paul in early Christianity had been even more significant. I had stumbled unawares into the minefield of New Testament scholarship, whose findings astounded me. In the convent, I had been introduced to the rudiments of modern biblical criticism while working for my theology diploma, but this had been a very ladylike syllabus, which had excluded most of the really challenging material. Now, reading in my flat in the weeks before my departure for Israel, while June was arguing with Channel 4 about my contract, I made some startling discoveries. A disturbing number of eminent scholars agreed that Jesus had no intention of founding a new religion. He had preached only to his fellow-Jews and there was nothing strikingly original about his teaching, which was in line with other strands of first-century Judaism. Jesus certainly never claimed to be God, but preferred the title 'Son of Man', which emphasized his humanity. After the scandal of his crucifixion, his traumatized disciples had had visions of him risen from the tomb and concluded that he was the long-awaited Jewish Messiah, who would shortly return to inaugurate the Kingdom of God on earth. But the early Christians still regarded themselves as forming an exclusively Jewish sect. It was St Paul, who had never known the historical Jesus, who had first marketed the faith for the non-Jewish world of the Roman Empire. But even Paul had not seen Jesus as divine in any simplistic way. When he called him 'Son of God', he used the phrase in its strictly Jewish sense: Jesus was an ordinary human being who had been given a special mission by God; as a result of his obedience and devotion, he had been elevated to a position of unique intimacy with God and given the title 'Lord' or *kyrios*. But (I now read) there is always a clear distinction in the New Testament between the *Kyrios Christos* and God, the Father.

This was startling information, but once I had been introduced to these ideas, I read the gospels and epistles with new eyes. All kinds of anomalies and contradictions in the text, which were easily overlooked when you read it piecemeal or heard it recited in a liturgical setting, now made sense. I could see why this had not been included in my diploma course, however. This was dynamite. It gravely undermined many of the theological assumptions of my Catholic years. I had realized that much Christian theology was man-made, but I had not appreciated how shaky were its very foundations. All my original ideas for the television series had to be revised. It was St Paul, not Jesus, who was the founder of Christianity, and even he would have been dismayed by some of the theological conclusions that were later drawn from his letters. I now discovered that Paul's epistles are the earliest extant Christian documents and that the gospels, all written years after Paul's own death, were penned by men who had adopted Paul's version of Christianity. Far from Paul perverting the gospels, the gospels, it seemed, owed their vision to Paul. The only Jesus we knew was the Jesus bequeathed to us by Paul. Further, it appeared that not all the epistles attributed to Paul in the New Testament were actually written by him. And this radically altered my view of Paul himself. Some of the most misogynist passages, for example, were almost certainly written by Christians some sixty years after Paul's death. Perhaps he wasn't the monster I had imagined.

John and I decided that we would call the series *The First*

Christian. After only a few weeks' exposure to modern New Testament criticism, I realized that I needed an expert adviser. I was completely unschooled, and, in my zeal to expose the truth, as I saw it, I could easily make serious mistakes. After some inquiries, John produced Michael Goulder of Birmingham University, a charming and learned scholar who had recently resigned his Anglican orders because he no longer believed in God. John assumed that he would, therefore, be a kindred spirit, but Michael quickly joined the ranks of those who thought that I should not be writing this series, because, he said, I simply did not know enough. And of course, he was quite right. He wrote John a long and extremely scathing letter about me, which John airily cast to one side. Michael was very, very tough. As I produced my draft scripts, he ripped them apart verbally over the telephone, sentence by jejune sentence, line by naïve line, and page by uninformed page. I needed this, and I learned fast. By the end we had become friends, and one of the best moments of the whole project was when Michael viewed the final version of the film and agreed to allow his name to appear alongside mine among the credits, saying that, much to his surprise, he could find no errors of fact. It was a baptism of fire, but I shall always be grateful to Michael for showing me not only how important it was but how rewarding it could be to insist on absolute accuracy in theological matters.

So by the time I flew out to Tel Aviv on that cold January day, I was convinced that my mission in life was to unmask the dogmatic intolerance of the churches. But there had been one slightly unsettling incident just a few weeks earlier. I had quickly become aware that if I wanted to understand St Paul, I needed to know a great deal more about Judaism. So far I had simply regarded it as a mere prelude to Christianity, superannuated and superseded by the later, more inspiring faith. I had accepted without question the portrait of Judaism in the New Testament, derived, in large part, I now realized, from Paul's early polemic with Jesus' disciples who had wanted Christianity to remain a strictly Jewish sect. From my earliest years, I had been taught that Judaism had become an empty faith: wedded to external observances and with no spiritual dimension, it was a religion that had lost its heart. Jews staggered under the burdensome requirements of the Law of Moses but could no longer understand the spirit that had originally inspired these now soulless commandments. No wonder Jesus had lambasted the Pharisees, comparing them to gleaming white tombs that looked beautiful from the outside but contained only corruption and decay! The Pharisees had constantly clashed with Jesus, castigated him for breaking the law by healing the sick on the sabbath or eating with people who did not observe their pointless purity laws. But I was now beginning to learn that many of Jesus' teachings about charity and loving-kindness were almost identical with those of the leading rabbis of his day. Clearly I would have to revise my childhood view of Judaism.

Nick put me in touch with Hyam Maccoby, who, like me, had done a piece for *Opinions*. He had delivered a swingeing attack on the New Testament view of the Pharisees, pointing out not only that they were among the most liberal Jews of their time but that in all likelihood Jesus had been a Pharisee himself. Michael Goulder was slightly dismissive of Hyam's ideas about Christianity, but I found Hyam's depiction of Judaism compelling and we agreed to meet for lunch. He worked as the librarian at the Leo Baeck College in north London, and I warmed to him immediately as he escorted me round the library, pulling books off the shelves, recommending some authors and warning me against others.

It was over egg-and-tomato sandwiches at a small greasy-spoon café near the tube station that Hyam delivered his bombshell. He was arguing that Jesus could well have belonged to the school of Rabbi Hillel, one of the leading Pharisees. Jesus had, after all, taught a version of Hillel's Golden Rule.

'You know the story?' I shook my head. 'Some pagans came to Hillel and told him that they would convert to his faith if he could recite the whole of Jewish teaching while he stood on one leg. So Hillel obligingly stood on one leg like a stork and said: "Do not do unto others as you would not have done unto you. That is the Torah. The rest is commentary. Go and learn it."'

'Jesus said, "*Do* unto others as you would have done unto you", didn't he?' I asked, stirring my large mug of milky coffee.

Hyam shrugged. 'Same difference.' He tended to talk very quickly and you had to listen hard to keep up. And these ideas were very strange and new. 'I think Hillel's version is *better* than Jesus', though. It takes more discipline to refrain from doing harm to others. It's easier to be a do-gooder and project your needs and desires on to other people.'

'When they might need something quite different.' Hyam nodded. But something was still troubling me. 'But how could Hillel say that his Golden Rule represented the *whole* of Jewish teaching? That everything else was just commentary?' I asked. 'What about faith? What about believing in God? What were those pagans supposed to *believe*?'

'Easy to see that you were brought up Christian.' Hyam didn't have a high opinion of Christianity, I noticed. 'Theology is just not important in Judaism, or in any other religion, really. There's no orthodoxy, as you have it in the Catholic Church. No complicated creeds to which everybody must subscribe. No infallible pronouncements by a Pope. Nobody can tell Jews what to believe. Within reason, you can believe what you like.'

I stared at him. I could not imagine a religion without belief. Ever since I had grown up and started to think, my Christian life had been a continuous struggle to accept the official doctrines. Without true belief you could not be a member of the Church, you could not be saved. Faith was the starting point, the *sine qua non*, the indispensable requirement, and for me it had been a major stumbling block.

'No official theology?' I repeated stupidly. 'None at all? How can you *be* religious without a set of ideas – about God, salvation and so on – as a basis?'

'We have orthopraxy instead of orthodoxy,' Hyam replied calmly, wiping his mouth and brushing a few crumbs off the table. '"Right practice" rather than "right belief". That's all. You Christians make such a fuss about theology, but it's not important in the way you think. It's just poetry, really, ways of talking about the inexpressible. We Jews don't bother much about what we believe. We just *do* it instead.'

'Or *not* do it – if you follow Hillel,' I quipped, and we were laughing as we left the café and headed home. I hadn't wanted to pursue the discussion any further. It was too big an idea and still made little sense to me. How could you live your faith unless you were convinced that God existed? How could you live a Christian life if you could not accept the official doctrines about Jesus? And yet I had to accept Hyam's description of the role of belief in the religious life of Jews. I needed to think about all this by myself, later. Right now I had scripts to write.

Joel and his assistant Danny were waiting for me outside the immigration hall at Ben Gurion Airport, near Tel Aviv. He greeted me with the air of hopeless scepticism that I remembered so well from our London meetings, and lumbered ahead of me to the car, pushing my luggage cart. I had to run to keep up with him, and found that I was shivering. I had not expected it to be so cold in the Holy Land and wondered if I had brought enough warm clothes.

'It will be colder in Jerusalem,' Joel assured me as he settled heavily in the back seat of the car and lit a cigarette. That was the only remark he addressed to me for the next forty minutes; my nervous attempts to make conversation were ignored and Joel remained silent, apart from barking out an occasional instruction to Danny in Hebrew. Danny was marginally more voluble, asking me about the flight, the weather in London, and if I had bought any duty-free items. After we had exhausted these scintillating topics, we all fell silent. I sat uneasily, wondering how on earth I was going to work with a man who would not even speak to me, but I stared, trying to look nonchalant, out of the window, watching the desolate plain give way to the hills, which seemed menacing in the darkness. Eventually, Joel broke his long silence and called out, 'Here it is!' and I could detect the pride that he tried to conceal beneath his gruff delivery. I looked. There beneath us were the lights of a city. So this was Jerusalem, the place that had been the central region of my interior geography ever since I was a small child. I waited to feel something, but the apartment blocks, the supermarkets and the small news agencies could have belonged to almost any modern city in southern Europe. Joel rapped out another order to Danny, who advanced what seemed to be an objection but was silenced by an explosive imprecation from Joel.

'We're going to take a brief tour before we go to your hotel,' he announced. 'It's *not* too late,' he added, clearly for Danny's benefit. 'You can't spend your first night in Jerusalem without seeing more than this shit!' He gestured out of the window. 'I want to get your imagination working. Give you some "inspiration" .' He spoke the last word in ironical inverted commas, but I could tell that he was serious. It was a good idea, and I sat back and waited for the commentary, the patter of the guided tour.

Nothing was forthcoming. We drove on in silence, broken only when Danny had a furious altercation with another driver at some traffic lights, leaning across me to yell at him out of the window, which he had yanked down to let in the cold city air. There was much clashing of brakes and shouting. Everybody in the adjacent car joined in, and Joel added his own clearly insulting contributions from the back seat. Finally the other car screeched off in high dudgeon.

'Bastards!' muttered Joel contemptuously. 'Wind up your window! It's freezing in here!' He sniffed. 'You know,' he said in a lighter tone, 'I think it's snowing. Karen!' he suddenly shouted expansively. 'You've brought the snow with you from London!'

I peered through my window. 'It doesn't look as if it's snowing to me.'

Joel guffawed – that is the only word for the sound he made. 'It's the holy snow of Jerusalem,' he snapped. 'You don't see, you just believe!'

I laughed too, because it *was* funny, but my laughter was lost in Joel's roars of mirth; I would learn that he was always convulsed by his own jokes. The atmosphere in the car lightened, and I could tell that – if only because I had occasioned a witty remark of his own – Joel felt more friendly towards me.

We continued our journey through the busy streets and then, suddenly, turned a corner. There, floodlit but somehow timeless, were the extraordinary walls of the Old City, built, as I knew from my preliminary reading, by the Ottoman Sultan Suleiman the Magnificent in the sixteenth century. We began to drive slowly round the circumference of the walled city, each turning revealing a new vista. There was the Tower of David, over there the modern basilica of Mount Zion, down below the Valley of Gehenna. This was a homecoming, after all. I had a strange sensation of being physically present in a place which had for so long been part of my inner landscape, a province of my own mind that now took on an objective life of its own. I could feel my personal geography shifting to take in this new reality, and yet also sensed that I had somehow caught up with myself and was about to discover something important. When we caught a glimpse of the golden Dome of the Rock, I involuntarily but audibly caught my breath, and as we veered away from the walls, I turned back to Joel to thank him. He was watching me and, almost in spite of himself, was smiling.

The purpose of this first visit was to find a way of putting my inevitably abstract, theological and historical ideas into a visual form suitable for television. The most important task right now was to find locations where I, as the presenter of the series, would film my 'pieces to camera', speaking directly to the audience. These had to be chosen with care. Each place had to have a clear relevance to the subject matter of the presentation delivered there, and our choice would affect the shape of our six hour-long films. Every morning Danny and Joel would collect me from the American Colony Hotel for a day's tour in Jerusalem or the surrounding countryside, visiting places that Joel thought I should see; during the second week we spent a few days in Galilee, in the north of Israel, looking at the sites connected with Jesus' ministry.

Joel could not drive. He was a recovered alcoholic and had lost his licence, but I would sit in the front of the car with Danny while Joel directed our tour from the back seat. There was no small talk, however. On the first morning, while we were driving out to the Mount of Olives, I had made another attempt at polite conversation, twittering in my English way to fill the awkward silence. After he had endured my pointless remarks – 'How beautiful the light is! How long have you lived in Jerusalem, Joel ... and where do *you* live Danny?' – for about ten minutes, sighing heavily and answering in curt monosyllables, Joel's patience finally came to an end.

'Karen!' he growled. 'If you have something to say, say it! If not, *sheket*!' The last word clearly meant 'Shut up!' I looked back at Joel inquiringly, surprised to find that I did not feel at all offended. Joel grinned. 'You are not in England now!' – a phrase that would often fall from his lips during the coming months. 'There is no need to be a polite lady here in Israel. We are not formal people. There is no point to speak if there is nothing to say.'

Curiously I found this liberating. After years of deference and formality, it was strangely peaceful to abandon these codes of politeness, at least for a while. I was quite content to sit in the car and gaze, enthralled by the biblical scenery, without having to think of stimulating topics of conversation.

For the first two days of my stay, the weather was cold. It didn't snow, after all, but there was a sharp wind and a sleety rain. But even though this didn't fit my expectation of sun-baked deserts, the sense of walking in an already familiar landscape persisted. It was like stepping into a myth. Here were the places I had struggled to imagine during all those meditations: the Garden of Gethsemane, the Via Dolorosa and Ein Karim, the home of John the Baptist. Jesus had probably walked up those steps leading to the Temple mount. He had certainly walked right here beside the Sea of Galilee. This was the best sightseeing I had ever done in my life. I was not simply letting the sights and sounds of the Holy Land sweep past me in an impressive panorama, but was in search of Jesus and Paul, trying to fit my thoughts and ideas with the landscape and the convoluted history of its famous sites. In the process these holy places entered my mind and heart in a way that they had never done when I had tried to re-create them in the 'composition of place' during meditation. I could understand why so many people felt possessive about the Holy Land. I was beginning to feel that it was *mine* too.

And yet the land was also a challenge, because the reality was nothing like my pious imaginings, nor would either Paul or Jesus have recognized it. When I had made the Stations of the Cross in the convent, I had never in my wildest dreams thought that I would one day sit at the fourth station – where Jesus met his mother on the road to Calvary – eating hummus and pita bread. But that is what we did one day, when Joel stopped at an Arab restaurant on the Via Dolorosa. Ahmed, a Palestinian who was taking us to Bethlehem and the West Bank, joined us there. Later that day we sat on the roof of the Basilica of the Nativity, drinking Arabic coffee, which Ahmed had brought in a flask, and smoking cigarettes, looking down on Manger Square below. My religious order had been dedicated to the infancy and childhood of Jesus. Bethlehem had been a constant symbol of our spiritual quest: like the Magi, we were to follow the star that would lead us to the holy child and his mother. Each one of our convents was a Bethlehem. But here I was, laughing with Joel and Ahmed, neither of whom had any time for religion, and having an impromptu picnic on the site of Jesus' birth. It showed me how far I had departed from those old ideals, and I could almost see my former self looking at this profane scene in astonishment.

I had a similar experience when Ahmed and his Jewish-Israeli wife picked me up at my hotel at five o'clock one morning and drove me down to Jericho. This was probably the road that Jesus had described in the parable of the Good Samaritan. Now, sitting between Ahmed and Miriam, watching the sun rise over the desert hills, with the Mendelssohn violin concerto blaring from the car radio, I felt happier than at any time in my life. Again, there was no polite conversation to break the mood. With my ears popping as we passed sea level and continued our descent to the Dead Sea, the deepest spot in the world, I gazed at the extraordinary beauty of the desert and felt moved as I had never been before by any landscape. I could not drag my eyes away from it and felt a great silence opening within me. There were no words and no thoughts; it was enough simply to be there. Perhaps other people had found this quietness in prayer, but there was no God here and nothing like the ecstasies experienced by the saints. Instead there was simply a suspension of self.

Later we sat with a Bedouin family who lived in the ruins of the deserted Palestinian refugee camp outside Jericho. Abu Musa gave Miriam and me a breakfast of pita bread and sour melted butter, while Ahmed rode the horse that the Bedouins looked after for him into the mountains. Then we had to drive home quickly, snaking swiftly up that mythical road, so that I would be ready to start work with Joel at nine o'clock. We re-entered Jerusalem, turned a corner and there on our right was the Dome of the Rock, blazing in the sunlight. Not only was it perfectly at one with the hills and stones, it seemed to bring all the elements of the environment together, completing them and giving them fresh significance. 'Strong!' Ahmed said briefly, and we all nodded. That was exactly the right word.

It was not simply my personal circumstances that had changed, but my religious landscape was also being transformed. In my convent meditations, Jews had scarcely figured in the scenes that I had tried so hard to conjure up. They were marginal figures, lurking in the wings in a rather sinister way. At best, they were simply foils to Jesus' superior insight: they asked Jesus trick questions but failed to catch him out; they made obtuse and heartless remarks, which showed how impervious they were to true spiritual values. But now that I was thinking about these scenes in modern Israel, Judaism had moved from the periphery to the foreground, and made sense of the lives and careers of both Jesus and Paul. When we visited the Western Wall, the last relic of the temple planned by King Herod, which was nearing completion in Jesus' lifetime, I stared fascinated at the crowds who were pressing forward to kiss the sacred stones. There were black-caftaned Orthodox, with their ear locks and huge fur hats, as well as men and women dressed in ordinary casual clothes. I watched a young Israeli soldier bind his *tefillin* to his arms with a thick strap as he bowed and prayed before the Wall. Judaism was not the superseded faith of my blinkered meditations. It had a life and dynamism of its own, and was as multifarious as Christianity. It had continued to grow and develop in ways that I had never considered since Jesus had died in this city some two thousand years ago.

As I worked on the scripts, I was entering more and more deeply into a Jewish perspective. I was now engrossed in the books that Hyam Maccoby had recommended, trying to imagine the religious ambience which Paul and Jesus had imbibed. There were elements that were both familiar and, at the same time, revealingly different. Hyam had been right, of course. This truly was a religion of doing rather than believing, and the discipline of living according to the Law was, I could see, very similar to our observance of the Rule in the convent. Or rather, in both cases, the *ideal* was the same. The 613 commandments of the Law brought God into the minutiae of daily life, whether one was eating, drinking, cooking, working or making love. No activity, no matter how mundane, was without religious potential. Each was what Christians called a sacrament: it was an opportunity to encounter the divine, moment by moment. Every time a Jew observed one of the commandments (*mitzvoth*), he or she was turning towards God, giving daily life a sacred orientation. Certainly, the Law could seem oppressive. Paul seemed to have found it so; it had ceased to project him into the divine presence, just as my convent Rule had seemed stifling to me after a time. But the Law could also bring joy. This was clear in the Psalms that described the Law as luminous and liberating. I was beginning to understand why Jesus' first disciples had been so angry when Paul, the brilliant newcomer, told them that God had now abrogated the Law and that Jesus had become God's primary revelation of himself to the world. They did not feel that Jesus had set them free from the Torah, but had experienced Paul's vision as a potential deprivation. They were fighting for something very precious that gave meaning and value to their lives.

I was also intrigued by the role of study in the religious life of Jews. As a woman, I could not visit the Orthodox *yeshivas* in Jerusalem where Jews studied Torah and Talmud, but Joel had some film of these noisy, lively sessions, which we were going to use in our series. I watched the men bent over the scrolls, swaying rhythmically in prayer, as they spoke the sacred words aloud and argued passionately with one another. Those gospel scenes suddenly sprang into new life. Those 'scribes and Pharisees' excoriated by the evangelists were not simply trying to trap Jesus when they questioned him about the greatest commandment of the Torah, about what Moses would say about paying tribute to the Romans, or about Sabbath observance. They were like these modern Jews in the *yeshivas*. This argumentation was a form of worship. Certainly the rabbis who compiled the Talmud, some of whom were Jesus' contemporaries, insisted over and over again that 'when two or three study the Torah together, the Divine Presence is in their midst' – words that were strangely echoed in one of Jesus' own maxims. Study of the Law was not a barren, cerebral exercise. It brought Jews into the presence of God. I might have liked that, I reflected, as I watched those films. Studying in that intense way might have suited me a great deal better than Ignatian meditation.

It seemed suddenly shameful to me that I had grown up in such ignorance of Judaism, the parent faith of Christianity. The more I read about first-century Judaism, the more intensely Jewish Jesus appeared, and even St Paul, who was such a rebel, was really arguing about a New Israel, a fresh way of being Jewish in the modern world of his day. I knew that because of this project, I would never again be able to think about Christianity as a separate religion. I would have to develop a form of double vision. Increasingly, Judaism and Christianity seemed to be one faith tradition which had gone in two different directions.

But there was a third factor. Every time we visited the Western Wall, my eyes were drawn upwards to the golden Islamic dome on the site formerly occupied by Herod's temple, which had been destroyed by the Romans. The Dome of the Rock, I was told, was the first major building to be constructed in the Muslim world. Here was another faith that, in its earliest days, had been proud to declare to the world that it was firmly rooted in Judaism. Ahmed and his family took me up to the Dome one Saturday, and I stared at the rock from which the prophet Muhammad was said to have ascended to heaven. It was also the rock on which the prophet Abraham had offered his son to God, Ahmed explained. Again, I felt ashamed of my ignorance. I knew nothing – nothing at all – about any of these traditions. I had no idea that Muslims venerated Abraham, but now Ahmed told me that the Qur'an revered all the great prophets of the past, even Jesus. And when we visited the Mosque of al-Aqsa at the southern end of Herod's huge platform, I felt immediately at home. There was light, space and silence. A bird flew in from outside: the mosque seemed to be inviting the world to enter, instead of shutting the profane world out. I watched Muslims sitting on the floor, study-ing the Qur'an – looking remarkably like the Jews studying Torah in the *yeshiva*, as their lips mouthed the sacred language. This, I realized, was a form of communion. By repeating words that God had in some sense spoken to Muhammad, Muslims were taking the Word of God into their very being. By doing what God had somehow done, they were symbolically positioning themselves in the place where God was.

My project, of course, demanded that I concentrate on Judaism and Christianity. I had no brief as yet to study Islam, but I found that in Jerusalem it was impossible to ignore this third member of the Abrahamic family. On my very first morning, I had been torn violently from sleep at dawn by the ear-splitting call to prayer, which exploded from the minaret beside the American Colony Hotel. I had sprung up in bed, dry-mouthed, with my heart beating wildly. Islam had erupted into my world as a reality that was raw, alien, shocking, intrusive and wholly unexpected. But after that first morning, the muezzin never woke me again, though the dawn call was still issued at exactly the same number of decibels. I had somehow managed to absorb and accommodate it. Indeed, I soon learned to love the strange Arabic chant as it echoed through the streets of Jerusalem and filled the valleys and hills around the Old City. The call to prayer was a constant reminder that whether Christians or Jews liked it or not, Islam was a part of their story too. Perhaps we were talking about a tradition that had gone not in two directions but in three.

Even though I was not studying Islam, I found, during this first visit, that I was spending more and more time in Muslim Jerusalem. My Israeli colleagues were becoming friendlier. I could see that Joel was now less pessimistic about my prospects, but they still regarded me as a prim English schoolteacher and were happy to part company with me at the end of a day's work. Danny would drive me back to the American Colony, screeching up to the entrance of the hotel with a flourish, clearly eager to get rid of me and begin his own evening.

'Thank you very much,' I had said on the first occasion, as I got out of the car.

'What for?' I looked at him questioningly. 'Why are you thanking me? Don't thank me! I *have* to drive you, whether I like it or not! It's my job!'

'OK,' I got out and slammed the door in what I hoped was a reasonable imitation of Israeli insouciance and strode into the hotel without a backward glance, smiling inwardly. I was always being told not to say 'please' or 'thank you'. When I had lunch with Joel and his colleagues, I learned that I just had to grab what I needed, even if that meant stretching across other people. 'You are not in England now!' Joel kept telling me, and even though I was far too English to leave 'please' and 'thank you' out of my vocabulary entirely, it was quite fun to lay aside the habit of deference for a time. I felt something within me relax and expand. But I saw little of my Israeli colleagues socially. Joel had dutifully invited me to dinner shortly after my arrival, and I had met his wife and baby son. But no further invitations came my way.

Ahmed and his Palestinian friends, though, clearly did not find me so dull, and almost every night somebody in East Jerusalem would call and invite me to dinner. I was so ignorant about the political situation that I saw nothing strange about crossing the line and entering the Arab districts of the city. I noticed that suddenly the Western buildings disappeared and that I seemed to enter the Third World. There were no streetlights, no street signs, and the taxi invariably got lost in Beit Hanina or Sheikh Jarrah. If the driver was an Israeli, he would become nervous and agitated.

'It's dangerous, lady! These people will kill you! Let me drive you back to your hotel.'

Today, of course, that would be sensible advice, but in 1983 the situation was less tense and, feeling perfectly safe, I would refuse to turn back. With much head-shaking and muttering, the driver would drop me outside a shop and drive off as though pursued by the hounds of hell, but always the Palestinian shop-keeper greeted me like a long-lost friend; even though he had never set eyes on me before, he would phone Ahmed or one of my other hosts, refuse to take any money for the call, and his wife would bring me a glass of hot sweet tea. Sometimes I would try to buy something from the store to make up for this, but to no avail. More often than not, the couple would give me the goods I had requested as a gift, so I learned not to make the offer. 'Please!' they would say, 'you are our guest!' Finally my friends would arrive and sweep me off to dinner.

After one of these evenings, Ahmed and three of his friends were driving me back to the hotel. The car radio was blaring out some tinny Arabic music, and two of the men on the back seat were drinking bottled beer. Suddenly the music stopped, there was an announcement, and the atmosphere in the car became very still. 'It's the Qur'an,' Ahmed told me tersely, but with eager anticipation, as though he were expecting a great treat. I was surprised. I knew that Ahmed was not a practising Muslim; in fact, he seemed to dislike religion. Had I been driving in London with beer-drinking secularists and found that we were about to be treated to a reading from the Bible on the radio, somebody would have lunged immediately for the 'off' button. But it was very different here. I listened to the chanted recitation as it filled the car. Periodically one of the men would make an involuntary exclamation of delight, and soon, feeling sorry for me, they tried to include me in the experience, by translating the text into English, the words tumbling over one another as they tried to express its complexity.

'This is *so* beautiful!' Ahmed kept saying in obvious excitement. 'I wish you could *hear* this!' He would then attempt another version of the words but broke off in frustration. 'It is that, but *more* than that. Too much to tell you!'

I was not merely impressed, but astonished. Somehow this scripture could still move these tough fifty-year-old men almost to tears, even though they never went near a mosque and saw religion as the bane of the Middle East. It was another impression to file away to think about later, when I had time.

These glimpses of other traditions were intriguing, but I was still convinced that God and I were through. And there were many aspects of Middle Eastern piety that fuelled my aversion. The offices of the film company were near Meah Shearim, one of the ultra-Orthodox quarters of Jerusalem, and the placards on the walls there, which equated Zionism with Hitler and which commanded the 'daughters of Israel' to dress modestly, repelled me – though my aversion was mild compared to the rage that the ultra-Orthodox inspired in Joel. Still worse was the Church of the Holy Sepulchre, the holiest place in the Christian world, where the atmosphere was poisoned by the vitriolic hatred of the various sects. Joel explained to me that since the seventeenth century, a local Muslim family had been deputed by the Ottoman authorities to keep the keys to the church and unlock the doors at carefully prescribed intervals, because the Christians kept locking their rivals out. There was nothing comparable to the aura of prayer and spirituality that I had sensed in the Aqsa Mosque. On my first visit to the church, a wizened Coptic monk had grabbed my arm as I had peered into the marble edifice surrounding Jesus' tomb, and produced what looked suspiciously like a pack of tarot cards. A polite refusal did not suffice: he was determined to tell my fortune on this holy spot, even if he had to drag me into the tomb with his own hands. Eventually Danny had to swear at him and gesture threateningly before he backed off. No, I wanted nothing to do with any of this.

As my stay drew to a close, Joel was beginning to think that we really might have an idea for a good series. We had started to work well together, sitting in small untidy offices, blue with cigarette smoke, drinking Coca-Cola and hammering out an outline. 'In the first programme of the series, we can alternate between Jesus and Paul,' Joel would suggest. 'We zigzag between shots of Tarsus and Israel. Here we have Paul's childhood in the Jewish Diaspora, and – in the meantime –' he cut to a shot of the synagogue in Capernaum, 'the other poor bastard is preaching in Galilee.' Again, I had to smile. Would I ever have imagined that I would one day be sitting at midnight in a grubby editing room in Jerusalem with a secularist, chain-smoking Jew, hearing Jesus referred to as a 'poor bastard'?

By the time I left, my Israeli colleagues had decided that I was worth talking to after all, and were astonished when I had to refuse their invitations to dinner or drinks because I was already engaged in East Jerusalem. Some of them, I gathered, had never been into the Arab neighbourhoods. But there was a new cordiality and respect. We had acquired one of the richest types of friendship, which comes from a submerging of self in a common project. I went home for a month to produce a final draft of the scripts, and when I returned I was greeted with enormous enthusiasm. Danny picked me up at the airport, this time talking volubly throughout the journey and telling me all the office gossip. 'Wake up, everyone!' he yelled as we tore down the hill into Jerusalem, 'Karen's back in town!'

It was just as well that I had never filmed a television series before, because I did not realize how unorthodox the shooting schedule was. We had no money. Channel 4 had given the film company a hundred thousand dollars, which sounded a lot to me, but which I now know was a laughably inadequate sum for a six-part series. The Israelis had agreed to this absurd contract because they saw it as their passport to British television. We could not afford to shoot new footage, and we had to cobble film together from the company's archives. There was no TelePromp-Ter, only the most rudimentary lighting, and when we went to film in Italy and Greece, the crew provided their services gratis and treated it as a vacation.

The inadequate budget affected my contribution in two ways. First there was simply not enough money to do more than a couple of 'takes' for any one of my presentations. Usually Joel and Yossi, the cameraman (also known as 'one-take Jo'), had to be satisfied with the first attempt. That meant that I had to be word-perfect, and make as few 'fluffs' as possible. Secondly, because we had so little footage, my own pieces-to-camera had to be much longer than is customary in a documentary, so that

282

we could use up more time. And the schedule was tight. We rushed helter-skelter from one location to another to shoot as much as possible before the light failed.

Because I had no experience, Joel had feared that this could not work but, in fact, I sailed through it all precisely because I thought that this was how it was always done, and after a slightly shaky start beside the statue of Artemis in the Israel Museum, we zipped through the schedule at top-speed, everybody looking progressively more cheerful until, by the end of the day, they were positively elated. Despite the pressures, it was the most relaxed filming I have ever done. There was no fussing with powder puffs, no tweaking of my hair, and no anguished discussion of my wardrobe – which last could have been because the crew had such a gloomy view of my appearance.

'Karen! You are not a pretty girl,' Joel said on the first morning. 'You have big teeth, and you walk clumsy. OK! What we can do? We will just have to build the film around this!'

Charming. But it was said with so little malice that it was impossible to take offence. Joel might have been remarking on the filmic qualities of a rock or a tree. And in any case, no one had time on this shoot to be upset by a chance remark.

'Karen!' Joel also announced on the first day. 'You are not in England now. Do not be a polite English lady. If you think I am unreasonable, tell me to get lost, to shut up – whatever you like!' For me, this was a novel invitation, and the first time I took Joel up on his offer, I was astonished at myself. We had just arrived in Caesarea, in the late afternoon, after a hectic day in Galilee. We had a considerable number of my pieces-to-camera to shoot before sunset, and tension was high. Joel was tired and anxious. When he snapped at me, rudely questioning the number of presentations we were about to do, I simply threw my script at him, told him to refresh his memory, and marched off to change my clothes behind a nearby rock.

'I was proud of you! Really!' Joel told me afterwards. ' "Refresh your memory" – it's a good phrase, I must remember it.'

I had never enjoyed anything so much. Before my neurologist had found the right medication for me, I would have found the tough schedule almost impossible, but now I felt wholly well – better, indeed, than I had felt for years. It was all such fun: hurtling along in the front seat of the van through glorious scenery, eating lunch beside the Sea of Galilee, free to think my own thoughts while the crew chatted with one another in Hebrew, or having the whole Acropolis to ourselves in Athens so that we could film the sun going down behind the Parthenon. To Joel's surprise, I bonded with the crew, who treated me with huge affection, almost like a mascot. And increasingly there was a mounting excitement: against all the odds, we were creating a good product. 'It is a religious programme in only one respect,' Joel said at the very end of the production. 'It is a miracle!'

But a part of me wondered how true that was. Certainly the film was iconoclastic. It demolished the assumptions of many Christians and was ruthless in its denunciation of what the churches had done with Paul's teaching. Yet as the project developed, I found that I felt very close to Paul. Michael Goulder's meticulous scholarship had disabused me of my early antipathy, and living with Paul day by day, and following (roughly) in his footsteps, I started to love the genius and pathos of the man. I was moved by his passion, his brilliance, his inventiveness, and the affection that he clearly felt for his converts. The Second Epistle to the Corinthians showed his extraordinary vulnerability, and when we finally got to Tre Fontane, just outside Rome, where (legend has it) Paul was executed by the Emperor Nero, I found that I was almost tearful. We were filming in a tiny, dark little chapel – a national monument and a place of pilgrimage – and there was no time for sentiment. The crew had rigged up some temporary and highly dangerous lighting for me. 'Karen! This really has to be one take only!' Joel shouted. 'We've got to get out of here before the whole place explodes!' So I hurried in and spoke about Paul's death. Was he a disappointed man at the end? He had really expected Jesus to return in glory in his own lifetime, and the new faith to spread to the ends of the earth. But he had died an obscure, anonymous death, and none of those extravagant hopes had been realized. If he had been able to foresee the next two thousand years of Church history, which he had set in motion, he would, I was certain, have come close to despair. I stood in the flickering light for a moment after Yossi had yelled, 'It's a wrap!' and realized that this had been another important journey. Paul, a difficult, prickly genius, had stormed his way into my affections, and I now felt so much at one with him that I could almost share his convictions. Almost – but not quite.

When *The First Christian* was screened in January 1984, it was a minor success. People liked the raw quality of the film, which, many felt, had freshness and originality. In secular Britain, my criticism of organized religion was also popular, and though, as expected, I received a lot of hate mail, a significant number of people wrote to tell me that after seeing the series, they felt that they could go back to church. I did not understand this. Had I not shown conclusively that the very foundations of Christian doctrine had been undermined by modern biblical scholarship? Why did people feel that their beliefs had been renewed by this onslaught? Again, I recalled Hyam Maccoby's insistence that intellectual assent was not the same as faith, and that theology was not very important for Jews. I still could not see how this would work in practice, yet it appeared that some of my Christian audience had come to a similar conclusion.

John had predicted that *The First Christian* would make me a television star. It did not. I was not sufficiently photogenic, and though the series got good ratings, religion could be only of minority interest in England. Even my friends rarely bothered to tune in. 'How can you be interested in this stuff?' they would ask in bewilderment. 'Who cares about it?' But I was finding it increasingly interesting – though strictly as a detached observer. After my return to London, I made two interview series. The first was called *Varieties of Religious Experience*. I talked to ten people from very different religious backgrounds about their faith. *Tongues of Fire* focused on poetry. Six poets – Craig Raine, D. M. Thomas, Seamus Heaney, Czeslaw Milosz, Derek Walcott and Peter Levi – read their favourite religious poems and discussed them with me.

These series were not very successful. Interviewing is an extremely difficult and underestimated skill, and I did not have it. I was too full of my own ideas, and was, therefore, unable to draw out my interviewee, and make the best of him or her. Often I arrogantly thought that I could give more interesting answers to the questions myself – which was absolutely the wrong attitude. It was fun to meet the interviewees and a privilege to meet the poets but the knowledge that I acquired while preparing for the programmes, mastering the rudiments of Judaism, Islam, Buddhism, Sufism and Kabbalah, remained superficial. Television is a transient medium. One week I would interview a rabbi, the next a Buddhist monk, and as soon as he had left the studio, I started to prepare for next week's faith healer. It was not like *The First Christian*, when I had lived with St Paul for nearly eighteen months and had learned to hear the emotional resonance of his ideas. My brief from John Ranelagh was to quiz my interviewees as though I were a news reporter, exposing the holes in their logic, and to interlard their reflections with sharp, incisive comments of my own.

This sceptical approach was evident in the two books that I published at this time. The first of these was a poetry anthology, called *Tongues of Fire*, which came out with the series. I chose the poems, and wrote short introductions to the various sections, exploring the similarity between religious experience and poetic creativity. This was potentially a fruitful line of inquiry but I concluded, in my own mind, that religion was *only* an art form, a purely natural activity, and could not therefore be seen as divine in any way. The second book was far more critical. *The Gospel According to Woman* developed some of the ideas in the piece that I had done for *Opinions*. Like *The Body of Christ*, it was a polemic, and traced the misogyny that had been the Achilles heel of Christianity. It was clever but inherently hostile to faith. In the crazed excesses of such theologians as Tertullian, Saint Jerome or Luther, and the lamentable neuroses of some of the women saints, Christianity appeared as unhealthy, unkind and unnatural in its rejection of women and sexuality. As I finished the book, I felt profoundly relieved to have shaken off the toils of religion once and for all.

In the spring of 1985, John asked me if I would like to do another series with Joel: this time on the crusades. Channel 4 had been so pleased with *The First Christian* that they were going to give us a proper commission this time. 'No more cutting corners, no more silly schedules, darling,' John promised. 'Proper, serious filming!' I was thrilled. I remembered what wonderful fun it had been last time and could hardly wait for the project to begin. Joel was also delighted. This time we would be a team right from the start, we promised each other. And with a decent budget, we could do wonders.

At first all went well. I flung myself into the research and quickly became fascinated by the topic. Joel and I spent many happy hours planning the series and considering possible locations. We toured France, Spain and southern Italy; we explored the crusader castles of Israel, and my publishers commissioned a book to come out with the series, to be entitled *Holy War*. It was soon clear that it was a rich subject. I discovered that the crusades had been crucial to the development of Europe and made a marked impression on the Western spirit. Even though we knew that the crusaders had committed fearful atrocities in the name of God, we still used the word 'crusading' in a positive context, talking about a crusade for justice or peace, or praising a crusading journalist who was bravely uncovering a salutary truth. The crusades had been the first co-operative act of the new Europe as it began to recover from the Dark Ages and struggled back on to the international scene. They had helped to weld Europeans together, but at terrible cost. These were brutal wars of religion. The crusaders had slaughtered thousands of Jews and Muslims with the cry 'God wills it!' on their lips. They represented the worst possible type of religion, and confirmed me in my determination to keep as far away from it as possible.

Besides studying the place of the crusades in Western history, I also had to look at them from the point of view of their victims. The first victims were the Jews of Europe. In 1096 a group of crusaders from Germany had decimated the Jewish communities along the Rhine valley, giving the inhabitants the brutal choice of death or baptism. Thenceforth, hatred of Judaism became a chronic disease in Europe. Every time a crusade was summoned to the Middle East to fight Muslims, Christians who could not accompany the expedition did their part by killing Jews at home. I began to read histories of the Western anti-Semitism that had culminated in Hitler's death camps. With two friends, I spent a long, cold day in our local cinema watching *Shoah*, Claude Lanzmann's chilling twelve-hour documentary about the Holocaust. How could we process this horror? And how could we make sure that nothing like this could ever happen again?

But the principal target of the crusaders was Islam, and now I had to come to terms with the third Abrahamic religion. Without knowing anything about it, I had always assumed that the Muslim faith was inherently violent and fanatical. It was a religion of the sword, and had established itself only by means of warfare. I had been instinctively moved by Islam when I had visited the Middle East, but I assumed that I would find the theology as repellent as the crusading ethos. Yet again – as with *The First Christian* – once I was confronted with the facts, I found the reality to be quite different. Islam might have become more intolerant during the last half-century; this seemed to be due to the peculiar strains of our modernity. In general, however, it had been far more respectful of other faiths than Christianity. During the crusades, Muslim generals, such as Nur ad-Din and Saladin who led the Islamic riposte, had behaved with greater restraint and compassion than their Christian counterparts. Increasingly, just as I had done with St Paul, I had to dismantle my old position, which I could now see was ignorant, prejudiced and deeply conditioned by the culture into which I happened to have been born. Westerners had *needed* to hate Islam; in the fantasies they created, it became everything that they hoped that they were not, and was made to epitomize everything that they feared that they were. Islam had become the shadow self of the West, and even in the 1980s, I noticed, we seemed to find it difficult to regard Muslim faith and civilization with fairness and objectivity. The stereotypical view of Islam, first developed at the time of the crusades, was in some profound sense essential to our Western identity.

This was a sobering discovery and it changed my thinking for ever. I would never again be able to assert blithely that West was best. Since Auschwitz, the civilized West had become the culture that had massacred its Jewish inhabitants, and this act of genocide tarnished all our other achievements. If we had cultivated a vicious hatred of both Judaism and Islam for so many centuries, what other mistakes had we made and what other misapprehensions had we nurtured? It suddenly seemed important to find out about other cultures and traditions. I was struck by the nihilism of the crusades. Instead of reaching out to the Jews in their midst, instead of trying to learn from Islam (a far more advanced civilization than their own), the crusaders had been unable to govern their fears and resentment. They had killed, maimed, burned, desecrated and destroyed what they were psychologically incapable of understanding. And in doing so, they had vitiated their own integrity and their own moral vision. Auschwitz showed where such calculated hatred could lead, but I realized that as long as Western people continued to accept the old distorted portrait of Islam, they would simply compound the original error. Perhaps this series could show the viewers that Islam was not the demon that haunted their imaginations, and that Muslims could be as flawed, imperfect, courageous and idealistic as their own heroes. If we could achieve this, we would do something important.

But this long exposure to the crusading ethos had another effect on me that was just as long lasting. It broke my heart. The sheer horror of what I was now forced to study day after day, month after month, and – as it turned out – year after year, breached the barricades I had erected to block out strong feeling. This material was so distressing that I could not approach it in the slick, cerebral spirit that had characterized my television work hitherto. As with St Paul, I began to feel emotionally involved. The story of the crusades was a hideous chronicle of human suffering, fanaticism and cruelty. I read of massacres in which the blood flowed up to the knees of the crusaders' horses; of Jews herded into their synagogues and burned alive; and of women and children raped and slaughtered. An Anglican bishop recently rebuked me during a radio discussion for my condemnation of crusading. It was simply Europe 'flexing its muscles' and 'getting a little carried away'. I was unable to reply, because I found this one of the most shocking remarks I had ever heard. These crimes were committed deliberately and in cold blood. The crusaders enjoyed hating their victims. When an eyewitness described the conquest of Jerusalem in July 1099, in which some forty thousand Jews and Muslims were massacred in two days, he crowed in delight that this was a 'glorious' day and the most important historical event since the crucifixion of Jesus. Living with this sorry tale of murderous bigotry was very different from living with St Paul. There was nothing inspiring about it. Instead, I was forced to confront the darkness of the human heart: we were beings who positively loved to hate our own kind.

My heart was beginning to thaw. For the first time in years, I was able to feel the pain of other human beings. Why had this happened now? One reason was certainly my improved health. Now that the drugs were effectively stabilizing my faulty brain rhythms, I no longer saw everything from a great distance or through a hazy screen. I felt as though I had been plugged in, like an electrical appliance, and suddenly come to life. To paraphrase my friend St Paul, instead of experiencing reality as through a glass darkly, I could now see it face to face. This meant that nothing now interposed itself between the material I was studying and my emotional and intellectual reflexes. It was also true that, working as I was in Israel, I was out of my usual environment, and could no longer operate on automatic pilot. Removed from the reflexive scepticism of Channel 4, I could not simply dismiss the crusaders as 'bonkers'.

This new sensitivity was not always comfortable, because I found that I could hear a kind of crusading aggression all around me in contemporary society. I heard it in Israel, when I listened to the Israelis and Palestinians condemning each other, wholly unable to appreciate each other's position. It was there again when British politicians attacked their opponents with bitter relish, and even in apparently civilized debates between intellectuals and literary critics on the radio. There was an edge of unpleasant self-righteousness, as people gleefully demolished their opponents. I heard it all the time in London, when even my most liberal friends inveighed wittily, and often unkindly, against this or that. I certainly heard it in Mrs Thatcher. So my study of the crusades changed me, making me determined always to listen to 'the other side' and at least try to understand where the enemy was coming from. Had the crusaders done that, a moral catastrophe could have been averted. Studying the crusades had confirmed me in my conviction that stridently parochial certainty could be lethal, especially in religious matters. We lived in a global age now, and it was dangerous to assume, without question, that 'we' had the monopoly of truth and justice.

We had started working on the television series in the summer of 1985, and the project was initially supposed to take a year – two at the most. Three years later, however, the film was still unfinished, for reasons that were never entirely clear to me. Something had gone badly wrong. I could hear it in Joel's muttered imprecations, and in the uneasy behaviour of the crew. Our old camaraderie had gone, to be replaced by a high level of tension. I would pack my suitcases, all ready to fly off for a period of shooting, and then – sometimes when I was actually waiting for the taxi to take me to Heathrow – I would get a call telling me that the filming had been indefinitely postponed. Sometimes a trip was curtailed in mid-schedule, which meant that I spent my days zigzagging erratically, back and forth between London, Israel and Europe. When we *were* able to shoot, the money came piece-meal, and there was always a bad moment at the end of the day when Joel and the producer, with their hearts in their mouths, went to the bank to see if the latest instalment of funds had arrived to get us through the next twenty-four hours. Joel asked John to send in a British producer to supervise the finances, but John, for his own reasons, refused to do this.

All this was very bad for the book, because the repeated inter-ruptions damaged my concentration. Books need solid blocks of time, not a week here or a fortnight there. When I did get a sustained period to work on the manuscript, I had to work too fast, and round the clock, because I was under pressure from the publishers to make sure that the book would be in print when the television series was screened. I felt strained, ill used and miserably aware that I was cutting corners. One night I felt so distraught that the whole house seemed to be shaken by the strong winds blowing outside. I got little sleep, but was at my desk as usual early the next morning. Shortly after nine o'clock, my mother telephoned. 'How are you getting on?' she asked, with obvious trepidation.

'Oh, not too bad,' I replied wearily. 'I've just finished the third draft of Chapter Three, and the first chapter . . .'

'No, no, no!' she interrupted impatiently. 'The *storm*! How is your house?' It was the night of the great hurricane of October 1987. 'Oh!' I said wonderingly, as she recited the catalogue of disasters – people killed, power lines down, trees uprooted, Kew Gardens irretrievably damaged, houses destroyed – and I then looked out at the devastation in my own street, 'I thought it was a little windy!'

By the summer of 1988, we had shot all my pieces-to-camera, but the production had come to a standstill. The company had exhausted its credit and we could neither film nor buy essential footage. Channel 4 declared the series bankrupt and pulled out. Three years' work had gone down the drain, and my television career was in ruins. I felt abandoned. Joel had cracked under the strain, gone back to drink and was sent to a rehabilitation centre. June had decided to close her literary agency. John had left Channel 4 to take up an appointment with Danish television. His successor had little time for me, clearly thought I was yesterday's news, and never fully explained what had happened. But the film that we had shot was confiscated pending a legal inquiry (which never in fact came to court).

I soon realized that my own reputation had been tainted by the mysterious and messy demise of the series. It was made very clear to me that I could not expect another commission, which frightened me because it seemed most unlikely that I would be able to make a living by writing alone. Aware that the project was in bad trouble, for two years I had begged Channel 4 to find out what was going on. Nobody had listened. I felt rather like a beached whale, since my television colleagues and acquaintances had fallen away overnight, as though my disgrace were contagious. Yet another door had slammed in my face. This was what always happened. Here I was, right back at the beginning, trying yet again to make the money I had managed to save last for as long as possible.

Significantly, I lost my voice. That is to say that, for about two years I found it impossible to speak in public – something that had never happened to me before and has never happened since. I suppose I felt that if nobody listened, or believed a word I said, it was pointless to talk. Shortly after Channel 4 had abandoned the series, *Holy War* was published and I had to promote it. As a television tie-in, *Holy War* without the film was like *Hamlet* without the Prince of Denmark, and there was naturally very little interest, but one day I did agree to travel to Maidstone in Kent, for a live interview with Southern Television. To my horror, I found it impossible to utter a complete sentence. My throat seized up, I was shaking like a leaf, I couldn't breathe, my chest contracted into a rigid knot, and I could only blurt a few words at a time, gasping between each broken phrase. Seeing the state I was in, the host quickly terminated the interview.

Previously when disaster had struck, I had not allowed myself to respond fully. Indeed, I had been unable to do so. On those other occasions, my state was not unlike that frozen condition described by Keats when he recalls 'the feel of not to feel it' in 'drear-nighted December'. But this time it was different. Thanks to my doctors, I was no longer neurologically impaired, no longer experiencing my emotions in a muffled way, no longer walled off from reality in remote Shalott. This time I let myself feel my outrage, frustration and dismay to the full. This time I also, as if for the first time, felt the distress that, perhaps, I should have experienced on those other occasions when my career had collapsed, or when my doctors had not listened to what I was trying to tell them. I was very angry, and though my rage may have seemed negative to friends who tried to talk me out of it, it was actually an advance. And (although I did not know this at the time) because the ability to experience pain and sorrow is the *sine qua non* of enlightenment, my spiritual quest could begin.

But how could I move forward? I seemed doomed to fail, fated to spend my entire life on the periphery. Indeed, I was even living in the back of beyond. When I left teaching, I had bought a Victorian cottage in north London. The little flat in Highbury had been marvellous when I was out at school all day, but I knew that I would go mad trying to write in one room, without a garden, balcony or fresh air. The only house I could afford was in a drab district in East Finchley in north London, at least a mile from the tube station and a thirty-minute walk from a parade of dismal shops. The cottage itself was pretty: I had it painted in vivid, jewel-like colours, and it looked warm and welcoming. But it was very difficult to live there without a car. Visitors complained that it was so far off the beaten track that they needed their passports when they came to see me, and a dear American friend habitually referred to my neighbourhood as 'Scotland'. I had always intended to move one day, but now I seemed stuck there for ever, miles from anywhere and anybody.

I had come to hate the long dull road which led to my house but which always seemed to be heading nowhere. Yet it was while I was toiling up this hill one day, weighed down with plastic bags of uninspiring groceries, that an idea came to me, and (again without realizing it) I turned another corner. I needed to cheer myself up, start a new project, and this time I should do something more positive. For three years I had steeped myself in the deadly hostility that had separated Jews, Christians and Muslims. Why not study something that they held in common? The Abrahamic faiths worshipped the same God, for instance. Why not study the way they had all seen this God over the centuries. Why not write a history of God?

❦ 8 ❧

TO TURN AGAIN

The decision to write *A History of God* seemed to come out of the blue, and it changed my life so radically that, if I were a traditional believer, I might be tempted to call it an inspiration. In Coleridge's poem the ancient mariner, adrift on a desolate ocean and apparently eaten up with bitterness and despair, found himself watching the water snakes coiling, writhing and gleaming around his becalmed ship:

> O happy living things! no tongue
> Their beauty might declare:
> A spring of love gusht from my heart,
> And I bless'd them unaware!
> Sure my kind Saint took pity on me,
> And I bless'd them unaware.

Redeemed by a spontaneous ecstasy that took him out of himself and towards his fellow creatures, the Mariner discovered that he could actually pray again. And immediately the albatross hanging around his neck like a millstone, the cause of all his misery, 'fell off, and sank / Like lead into the sea'.

The Mariner attributes this impulse of love to the prompting of his patron saint, but Coleridge, who was, I believe, the first person to use the word 'unconscious' in its modern, psychological sense, stresses that it came upon him 'unaware'. The Mariner did not know what he was doing but was saved by the hidden workings of his psyche, which knew instinctively what was best for him. My own experience was similar, but while the Mariner was redeemed in an instant, as tends to happen in myths and fairy tales, it took me much longer to go through the process. I too was 'unaware' of what was happening to me. There was no sudden road-to-Damascus illumination, and it was only in retrospect that I realized that the decision to write about God had been a defining moment. With no clear understanding of what I was about, I had taken the first step down a path that would lead me in a wholly unexpected direction.

At the time, however, I simply grabbed at the idea as a pragmatic expedient. I was desperate to get to work on something – anything – to convince myself that I still had a future. I expected this new book to follow the somewhat sceptical line of its predecessors. God, of course, did not exist, but I would show that each generation of believers was driven to invent him anew. God was thus simply a projection of human need; 'he' mirrored the fears and yearnings of society at each stage of its development. Jews, Christians and Muslims had all produced the same kind of God because they had similar desires and insecurities, but increasingly, in the clear light of rational modernity, people were learning how to do without this divine prop. That was my idea at the outset, but even then I expected some surprises. By this time I had enough experience to know that the finished work was always different from my original proposal. And I was also determined not to fall into the trap of making the book merely a clever, shallow rebuttal of God's existence. That would not only be boring and predictable, but also inappropriate. This could not be a wholly cerebral book, because images of God had, surely, much to tell us about the pathos of human aspiration.

Nobody thought much of the idea, however, and it was a long time before my new agent found a publisher. 'It can't be done,' said one of the editors who saw my synopsis. 'It's impossible to condense such a huge idea into a single volume.' 'Who's going to read it?' asked another. 'Religious people won't want to hear that their God is on a par with the gods of other faiths, and unbelievers won't be interested.' 'It's so *religious*!' sighed a friend who worked in one of the houses that had rejected the book. 'Karen, don't write this book now! You need to do something more mainstream.' More secular, she meant. 'You read English at college. Perhaps you could do something literary? A new biography of Fanny Burney or George Eliot.' 'What about a travel book?' Charlotte asked. 'You enjoyed the travel you did with the Israelis, didn't you? Why not go on a journey to somewhere important. Japan, for instance. What about a look at modern Japan?' Anything, it seemed, would be better than God.

This was sensible advice. After all, I wasn't a believer, so why let my career be hamstrung by this religious stuff? The book on the crusades had been a disaster and the dismal sales figures would not endear me to a future publisher. Better to make it clear that I had turned over a new leaf and abjured my unprofitable past. Yet despite the lack of encouragement, I refused to relinquish the project. Why? It was not as though I were passionately in love with the subject. I had rarely read a book about God that was not, at least in part, abstract and dull. Why should my own be any different? I had no training in philosophy or metaphysics, and might write something hopelessly naïve. And why go on producing religious books in Britain, where only about six per cent of the population attended a service on a regular basis?

It seemed a doomed and even a self-destructive project. Many found the very idea hilarious. 'Hi, Karen – how's God?' they would ask, as though inquiring about a mutual acquaintance. Others raised their eyebrows in mild disapproval. 'Do you think you can find anything new to say? Do we really need yet *another* book about God?' After the fiasco of the crusades, my confidence was at such low ebb that these objections really struck home. I could already hear the ridicule and scorn of the reviewers. The general assumption was that nobody in the late twentieth century should take God seriously – least of all me. After all, this wretched God had lured me into a convent; his mythical perfection had made me chronically dissatisfied with myself; and his apparent indifference toward me had left me feeling spurned and hopeless. Who needed him? I had often declared that I had finished with God, and was much the better for it. Yet still, despite all the evidence I had so painfully amassed to the contrary, at some inchoate, unconscious level, I felt that God and I had unfinished business – even though I didn't believe that he existed.

Writing *Through the Narrow Gate* had reawakened that old longing for a more intense existence, shot through with transcendent meaning. This had quickly been submerged in the sceptical climate of the television world, but had surfaced occasionally at infrequent intervals. I remembered my drive from Jerusalem to Jericho, watching the sunrise over the surrounding desert. I saw again the Orthodox Jews arguing so passionately about God in the *yeshiva*, and the Muslim cleric studying the Qur'an in the al-Aqsa mosque. I recalled my emotional identification with St Paul at Tre Fontane, when my voice had wobbled (just a little bit) when I had quoted his words: 'Now we see as through a glass darkly – but then, face-to-face!' Even though I considered faith a chimera, religion could still catch me unawares. Whatever my friends thought, God was not – quite – a joke. If I wanted to stay in the swing of things in London, it would be much more sensible to write a life of Fanny Burney. But despite the dismal predictions of the publishers, something in me refused to give up my God book. Maybe, like the Mariner, I was moving toward a salvation of sorts 'unaware', my unconscious mind reaching out for what it knew I needed.

In deciding to write about God, I knew that I was setting off on a lonely path, even though, in a sense, that was the last thing I wanted. On the other hand, I reflected, when I had come to an apparent dead-end in the past, my life had sometimes taken a turn for the better. 'Because I do not hope to turn again,' Eliot had reflected in *Ash-Wednesday*, 'consequently I rejoice'. Like the Mariner in his doomed ship, I seemed hopelessly adrift right now, but this had happened to me every five or six years, with uncanny regularity. I had spent twenty years trying to fit into one environment, one career after another, to no avail. Perhaps I should simply stop trying to enter the mainstream. Instead of fighting against the bias in my life that pushed me outside the group and beyond the norm, maybe I should just go with it, and see what happened.

The great myths show that when you follow somebody else's path, you go astray. The hero has to set off by himself, leaving the old world and the old ways behind. He must venture into the darkness of the unknown, where there is no map and no clear route. He must fight his own monsters, not somebody else's,

301

explore his own labyrinth, and endure his own ordeal before he can find what is missing in his life. Thus transfigured, he (or she) can bring something of value to the world that has been left behind. But if the knight finds himself riding along an already established track, he is simply following in somebody else's footsteps, and will not have an adventure. In the words of the Old French text of *The Quest of the Holy Grail*, if he wants to succeed, he must enter the forest 'at a point that he, himself, had chosen, where it was darkest and there was no path'. The waste land in the Grail legend is a place where people live inauthentic lives, blindly following the norms of their society and doing only what other people expect.

The myth of the Holy Grail was a watershed in the spiritual development of the West. It turned the crusading ethos on its head. Instead of marching to their adventure in the huge, massed armies of the crusades, the Grail knights embarked on a solitary quest, riding into the forest alone. The destination of the Grail knights is not the earthly city of Jerusalem but the heavenly city of Saras, which has no place in this world. The forest represents the interior realm of the psyche, and the Grail itself becomes a symbol of a mystical encounter with God. By the thirteenth century, when the Grail legend began to take root in Europe, the people of the West were finally ready to develop a more spiritualized form of Christianity. And when I started to work on *A History of God*, I too began to focus on my inner life. This was not initially a conscious choice but, whether I liked it or not, I was now much more alone than before. Henceforth I would often be very busy indeed – researching, writing, lecturing, travelling, having fun, seeing friends – but increasingly that was no longer where the action was. There were plenty of events in my external life, but I cannot, at least at present, find a narrative there. The real story was unfolding, at first imperceptibly and by slow degrees, within myself.

When I entered my convent, I thought I had embarked on a mystical adventure like that of Percival and the other knights of the Grail, but instead of finding my own path, I had to follow somebody else's. Instead of striking out on my own, I had conformed to a way of life and modes of thought that had often seemed alien. As a result, I found myself in a waste land, an inauthentic existence, in which I struggled mightily but fruitlessly to do what I was told. Even after I left the convent, I continued to follow goals that were not right for me, 'desiring this man's gift and that man's scope'. I had too clear a preconceived idea of what I was supposed to be, and was not open to new possibilities. So again I got lost in the waste land. I had been repeatedly warned, for example, that I was not suited to the academic life, yet I had ploughed stubbornly on. I longed to be like everybody else, with a warm family life and a successful career. But I was no more suited to university or school teaching than to the glitzy lifestyle of the television personality. No wonder each of these enterprises had ended in disaster. These were professions that brought fulfilment to other people, but they were not for me. Now circumstances had forced me to find my own track and enter the forest at a point that I myself had chosen, where there was no established path.

I cannot pretend, however, that at the time I felt like an intrepid knight, striding heroically into the darkness. Instead, it seemed to me that I was being driven away from 'the usual reign' against my will, and I kept turning back resentfully, casting envious glances at the receding world. I had no idea that I was about to 'turn again', and experience what the Greeks call *metanoia* or 'conversion'. That was the last thing I wanted, and if anybody had told me that it was on the cards, I would probably have abandoned the God book immediately and started forthwith on that biography of Fanny Burney. It is only now, after over a decade of study, that I can understand what happened.

Hyam Maccoby had given me a clue six years earlier, when we sat together, eating egg-and-tomato sandwiches in the little café near Finchley Central tube station. He had told me that in most traditions, faith was not about belief but about practice. Religion is not about accepting twenty impossible propositions before breakfast, but about doing things that change you. It is a moral aesthetic, an ethical alchemy. If you behave in a certain way, you will be transformed. The myths and laws of religion are not true because they conform to some metaphysical, scientific or historical reality but because they are life-enhancing. They tell you how human nature functions, but you will not discover their truth unless you apply these myths and doctrines to your own life and put them into practice. The myths of the hero, for example, are not meant to give us historical information about Prometheus or Achilles – or for that matter about Jesus or the Buddha. Their purpose is to compel us to act in such a way that we reveal our own heroic potential.

In the course of my studies, I have discovered that the religious quest is not about discovering 'the truth' or 'the meaning of life', but about living as intensely as possible in the here and now. The idea is not to latch on to some superhuman personality or to get to heaven, but to discover how to be fully human – hence the images of the perfect or enlightened man, or the deified human being. Archetypal figures such as Muhammad, the Buddha and Jesus become icons of fulfilled humanity. God or Nirvana is not an optional extra tacked on to our human nature. Men and women have a potential for the divine, and are not complete unless they realize it within themselves. A passing Brahmin priest once asked the Buddha whether he was a god, a spirit or an angel. None of these, the Buddha replied: 'I am awake!' By activating a capacity that lay dormant in undeveloped men and women, he seemed to belong to a new species. In the past, my own practice of religion had diminished me, whereas true faith, I now believe, should make you more human than before.

Thus, the myth of the hero shows that it is psychologically damaging to live in the waste land. If you slavishly follow somebody else's ideas, you will be impoverished and impaired. I had certainly found this to be the case in my own life. Blind obedience and unthinking acceptance of authority figures may make an institution work more smoothly, but the people who live under such a regime will remain in an infantile, dependent state. It is a great pity that religious institutions often insist on this type of conformity, which is far from the spirit of their founders, who all, in one way or another, rebelled against the status quo. The heroes of myth and religion do not preach unbridled individualism, of course. There are, as I would discover, checks and restraints. But unless you act upon this heroic myth and allow it to change your behaviour, it will remain opaque and incredible.

In 1989, when I started to research *A History of God*, I didn't know any of this. For me, religion was still essentially about belief. Because I did not accept the orthodox doctrines, I considered myself an agnostic – even an atheist. But by unwittingly putting into practice two of the essential principles of religion, I had already, without realizing it, embarked on a spiritual quest. First, I had set off by myself on my own path. Second, I had at last been able to acknowledge my own pain and feel it fully. I was gradually, imperceptibly being transformed.

All the world faiths put suffering at the top of their agenda, because it is an inescapable fact of human life, and unless you see things as they really are, you cannot live correctly. But even more important, if we deny our own pain, it is all too easy to dismiss the suffering of others. Every single one of the major traditions – Confucianism, Buddhism and Hinduism, as well as the mono-theisms – teaches a spirituality of empathy, by means of which you relate your own suffering to that of others. Hyam had quoted Hillel's Golden Rule, which tells you to look into your own heart, find out what distresses you, and then refrain from inflicting similar pain on other people. That, Hillel had insisted, was the Torah, and everything else was commentary. This, I was to dis-cover, was the essence of the religious life.

In 1989, my heart newly sensitized to pain, I found that I was constantly jolted out of my bitter, frustrated introspection by the spectacles of suffering that assailed me every time I turned on my television or opened a newspaper. I knew what it was like when people ignored your needs, but my little woes paled into insignifi-cance when compared with the suffering of the Lebanese, the people of El Salvador or South Africa. I was beginning to act according to the Golden Rule, even though my new awareness of the world's pain did not seem 'religious' to me, because I didn't associate religion with this type of sympathy. But it was not sufficient simply to emote in front of the television screen. This habit of empathy had to become a regular part of my life, and it had to find practical expression. It could easily degenerate into self-indulgence, and would not have changed me had I not acted upon it.

These were momentous months. During the autumn and winter of 1989 one communist government in the former Soviet Union fell after another. Crowds smashed the Berlin Wall and danced upon this hated symbol of a divided Europe. On 22 December, the Brandenburg Gate was ceremonially opened, uniting East and West. The world that had come into being after the Second World War seemed to be undergoing radical change. I was still feeling frightened, and depressed about my own circumstances, but it was impossible not to feel stirrings of hope. The Berlin Wall had seemed an unshakable reality; it had been an image of nearly everything that had gone wrong in Europe, but now it was no more. If unthinkable change could take place on this scale, could not something – anything – move for me?

And, indeed, it did, when my new agent, Felicity Bryan, managed at about this time to find a publisher for *A History of God*. Helen Fraser of Heinemann, who had been at St. Anne's with me and had even made a brief appearance in *Through the Narrow Gate*, offered a modest advance, and we agreed that I would submit the manuscript some time in 1992. We decided to wait until after the book was finished before trying to find an American publisher, when Felicity felt that we would have a better chance. I was delighted. With the money that I was beginning to earn from reviewing and writing the occasional article, I could just keep afloat financially. But most important, I felt that I now had a future. I settled down to work with a greater sense of purpose and direction, looking forward to two years of uninterrupted research. But in February 1990, this tidy program was interrupted by a new confrontation with the Islamic world.

Fresh from my study of the Crusades, I found myself preoccupied by one news story in particular. Everybody in literary London was talking about the plight of Salman Rushdie, who was now approaching the end of his first year in hiding. His novel *The Satanic Verses*, which included a portrait of the Prophet Muhammad that many Muslims found blasphemous, had caused riots in Pakistan, and Muslims in Bradford, in northern England, had ceremonially burned the novel, raising the fearful spectre of the Inquisition and the book-burnings of the Nazis. On 14 February 1989, Ayatollah Khomeini had issued his *fatwah*, condemning Rushdie and his publishers to death. In hiding, Rushdie had become a martyr for the sacred principle of free speech, and the *fatwah* was a prime example of the cruel religious certainty that I had come to loathe. Of course I believed that Rushdie had the right to publish what he chose.

But I was also shocked by the raw pain experienced by the more thoughtful Muslims who condemned the *fatwah* and the book-burning, but tried to explain to us why the novel had occasioned such outrage. They spoke of this insult to their Prophet in startling imagery – as a violation, a rape, or as a knife through the heart. Even though this reaction seemed initially excessive, it struck a chord with me. I myself had felt violated and undermined when people had preferred their own fictitious interpretations to my own version of events that were central to my life and identity. And I remembered the Golden Rule. If I had felt this type of pain, I should not inflict it on others. How would we in the West like our traditions misrepresented in this manner? *The Satanic Verses* itself was a brilliant and sympathetic study of the way this kind of prejudice turned people into monsters. And I felt a pang of fear for the future.

I disliked the crusading certainty of Ayatollah Khomeini, yet I was also disturbed by the shrill rhetoric of some of Rushdie's champions. Did we not believe in the importance of truth and accuracy in our dealings with others? But some London literati who had begun by attacking the Ayatollah and the Bradford Muslims very quickly segued into a denunciation of Islam itself, and what they said was dangerously over the top. Muslims were compared to Nazis and told to go back to their countries of origin.

Islam was described as a bloodthirsty religion, and the Qur'an was said to preach a God of vengeance, who ruled by terror and threat. I knew that this was not correct, and could not see how it was acceptable to defend a liberal position by promoting a bigotry that, in view of our recent history, we Europeans could ill afford.

On the first anniversary of the *fatwah*, there was yet more media ferment. I had written a short opinion piece in the Books Section of the *Sunday Times*, showing that Rushdie's portrait of 'Mahound' corresponded exactly with Islamophobic myths that had first been promoted by the crusaders. On the day that the essay was published, I looked bleakly through the newspapers. My little contribution seemed a minnow beside the more authoritative articles by the literary heavyweights, and I felt suddenly overcome by a cold, pervasive dread. By failing to live up to our own standards of tolerance and compassion, by assuming that all Muslims were as vengeful as the Ayatollah, and that their religion was inherently violent and evil, we were laying up a store of trouble for ourselves in the future. Rightly or wrongly, many Muslims throughout the world believed that the West despised them. The tone of these articles would confirm them in their suspicions, and provoke some to extremism. Of course, we must defend the principle of free speech, but after Auschwitz we could not afford to indulge an old crusading prejudice which was manifestly untrue.

Rushdie's portrait of 'Mahound' performed an important function in his novel. It was presented as fiction and delusion, as part of the theme of distortion and 'monsterization'. But the writers who were denouncing Islam so vehemently in the papers this morning presented their views as hard, incontrovertible fact. Most of their readers would not know the true story of Muhammad, and many would probably accept *verbatim* this inaccurate depiction of

Islam, thus compounding the problem. The trouble was, I said to myself as I sadly returned to the pile of newspapers, there was no accessible life of the Prophet to act as a counter-narrative. The traditional Muslim biographies of Muhammad were written in a foreign idiom that could appeal only to a believer from the Arab world or the Indian subcontinent. It really was too bad that nobody had written a life of the Prophet to which Western people could relate.

Then it hit me. Perhaps I should write it myself. I resumed my pacing, but this time thinking furiously. My book could set the Prophet in the context of his time, and I could angle it to a Western person who was confused by the controversy and had an inbuilt cultural suspicion of Islam. In the West we took it for granted that Islam was the religion of the sword; I myself had assumed that it was an inherently violent religion until I had started to study Islam seriously. In the new book, I could deal with this question when telling the story of Muhammad's war with Mecca. When I described the Prophet's relationship with his wives, I could discuss the position of women in Islam. I could look into the real meaning of the episode of the so-called Satanic verses that had inspired Rushdie's novel, talk about the nature of scripture and what was entailed in the concept of divine inspiration. Feeling more excited and positive than I had felt for a long time, I went upstairs to my study, typed out an eight-page proposal, and faxed it to Felicity Bryan so that she could see it as soon as she came into the office on Monday morning.

I was eager to begin, but it was months before we could find a publisher. Once again, most people who saw the proposal turned it down flat, convinced that the topic was too dangerous and that I would be joining Rushdie in hiding. There were the usual gloomy jeremiads. 'Muslims won't like it, you know,' a friend warned me solemnly. 'They'll see it as provocative to have not only a West-erner, but a Western *woman*, writing about their Prophet!' Others could not see why I wanted to get involved at all. I would appear to be siding with Islam, a position that would put me even further beyond the pale in London at the present time. It was just not politically correct right now. Finally, however, Liz Knights of Gol-lancz saw that the project had possibilities, and offered a small advance. Because I felt that time was of the essence, I agreed to deliver the manuscript on New Year's Day 1991.

Like *The First Christian* and *The Gospel According to Woman*, *Muhammad* began as a polemic. I wanted to refute the accusations of Rushdie's partisans and set the record straight. But during the research and writing, something else happened. Rather to my surprise, I found myself as strongly drawn to Muhammad as I had been to St Paul. 'Your book is a love story,' the Pakistani scholar Akbar Ahmed told me years later. 'If you had met the Prophet, you would have consented to be his fifteenth wife!' I am not sure about that, but I did find real pathos in his story. Muham-mad lived in a dark and violent time, not dissimilar to our own. Because we know more about him than about the founder of almost any other major tradition, he emerges from the sources as far more human than either Jesus or the Buddha. We see him laughing, carrying his grandchildren on his shoulders, and weeping over the death of his friends. Above all, we see him struggling, sometimes literally sweating with the effort of bringing his people out of an apparently hopeless situation. We see his doubts, his grief, his moments of despair and terror. All this reminded me that religion is born of desperation, horror and vulnerability as well as from moments of sublime insight.

Even though I did not realize it fully at the time, my research was taking on a more 'religious' character. I was working at top

311

speed, with one eye on the clock, yet I was approaching my subject in an entirely different spirit. This time, there were no witty, sophisticated friends around telling me that it was all bonkers. I was working entirely on my own. With the plight of poor Rushdie constantly before us, Liz and I were acutely aware that the subject was highly sensitive, even explosive, and must not be approached with anything that could be construed as levity. There must be no slick remarks this time, no witty, biting polemic as in *The First Christian*. When I was writing television tie-ins, it had always been essentially 'my' show. I was not an established scholar, after all, so my books and programmes were always presented as a highly personalized view. 'I' – a contentious and, we hoped, entertaining 'personality' – was very much to the fore. That would not work for *Muhammad*. In this dangerous climate, 'I' had to stay in the background. This was not a policy adopted for idealistic reasons but was an editorial necessity. Yet editing out ego is, I now realize, an essential prerequisite for religious experience. Again, I had unwittingly started to practise one of the most universal religious principles, one that is central to all the world faiths.

Further, I had to make a daily, hourly effort to enter into the ghastly conditions of seventh-century Arabia, and that meant that I had to leave my twentieth-century assumptions and predilections behind. I had to penetrate another culture and develop a wholly different way of looking at the world. It required a constant con-centration of mind and heart that was in fact a type of meditation, and one that suited me far better than the Ignatian method that I had followed in the convent to so little effect. It now strikes me that while I was writing *Muhammad* I was learning the disciplines of ecstasy. By this, of course, I do not mean that I fell into a trance, saw visions or heard voices. Had I done so, I would never have got the book finished in time. The Greek *ek-stasis*, it will be recalled, simply means 'standing outside'. And 'transcendence' means 'climbing above or beyond'. This does not necessarily imply an exotic state of consciousness. For years I had longed to get *to* God, ascend *to* a higher plane of being, but I had never considered at sufficient length what it was that you had to climb *from*. All the traditions tell us, one way or another, that we have to leave behind our inbuilt selfishness, with its greedy fears and cravings. We are, the great spiritual writers insist, most fully ourselves when we give ourselves away, and it is egotism that holds us back from that transcendent experience that has been called God, Nirvana, Brahman or the Tao.

What I now realize, from my study of the different religious traditions, is that a disciplined attempt to go beyond the ego brings about a state of ecstasy. Indeed, it *is* in itself *ekstasis*. Theologians in all the great faiths have devised all kinds of myths to show that this type of *kenosis* or self-emptying is found in the life of God itself. They do not do this because it sounds edifying, but because this is the way that human nature seems to work. We are most creative and sense other possibilities that transcend our ordinary experience when we leave ourselves behind. There may even be a biological reason for this. The need to protect ourselves and survive has been so strongly implanted in us by millennia of evolution that, if we deliberately flout this instinct, we enter another state of consciousness. This is a purely personal speculation. But the history of religion shows that when people develop the kind of lifestyle that restrains greed and selfishness; they experience a transcendence that has been interpreted in different ways. It has sometimes been regarded as a supernatural reality, sometimes as a personality, sometimes as wholly impersonal, and sometimes as a dimension that is entirely natural to humanity, but however we see it, this ecstasy has been a fact of human life.

While writing *Muhammad* I had to make a constant, imaginative attempt to enter empathically into the experience of another. This was a kind of ecstasy. For six months I was intent all and every day on trying to understand a man's search for sanctification. Even though I was not a 'believer', I had to think myself into a religious frame of reference, and enter the mind of a man who believed that he was touched directly by God. Unless I could make that leap of sympathy, I would miss the essence of Muhammad. Writing his life was in its own way an act of *islām*, a 'surrender' of my secular, sceptical self, which brought me, if only at second hand and at one remove, into the ambit of what we call the divine.

During these months, I often recalled my conversation with Hyam. I noticed that the Qur'an spends very little time imposing an official doctrine; it propagates no creed, and is rather dismissive of theological speculation. Like Judaism, Islam is not especially bothered about belief: the word *kafir*, often translated 'unbeliever', really means one who is ungrateful to God. Instead of accepting a complex creed, Muslims are required to perform certain ritual actions, such as the *hajj* pilgrimage and the fast of Ramadan, which are designed to change them. One of the first things the Prophet asked his converts to do when he began to preach in Mecca was to prostrate themselves in prayer several times a day, facing the direction of Jerusalem. Arabs did not approve of kingship, and it was hard for them to grovel on the ground like a slave, but the posture of their bodies in the characteristic prostrations of Islamic prayer taught them, at a level deeper than the rational, what was required in the act of *islām*, the existential surrender of one's entire being to God. For a set time each day, they had to lay aside that egotistic instinct to prance, strut, preen and draw attention to themselves. The physical discipline was meant to affect their inner posture.

Second, Muslims were commanded to give alms (*zakat*: 'purifi-cation') to the poorer and more vulnerable citizens of Mecca. It seems that initially Muhammad called his religion not Islam but *tazakkah*, an obscure word, related to *zakat*, which is probably best translated 'refinement'. Muslims had to cultivate within them-selves a caring, generous spirit that made them want to give graciously to all, just as God himself did. By concrete acts of compassion, performed so regularly that they became engrained, Muslims would find that both they and their society would be transformed. As long as people are motivated solely by self-interest, they remain at a bestial level. But when they learn to live from the heart, becoming sensitive to the needs of others, the spiritual human being is born. Instead of the chaos, violence and grasping barbarism of the pre-Islamic period in Arabia, there would be spiritual and humane refinement. Repeated actions would lead to the cultivation of a new awareness. The point is that this was not a belief system, but a process. The religious life designed by Muhammad made people act in ways that were supposed to change them for ever. Without fully understanding what I was doing, I too had started to behave in a different way.

Muhammad had been intended in part as a gift to the Muslim community, but I was astonished by the generosity of their response when the book was published in the autumn of 1991. None of the pessimistic predictions came to pass, and Muslims in Britain and in the United States (where the book appeared the following year) took it to their hearts. But on the international stage, relations with the Muslim world were rapidly deteriorating. Two short weeks after I had delivered the manuscript to the publishers, the United States-led coalition began the air offensive 'Desert Storm' against Iraq. There were rigged elections in Algeria, when, with the tacit approval of the West, the secularist National

Liberation Front suppressed FIS, the Islamic party which was set to win in the polls. The result was a hideous civil war. And at about the same time, fighting broke out in Yugoslavia between Serbs and Croats. Once again we would see concentration camps in Europe, but this time the victims were Muslim.

We seemed to be heading into a period of great darkness. In the ensuing years, as violence and religious extremism escalated in one region after another, especially in the Middle East, I found myself preoccupied by the problems of the Muslim world and its relationship with the West. No longer did news stories seem remote events that might as well be happening on another planet. The dread that had impelled me to write *Muhammad* would not go away. I wrote more books – about Islam, Jerusalem and fundamentalism – because I felt instinctively that we were embarked on a dangerous course, that Muslims and Westerners were increasingly unable to understand each other, and were all hurtling toward some nameless horror.

Muhammad introduced me to a different world. I began to be invited to inter-faith gatherings, and gained a new circle of friends. I was surprised and moved that I – a woman and a *kafir* – should be invited to speak to Muslims on the occasion of their Prophet's birthday, and wondered if Christians would be prepared to invite a Muslim to address their congregation on Christmas Day – the birthday of the Prophet Jesus, who is, of course, greatly revered in Islam.

These gatherings were not entirely an unmixed delight, however. I had no problem accommodating Muslim faith but, as an uptight Westerner who hates to be late, I sometimes had difficulty coming to terms with the relaxed oriental attitude to punctuality. I once got up to speak at the time when my host had suggested that I order the taxi to take me home. And what was a wine-loving lady like me doing at a dinner where you could hope only for a stiff mineral water on the rocks? On one occasion, I sat on the high table next to an eminent Sufi sheikh who, to the dismay of his followers in the hall, refused to address a single word to me. Eventually I gave up and turned to my other neighbour, an ambassador from one of the Muslim countries, who was a delight. As the evening ground on, lecture following lecture, he leaned toward me confidentially. 'Tell me, what is your advice?' he muttered. 'Should I speak for a long or short time?' 'Oh – as short as you possibly can!' I whispered back. 'Look at them!' Hundreds of people on the floor below were gazing in our direction with the glazed, punch-drunk expression of those who have listened to too many speeches. The ambassador, who was to sum up the proceedings, was introduced with a long, elaborate encomium. He approached the mike, and glanced back at me. 'Short!' I mouthed back. He certainly took me at my word. 'Thank you very much and all the best!' he cried, and sat down, to the consternation of our hosts but to thunderous applause from the floor.

On one such occasion I met Rabbi Dr Jonathan Magonet, principal of the Leo Baeck College, the chief academy for Reform Judaism in Europe, which happened to be near my house in Finchley. He later asked me if I would like to teach Christianity to his fourth-year rabbinical students. I agreed, and found that I looked forward to the classes. It was fun to teach future rabbis about the Trinity and the Incarnation, and the students were wonderful: open and enthusiastic, welcoming me for the most part with genuine affection. And I noticed that during these classes, feeling loved and appreciated, I became a more lovable person and that my ideas flowed more freely. It was an important lesson.

But these outside events were a rarity. After completing

317

Muhammad, I had returned to my book about God. Most of my days were spent in a silence that also had a transforming effect. When I had been working in television, the phone was constantly ringing. I had to go to endless meetings to discuss shooting schedules and talk for hours at a time with colleagues about the concept. But now, researching *A History of God*, I found that the telephone rarely rang, and I would sometimes go for two or three days at a time without speaking to anybody. I was alone with my books. I would get up each morning, eat breakfast and drink a cup of coffee while I walked around my long, narrow garden, examining the plants or my elderly apple trees, and then go up to my study. The street outside my window was deserted; the clock on my desk ticked steadily, hypnotically, and nothing came between the words on the page and me.

At first this silence had seemed a deprivation, a symbol of an unwanted isolation. I had resented the solitude of my life and fought it. But gradually the enveloping quiet became a positive element, almost a presence, which settled comfortably and caressingly around me like a soft shawl. It seemed to hum, gently but melodiously, and to orchestrate the ideas that I was contending with, until they started to sing too, to vibrate and reveal an unexpected resonance. After a time I found that I could almost listen to the silence, which had a dimension all of its own. I started to attend to its strange and beautiful texture, which, of course, it was impossible to express in words. I discovered that I felt at home and alive in the silence, which compelled me to enter my interior world and walk around there. Without the distraction of constant conversation, the words on the page began to speak directly to my inner self. They were no longer expressing ideas that were simply interesting intellectually, but were talking directly to my own yearning and perplexity. I was no longer just grabbing concepts and facts from my books, using them as fodder for the next interview, but learning to listen to the deeper meaning that lay quietly and ineffably beyond them. Silence itself had become my teacher.

This, of course, is how we should approach religious discourse. Theology is – or should be – a species of poetry, which, read quickly or encountered in a hubbub of noise, makes no sense. You have to open yourself to a poem with a quiet, receptive mind, in the same way as you might listen to a difficult piece of music. It is no good trying to listen to a late Beethoven quartet or read a sonnet by Rilke at a party. You have to give it your full attention, wait patiently upon it, and make an empty space for it in your mind. And finally the work declares itself to you, steals deeply into the interstices of your being, line-by-line, note-by-note, phrase-by-phrase, until it becomes part of you. Like the words of a poem, a religious idea, myth or doctrine points beyond itself to truths that are elusive, that resist words and conceptualization. If you seize upon a poem and try to extort its meaning before you are ready, it remains opaque. If you bring your own personal agenda to bear upon it, the poem will close upon itself like a clam, because you have denied its unique and separate identity, its own inviolable holiness. I had found this to be true in my study of literature. As soon as I had stopped trying to use it to advance my career, it began to speak to me again. Now I was having exactly the same experience with theology.

The religious traditions have all stressed the importance of silence. They have reminded the faithful that these truths are not capable of a simply rational interpretation. Sacred texts cannot be perused like a holy encyclopaedia, for clear information about the divine. This is not the language of everyday speech or of logical, discursive prose. In some traditions, words are thought to contain the sacred in their very sound. When Hindus chant the syllable *aum*, its three distinct phases evoke the essence of the gods Brahma, Vishnu and Shiva, while the silence that follows when the reverberation of the chant has finally died away expresses the attainment of Brahman, the supreme but unspeakable reality. Other scriptures are chanted or sung in a liturgical setting that separates them from profane speech and endows them with the non-conceptual attributes of music. You have to listen to them with a quietly receptive heart, opening yourself to them either in ritual or through yogic disciplines designed to abolish secular modes of thought. That is why so many of the faiths have developed a form of the monastic life, which builds a disciplined silence into the working day.

In the convent, I had spent most of my time in silence, but it had been too busy – noisy with tension and anxiety, anger and irritation. The constant reprimands made me hyperconscious of my own performance, and so instead of getting rid of self, I had become embedded in the egotism that I was supposed to transcend. Now I was beginning to understand that a silence that is not clamorous with vexation and worried self-regard can become part of the texture of your mind, can seep into you, moment by moment, and gradually change you. The study of texts for *A History of God* had become very different from the research I had done during my years in television, when I had been reading and amassing information at breakneck speed to keep one step ahead of the production team. At that time, I had remained trapped on the cerebral level, as though I were reading a guidebook or an instruction manual. Instead of allowing these images and dogmas to percolate slowly, drop by drop, into the deeper, unconscious levels of my mind, I had grasped prematurely at what I thought they meant.

I had also been engaged in a crusade during my time in television. I use that word deliberately because, however well intentioned, my work had an aggressive edge. I wanted to show that religion was indeed bonkers, partly in order to free myself once and for all from a system that had exerted such a baleful influence on my life. I had read in order to debunk. Egged on by colleagues and friends who found the very idea of faith risible, I had too often reached for the witty, deflationary phrase or the sparkling put-down while explicating a theological point. And instead of losing myself in my work, I had been engaged in what amounted to constant self-advertisement. Even in *Muhammad*, when I had deliberately eschewed this habit of superficial cleverness, I had been writing a polemic and had an agenda. True, it was a benevolent polemic, one that tried to build up rather than demolish, but an argument had constantly been in progress in my head as I anticipated the hostile point of view that I wanted to counter. I had not let the ideas speak quietly for themselves or come to me in their own good time.

Now I found myself in a position where I had no agenda. There was no point in thinking up barbed remarks about a Jewish mystical idea or revealing the hopeless irrationality of a Greek Orthodox doctrine, because there was nobody to hear it. In the past, my literary agent and publishers had wanted me to be ceaselessly entertaining and topical in order to make the seriously uncool subject of religion accessible. But my new agents and publishers seemed content to let me be an egghead, and nobody wanted to talk about God at a London dinner party. I could immerse myself in the silence, allow it to open up wide spaces in my head, and listen to the undercurrent of these new ideas.

This, I am now convinced, is the only way to study religion. I think that I was lucky not to have studied theology or comparative religion at university, where I would have had to write clever papers and sit examinations, get high marks, and aim for a good degree. The rhythm of study would have been wrong – at least, for me. In theology, I am entirely self-taught, and if this makes me an amateur, that need not necessarily be all bad. After all, an amateur is, literally, 'one who loves', and I was, day by solitary day, hour by silent hour, falling in love with my subject. I discovered that I could scarcely wait to get to my desk each morning, open my books and pick up my pen. I anticipated this moment as eagerly as a tryst with a lover. I would lie in bed at night waiting for sleep, delightedly reviewing what I had learned that day. Occasionally, while sitting at my desk or poring over a dusty tome in the British Library, I would experience mini-seconds of transcendence, awe and wonder that gave me some sense of what had been going on in the mind of the theologian or mystic I was studying. At such a time I would feel stirred deeply within, and taken beyond myself, in much the same way as I was in a concert hall or a theatre. I was finding in study the ecstasy that I had hoped to find in those long hours of prayer as a young nun. When I shared this with my students at the Leo Baeck College, Rabbi Lionel Blue, my boss in the comparative religion department, told me with amusement that this was very Jewish. It was what Jews experienced when they studied Torah or Talmud. I also learned that St Benedict instructed his monks to spend part of the day in *lectio divina* (divine study), during which they would experience moments of *oratio* or prayer.

I was, moreover, discovering that many of the great theologians and mystics whose work I was studying would have found the idea of a purely academic degree in theology rather odd. In the Greek Orthodox tradition, you could not be a theologian unless you were also a contemplative and participated daily in the liturgy.

In Islam, after the formative career of the eleventh-century theologian al-Ghazzali, philosophy and theology became inseparable from spirituality. In Judaism, the study of Torah and Talmud had never been as goal-directed as some modern scholarship. Yeshiva education was not a matter of acquiring information about Judaism, the process of study itself was just as important as the content, and was itself transforming: the heated arguments, the intensive interaction with a teacher, the question-and-answer methodology all propelled students into a heightened awareness of the divine presence.

Indeed, studying English literature at university may have been a fruitful preparation, because increasingly I was coming to see that theology, like religion itself, was really an art form. In every tradition, I was discovering, people turned to art when they tried to express or evoke a religious experience: to painting, music, architecture, dance or poetry. They rarely attempted to define their apprehension of the divine in logical discourse or in the scientific language of hard fact. Like all art, theology is an attempt to express the inexpressible. As T. S. Eliot had said of poetry, it is a 'raid on the inarticulate'. Until art was made accessible to the masses – in the printed book, the gramophone record, the compact disc or the public museum – most people would have experienced the ecstasy of art only in a religious context. Like great art, the best theology tends to be universalistic. Ethnic, tribal or ideological polemic is as out of place in theology as in Soviet realist art. If you are bent on proving that your own tradition alone is correct, and pour scorn on all other points of view, you are interjecting self and egotism into your study, and the texts will remain closed. I found this idea beautifully expressed by the influential twelfth-century Muslim mystic and philosopher Ibn al Arabi:

Do not attach yourself to any particular creed exclusively, so that you may disbelieve all the rest; otherwise you will lose much good, nay, you will fail to recognize the real truth of the matter. God, the omnipresent and omnipotent, is not confined to any one creed, for, he says, 'Wheresoever ye turn, there is the face of Allah.' Everyone praises what he believes; his god is his own creature, and in praising it he praises himself. Consequently he blames the beliefs of others, which he would not do if he were just, but his dislike is based on ignorance.

(From R. A. Nicholson, ed., *Eastern Poetry and Prose*, 1922)

This was becoming my own experience. I was writing about the three Abrahamic faiths, but could not see any one of them as superior to any of the others. Indeed, I was constantly struck by their profound similarity. I was equally delighted by the insights of Jewish, Muslim and Christian thinkers, none of them had a monopoly on truth. Working in isolation from one another, and often in a state of deadly hostility, they had come up with remarkably similar conclusions. This unanimity seemed to suggest that they were on to something *real* about the human condition.

At quite an early stage in my research, I was fortunate to come across a phrase that sprang out at me from a footnote in Marshall G. S. Hodgson's magisterial work *The Venture of Islam* (1974). It seemed to sum up my experience during the last year and showed me how a religious historian should proceed. I immediately copied out the passage and pinned it to the noticeboard beside my desk. I tried to read it every day, especially when I felt weary or jaded with the effort of penetrating minds that sometimes seemed light-years from my own circumstances. Hodgson is discussing the esoteric tradition in Islam, and cautions his readers not to approach it patronizingly, from a position of enlightened rationality. He cites what the eminent Islamist Louis Massignon had called the psycho-sociological 'science of compassion'.

> The scholarly observer must render the mental and practical behavior of a group into terms available in his own mental resources, which should remain *personally felt*, even while informed with a breadth of reference which will allow other educated persons to make sense of them. *But this must not be to substitute his own and his readers' conventions for the original, but to broaden his own perspective so that it can make a place for the other.* Concretely, he must never be satisfied to cease asking 'but why?' until he has driven his understanding to the point where he has an *immediate, human grasp* of what a given position meant, such that every nuance in the data is accounted for and withal, given the total of presuppositions and circumstances, *he could feel himself doing the same.* [My italics.]

Compassion does not, of course, mean to feel pity or to condescend, but to *feel with*. This was the method I had found to be essential while writing *Muhammad*. It demanded what St Paul had called a *kenosis*, an emptying of self that would lead to enlargement and an enhanced perspective. And I liked Hodgson's emphasis on the importance of feeling and emotion. It was not enough to understand other people's beliefs, rituals and ethical practices intellectually; you had to feel them too and make an imaginative, though disciplined, identification.

This became my own method of study. Henceforth I tried not to dismiss an idea that seemed initially alien, but to ask repeatedly 'Why?' until, finally, the doctrine, the idea, or the practice became transparent and I could see the living kernel of truth within – an insight that quickened my own pulse. I would not leave an idea until I could to some extent experience it myself, and understand why a Jew, a Christian or a Muslim felt in this way. I found that one of my new luminaries, the late Canadian scholar Wilfred Cantwell Smith, himself a Christian minister, had made his students live according to Muslim law when he was teaching Islamic studies at McGill University. They had to pray five times a day, prostrating themselves in the direction of Mecca, observe the fasts and dietary laws, and give alms. Why? Because, Cantwell Smith believed, you could not understand the truth of a religion by simply reading about its beliefs. The tradition became alive only when you lived it and observed those rituals that were designed to open a window on transcendence.

But (I can almost hear an exasperated reader ask), What *is* this truth? Does this woman believe in God or not? Is there, or is there not, anything out there? Does she believe that the God of the Bible exists? Does she, or does she not, worship a personal God? These are surely the truth claims of religion, and all this talk about compassionate empathy and religion as an art form is merely a distraction from the real issue. To believe or not to believe: that is surely *the* religious question, is it not?

Well . . . no. To my very great surprise I was discovering that some of the most eminent Jewish, Christian and Muslim theologians and mystics insisted that God was not an objective fact, was not another being, and was not an unseen reality like the atom, whose existence could be empirically demonstrated. Some went so far as to say that it was better to say that God did not exist, because our notion of existence was too limited to apply to God. Many of them preferred to say that God was Nothing, because this was not the kind of reality that we normally encountered. It was even misleading to call God the Supreme Being, because that simply suggested a being like us, but bigger and better, with likes and dislikes similar to our own. For centuries, Jews, Christians and Muslims had devised audacious new theologies to bring this point home to the faithful. The doctrine of the Trinity, for example, was crafted in part to show that you could not think about God as a simple personality. The reality that we call 'God' is transcendent; that is, it goes beyond any human orthodoxy, and yet God is also the ground of all being and can be experienced almost as a presence in the depths of the psyche. All traditions went out of their way to emphasize that any idea we had of 'God' bore no absolute relationship to the reality itself, which went beyond it. Our notion of a personal God is one symbolic way of speaking about the divine, but it cannot contain the far more elusive reality. Most would agree with the Greek Orthodox that any statement about God had to have two characteristics. It must be paradoxical, to remind us that God cannot be contained in a neat, coherent system of thought; and it must be apophatic, that is, it should lead us to a moment of silent awe or wonder, because when we are speaking of the reality of God we are at the end of what words or thoughts can usefully do.

Cantwell Smith was one of the first theologians to make all this clear to me, in such books as *Faith and Belief* and *Belief in History*. I remember the extraordinary sense of relief I felt when I read in his somewhat dry, scholarly prose that our ideas of God were man-made; that they could be nothing else; that it was a modern Western fallacy, dating only from the eighteenth century, to equate faith with accepting certain intellectual propositions about God. Faith was really the cultivation of a conviction that life had some ultimate meaning and value, despite the tragic evidence to the contrary – an attitude also evoked by great art. The Middle English word *beleven* originally meant 'to love', and the Latin *credo* ('I believe') probably derived from the phrase *cor do*

('I give my heart'). St Anselm of Canterbury had written '*Credo ut intellegam*', usually translated: 'I believe in order that I may understand.' I had always assumed that this meant that I had to discipline my rebellious mind, and force it to bow to the official orthodoxy, and that, as a result of this submission, I would learn to understand a higher truth. This was the foundation of my training in the convent. But no, Cantwell Smith explained. *Credo ut intellegam* should be translated: 'I commit myself in order that I may understand.' You must first live in a certain way, and then you would encounter within a sacred presence that monotheists call God, but which others have called the Tao, Brahman or Nirvana.

But did that mean that we could think what we liked about God? No. Here again, the religious traditions were in unanimous agreement. The one and only test of a valid religious idea, doctrinal statement, spiritual experience or devotional practice was that it must lead directly to practical compassion. If your understanding of the divine made you kinder, more empathetic and impelled you to express this sympathy in concrete acts of loving-kindness, this was good theology. But if your notion of God made you unkind, belligerent, cruel, or self-righteous, or if it led you to kill in God's name, it was bad theology. Compassion was the litmus test for the prophets of Israel, the rabbis of the Talmud, for Jesus, for Paul and for Muhammad, not to mention Confucius, Lao tzu, the Buddha or the sages of the *Upanishads*. In killing Muslims and Jews in the name of God, the crusaders had simply projected their own fear and loathing on to a deity which they had created in their own image and likeness, thereby giving this hatred a seal of absolute approval. A personalized God can easily lend itself to this type of idolatry, which is why the more thoughtful Jews, Christians and Muslims insisted that while you could begin by thinking of God as a person, God transcended personality as 'he' went beyond all other human categories.

I wrote the book with mounting excitement. It represented a quest and liberation for me. No wonder I had found it impossible to 'believe' in God; no wonder my attempts to bludgeon myself into orthodox 'faith' had led only to sterility, doubt and exhaustion. No wonder I had never experienced this God in prayer. Some of the best mystics would have told me that instead of waiting for God to condescend to me, I should create my own theophanies, just as I cultivated an aesthetic sense that enabled me to experience the transcendence of art. The personalized God might work for other people, but 'he' had done nothing for me. I was not a chronic failure, but had simply been working with a spirituality and theology that were wrong for me. My approach had been misguided. Because I had assumed that God was an objective fact, I had thought about God using the same kind of logical, discursive reflection that I employed in my secular life. Rational analysis is indispensable for mathematics, medicine or science, but useless for God. The nuns were not to blame for teaching me to pray in this way, because (I now discovered) the whole of Western theology had been characterized by an inappropriate reliance upon reason alone, ever since the scientific revolution of the sixteenth and seventeenth centuries. Rationalism had achieved such spectacular results that empirical reason came to be regarded as the sole path to truth, and Western people started to talk about God as an objective, demonstrable fact like any other. The more intuitive disciplines of mythology and mysticism were discredited. This was the cause of many of the religious problems of our day, including my own.

It was, therefore, with huge exhilaration that I completed my book one hot and sultry afternoon in July 1992 and sent the manuscript off to my publisher. There was a sense of wonder and delight as all the ideas I had gathered fitted together, and a heady freedom as the load that I had carried around for thirty years fell from my shoulders. I no longer needed to think about religion as a source of sorrow and secret shame. I felt physically lighter, as though I could float, as though I could now do anything at all. This euphoria was short-lived. Pride came before a fall. I was due to go to Cambridge the following morning, to spend a week with Sally in a little apartment in Clare College. We did this every year, and it was always fun. Still enchanted with myself, while packing my suitcase I sprang – weightlessly, I thought – up a short flight of steps, misjudged it, came crashing down to earth, and broke my big toe in two places. I got little sympathy, of course. There is an indignity about a broken toe that people find hilarious. Two weeks later, I even detected my mother's lips twitching as I hobbled across the room.

My life changed after the publication of *A History of God*. The book was a success, especially in the United States and the Netherlands, and I began to travel widely. But my work continued to revolve around the same issues, particularly around the centrality of compassion. When I wrote an essay about Genesis in *In the Beginning*, I found that the struggle to achieve harmonious relations with our fellows brings human beings into God's presence; that when Abraham entertained three strangers, making room for them in his home and giving them all the refreshment he could on their journey, this act of practical compassion led directly to a divine encounter. In my history of Jerusalem, I learned that the practice of compassion and social justice had been central to the cult of the holy city from the earliest times, and was especially evident in Judaism and Islam. I discovered that in all three of the religions of Abraham, fundamentalist movements distort the tradition they are trying to defend by emphasizing belligerent elements and overlooking the insistent and crucial demand for compassion.

The theme of compassion kept surfacing in my work, because it is pivotal to all the great religious traditions at their best. But it was my short biography of the Buddha that showed me why this was so. I knew that I could never be a yoga practitioner. The classical yoga, which brought the Buddha to enlightenment, is immeasurably more rigorous than most of the yoga practised in the West today. I still quailed at the thought of any formal meditation, let alone this fearsome discipline designed to cancel profane consciousness by a ruthless onslaught on the egotism that pervades our lives. But all was not lost, because the practice of compassion, the Buddha had taught, could also effect *ceto-vimutti*, the 'release of the mind' from the toils of self-seeking that is synonymous in the Buddhist scriptures with the supreme enlightenment of Nirvana. In monotheistic terms, this compassion could bring us directly into the presence of God. It was a startling moment of clarity for me. Compassion has been practised by all the great faiths because it has been found to be the safest and surest means of attaining enlightenment. It dethrones the ego from the centre of our lives and puts others there, breaking down the carapace of selfishness that holds us back from an experience of the sacred. And it gives us ecstasy, broadening our perspectives and giving us a larger, enhanced vision. As a very early Buddhist poem puts it: 'May our loving thoughts fill the whole world; above, below, across – without limit; a boundless goodwill towards the whole world, unrestricted, free of hatred and enmity' (Sutta Nipata, 118). We are liberated from personal likes and dislikes that limit our vision, and are able to go beyond ourselves.

This insight was not confined to Buddhism, however. The late

Jewish scholar Abraham Joshua Heschel once said that when we put ourselves at the opposite pole of ego, we are in the place where God is. The Golden Rule requires that every time we are tempted to say or do something unpleasant about a rival, an annoying colleague or a country with whom we are at war, we should ask ourselves how we should like this said of or done to ourselves, and refrain. In that moment we would transcend the frightened egotism that often needs to wound or destroy others in order to shore up the sense of ourselves. If we lived in such a way on a daily, hourly basis, we would not only have no time to worry overmuch about whether there was a personal God 'out there', we would achieve constant ecstasy, because we would be ceaselessly going beyond ourselves, our selfishness and greed. If our political leaders took the Golden Rule seriously into account, the world would be a safer place.

I have noticed, however, that compassion is not always a popular virtue. In my lectures I have sometimes seen members of the audience glaring at me mutinously: where is the *fun* of religion, if you can't disapprove of other people! There are some people, I suspect, who would be outraged if, when they finally arrived in heaven, they found everybody else there as well. Heaven would not be heaven unless you could peer over the celestial parapets and watch the unfortunates roasting below.

But I have myself found that compassion is a habit of mind that is transforming. The science of compassion which guides my studies has changed the way I experience the world. This has been a pattern in my life. Once I had started to study seriously at Oxford, I found that I could no longer conform to convent life. The attitudes that you learn at your desk spill over into your everyday existence. The silence in which I live has also opened my ears and eyes to the suffering of the world. In silence, you begin to hear the note of pain that informs so much of the anger and posturing that pervade social and political life. Solitude is also a teacher. It is lonely; living without intimacy and affection tears holes in you. St Augustine of Hippo said somewhere that yearning makes the heart deep. It also makes you vulnerable. Silence and solitude strip away a skin, they break down that protective shell of heartlessness which we cultivate in order to prevent ourselves from being overwhelmed by the suffering of the world that presses in upon us on all sides.

This is not always comfortable; in fact, it has become something of a social liability, because I find myself more and more distressed by the disdain that so often peppers social conversation. I know how this puts a splinter of ice into the heart of the disdained. I tremble for our world, where, in the smallest ways, we find it impossible, as Marshall Hodgson enjoined, to find room for the other in our minds. If we cannot accommodate a viewpoint in a friend without resorting to unkindness, how can we hope to heal the terrible problems of our planet? I no longer think that any principle or opinion is worth anything if it makes you unkind or intolerant. Of course toleration has its limits. We should cry out against injustice and cruelty wherever we find it, as the prophets did, especially when it occurs in our own society or on 'our' side. It may be politically expedient to ignore the beam in our own eye while decrying the splinter in the eye of our enemy, but I do not see how it can be a religious option.

But this pain is a small price to pay for the spirituality of empathy. Paradoxically, what I have gained from this identification with suffering is joy. This was something that I did not expect. And this habit of looking outside myself into the heart of another has put me outside the prism of myself. This 'ecstasy' may not last for long, but while it lasts you experience an astonishing freedom. Self, after all, is our basic problem. When I wake up at three in the morning, and ask myself, 'Why does this have to happen to me? Why cannot I have what X has? Why am I so unloved and unappreciated?' – and I still have plenty of moments like this – I learn that ego is at the heart of all pain. When I get beyond this for a few moments I feel enlarged and enhanced – just as the Buddha promised.

It is important for me to do this, because my solitary lifestyle could imprison me for ever in selfishness. In a relationship, you constantly have to go beyond yourself. Each day you have to forgive something, each day you have to put yourself to one side to accommodate your partner. Looking after somebody else means that you have to give yourself away. But I never have to do this. Because I travel such a lot, I cannot even have an animal to look after. So my science of compassion does for me what a husband, lover, child or even a dog might have done in a different life.

I am not for one moment claiming that I have now arrived on a pinnacle of compassion and view the entire world with calm benevolence. I still have a sharp tongue, I still feel intense irritation when a minor official is rude, or when I encounter inefficiency and stupidity. I still feel despondent, when I receive hate mail or am publicly attacked. I have encountered a lot of ugly opposition since 11 September. When I have tried to explain the true nature of Islam, some Americans have said to me what they would like to say to Osama bin Laden, and that hurts. For two days last summer, when people were even circulating lies about my personal life, I retired to my room, unwilling even to go outside. I was like Jonah at the end of the book that bears his name, when he went into a sulk, flounced off to sit under a tree, and told God that he no longer wanted to be a prophet.

So I am still a flawed, insecure human being, who doesn't like it when people bruise my ego. But this is valuable too. I have been enormously moved by the love I have experienced as a result of my work, especially in the United States. But this more abrasive type of encounter is a reminder that you must not practise the spirituality of empathy simply in order to get something for yourself. I am sure that this is what Jesus meant when he told people to love their enemies. You have to be prepared to extend your compassionate interest where there is no hope of a return. This is probably what T. S. Eliot meant when he prayed, 'Teach us to care and not to care' – without interjecting yourself into your concern. And abuse feeds back into the Golden Rule. It reminds me what it is like for people in our world who are constantly reviled and misrepresented. I have also noticed that when I am full of resentment, anger or egotistic distress, I cannot work properly. The texts do not open themselves to me. It seems that the inner dynamic of all these great religious traditions can work effectively only if you do not close your mind and heart to other human beings.

For years, however, when travelling around the world and talking about these matters, I often felt rather a fraud. People would ask my advice about spiritual practice, clearly thinking that I was more enlightened than I really was. After all, I wasn't a truly religious person. I never went near a church and did not belong to an official religious community. I could not really believe that the seconds of *oratio* that I experienced at my desk amounted to a real contact with the sacred. It was surely just a moment of delight in work that absorbed me. I was not directing prayer *to* anything or anybody. There was still emptiness where the personalized God used to be.

It was Fred Burnham, the director of Trinity Institute, Wall Street, who made me rethink this. We had both spent a week at

335

Chautauqua, that quintessentially American utopia in New York State, in the summer of 2001, just two months before the catastrophe of 11 September, in which Fred was nearly killed. Each afternoon I had lectured on the theme of 'The Human Person' in the Hall of Philosophy, and Fred had come from Trinity to introduce me and to moderate the sessions. On our last evening, sitting on the porch of the Hall of Missions, Fred with a vodka on the rocks and I with a glass of Kendal-Jackson chardonnay, Fred had said: 'You always claim that you have never had a religious experience. But I disagree. I think you are constantly living in the dimension of the sacred. You are absorbed in holiness all the time!'

I waved this aside, thinking that Fred was telling me that I was a holy person. But Fred is not given to such exuberant or inaccurate remarks, and that was not what he meant. His words stayed with me, and now I see what he was getting at. In so far as I spend my life immersed in sacred writings, living with some of the best and wisest insights that human beings have achieved, constantly moved and stirred by them, I am indeed in constant contact with holiness. The fact that my 'prayer' seems directed toward no person, no end, is something that many of the theologians I have studied had experienced. This, after all, was what I had been writing and talking about for the past seven years. I had constantly explained that the greatest spiritual masters insisted that God was not another being, and that there was Nothing out there. Yet for all this, at some level I had not relinquished the old ideas. I was still seduced by the realistic supernatural theism that I thought I had left behind, still childishly waiting for that clap of thunder, that streak of lightning, and the still, small voice of calm whispering in my ear. I thought that I had renounced 'the blessèd face', but I was still hankering to drink 'where trees flower, and springs flow'.

I had not truly accepted the hard, irreducible fact that 'there is nothing again'.

The Greek Fathers of the Church had loved the image of Moses going up the mountain and on the summit being wrapped in an impenetrable cloud. He could not see anything but he was in the place where God was. This Cloud of Unknowing was precisely that. It offered no knowledge: 'I know I shall not know,' as Eliot had put it. I had been expecting the thick mist to part, just a little, and had not really known, with every fibre of my being, that I would never know, would never see clearly. I was still hankering for the 'one veritable transitory power'.

And yet the very absence I felt so acutely was paradoxically a presence in my life. When you miss somebody very intensely, they are, in a sense, with you all the time. They often fill your mind and heart more than they do when they are physically present. That was the sort of contradiction that the Greek Fathers liked, but the ancient Greeks had known this too. The masked god Dionysus is everywhere and nowhere. He is always somewhere else. Yet at the same time he is manifest on earth in a bull, a lion or a snake. He both reveals and conceals himself in the mask that is his symbol. The wide, staring eyes of the mask fascinate and attract, but the mask is empty. At the crucial moment of Euripides' *Bacchae*, the supreme epiphany of Dionysus is not an apparition but a sudden disappearance. The god vanishes abruptly – yet a great silence descends upon the earth in which his presence is felt more strongly than ever before. If we try to hold on to our partial glimpses of the divine, we cut it down to our own size and close our minds. Like it or not, our human experience of anything or anybody is always incomplete: there is usually something that eludes us, some portion of experience that evades our grasp. We used to think that science would answer all our questions and solve all the mysteries, but the more we learn, the more mysterious our world becomes.

Yet we do have glimpses of transcendence, even though no two experiences of the divine are the same. All the traditions insist that the sacred is not merely something 'out there', but is also immanent in our world. Again, I had not taken my texts sufficiently seriously. I had often quoted the famous story from the *Upanishads*, in which the sage Uddalaka makes his son Svetaketu aware of the omnipresence of the divine by telling him to dissolve a lump of salt in a beaker of water. In the morning, the lump has disappeared, but though the salt is now invisible, it pervades the entire beaker and can be tasted in every sip. 'My dear child,' Uddalaka concludes, 'it is true that you cannot see Brahman here, but it is equally true that it *is* here. This first essence – the whole universe has as its Self. That is the Real. That is the Self. That *you* are, Svetaketu'. Our task is to learn to see that sacred dimension in everything around us – including our fellow men and women.

That, I think, is the meaning of the story of the apparition of Jesus on the road to Emmaus. The two disciples are depressed; Jesus has just died a terrible and disgraceful death, and this has dashed all their hopes. A stranger joins them on the road and engages them in conversation. He discusses the scriptures with them, showing that the Messiah had to suffer before his glorification. That evening the three dine together, and the stranger breaks bread. In that instant, they recognize that he is Jesus but just as they realize this he disappears, like Dionysus. The story recalls the oft-repeated rabbinical teaching about the divine becoming present whenever two or three people study Torah together. Even though the disciples were not aware of it, the Presence was with them while they were reviewing the scriptures together on the road. Henceforth, we will catch only a fleeting glimpse of it – in the study of sacred writings, in other human beings, in liturgy, and in communion with the stranger. But these moments remind us that our fellow men and women are themselves sacred; there is something about them that is worthy of absolute reverence, is in the last resort mysterious, and will always elude us.

Perhaps in our broken world, we can only envisage an absent God. Since 11 September I have found myself drawn to the powerful mythology of the Jewish Kabbalah, which imagines God as originally a sacred emptiness, sees creation as a massive error, the world shattered and dense with evil, and offers no easy solution. Everything is a bewildering puzzle. One Kabbalistic text tells us that when the temple of Jerusalem was destroyed, the Holy King departed from the earth and no longer dwelt in our midst. Maybe God vanished also, like Dionysus, after the destruction of the World Trade Center, an atrocity that was committed in God's name. The events of 11 September were a dark epiphany; a terrible revelation of what life is like if we do not recognize the sacredness of all human beings, even our enemies. Maybe the only revelation we can hope for now is an experience of absence and emptiness. We have seen too much religious certainty recently. Maybe this is a time for honest, searching doubt, repentance, and a yearning for holiness in a world that has lost its bearings.

The best theologians and teachers have never been afraid to admit that in the last resort there may be 'Nothing' out there. That is why they spoke of a God who in some sense did not exist. It is why the Buddha refused to comment on the metaphysical status of a Buddha after death, and why Confucius would not speak of the Tao. What is vital to all of the traditions, however, is that we have a duty to make the best of the only thing that remains to us – ourselves. Our task now is to mend our broken world; if religion cannot do that, it is worthless. And what our world needs now is not belief, not certainty, but compassionate action and practically expressed respect for the sacred value of all human beings, even our enemies.

September 11 changed my life once again. Suddenly my subject had acquired a terrible new relevance. I wish with all my heart that it had not happened in this way. I have spent most of the months since that fearful day in the United States, trying to share my understanding of Islam and fundamentalism. I have spoken to senators and congressmen, to members of the State Department and at the United Nations.

I see this as a form of ministry. The September apocalypse was a revelation – an 'unveiling' of a reality that had been there all the time but which we had not seen clearly enough before: we live in one world. What happens in Gaza or Afghanistan today will have repercussions in New York or London tomorrow. We in the First World cannot continue to isolate ourselves in our wealth and good fortune. If we do that, those who feel dispossessed or excluded will come to us, in a terrible form. The study of other people's religious beliefs is now no longer merely desirable, but is necessary for our very survival. And so I spend a great deal of my time helping people to understand Islam, showing that we cannot judge the faith of 1.2 billion Muslims by the extremists, and also indicating that our own short-sighted actions and policies in the past have contributed to the situation. Nothing excuses the atrocities of that fateful day, but the Buddhists are right to remind us that the laws of *karma* are always a factor in human life: our deeds have consequences that we could never have predicted at the time.

It has been a great privilege to contribute to the debate in this way, but I miss my study and silence as others might miss a beloved person. I once reviewed a book about hermits, which showed that the more solitary a person becomes, the more he or she is drawn into public life. Crowds of people descended upon St Antony, the fourth-century ascetic who lived in the deserts of Egypt, demanding his help and advice. In our own day, the Trappist monk Thomas Merton had much the same experience. In a very minor way, this has happened to me, but I have to understand that after the revelation of 11 September I too cannot isolate myself from the problems of the world.

There is, perhaps, something about the dynamic of a solitary lifestyle that propels an anchorite back to the world. I am still an outsider. In the United States, despite the warmth and generous appreciation that I enjoy there, I am a stranger and a foreigner. But when I go back to London, I remain on the periphery, because my interest in religion and spirituality leaves most of my fellow-countrymen cold. This feeling of being always on the outside has been an important element in my journey, and yet, despite this, I have, if only for a few months, come close to the centre of things in a way that would have been inconceivable when I left my convent thirty-four years ago. In the words of the late Joseph Campbell, we have to 'follow our bliss', find something that wholly involves and enthrals us, even if it seems hopelessly unfashionable and unproductive, and throw ourselves into this, heart and soul. As the foundress of my religious order used to say: '*Do* what you are doing!' My 'bliss' has been the study of theology. For other people it may be a career in law or politics, a marriage, a love affair or the raising of children. But that bliss provides us with a clue: if we follow it to the end, it will take us to the heart of life.

My life has kept changing, but at the same time I have constantly found myself revolving round and round the same themes, the same issues, and even repeating the same mistakes. I tried to break away from the convent but I still live alone, spend my days in silence, and am almost wholly occupied in writing, thinking and speaking about God and spirituality. I have come full circle. This reminds me of the staircase in Eliot's *Ash-Wednesday*, which I picture as a narrow spiral staircase. I tried to get off it and join others on what seemed to me to be a broad, noble flight of steps, thronged with people. But I kept falling off, and when I went back to my own twisting stairwell I found a fulfilment that I had not expected. Now I have to mount my staircase alone. And as I go up, step by step, I am turning, again, round and round, apparently covering little ground, but climbing upwards, I hope, towards the light.